DAN'S WAR

ON POVERTY

A Grassroots Crusade for Social Justice

Ann
Patton

THE DAN ALLEN CENTER FOR SOCIAL JUSTICE
AND APLCORPS BOOKS, LLC.

Publication of Dan Allen's story was made possible by geneous contributions and grants to the Dan Allen Center for Social Justice, Inc. The Center and the author wish to thank the book's sustaining sponsors, whose names are listed on the Center's website, www.danallencenter.org. Their help and dedication exemplify the good will and *caritas* that can heal our society and eliminate poverty and injustice.

Library of Congress Cataloging-in-Publication Data
Library of Congress Control Number: 2011918850

ISBN: 978-0-9839131-1-5
ISBN: 978-0-9839131-0-8 Pbk.

Published by Dan Allen Center for Social Justice and APLcorps Books LLC, Tulsa, Oklahoma.

Manufactured in the U.S.A.

The paper in this book meets the guidelines for permanence and durability of the Government Paper Specification Standards of the American National Standards Institute.

1 2 3 4 5 6 7 8 9 10

Cover design by Larry Silvey.

Cover photo by Stephen Crane, *Tulsa World.*

Book design by Joe Williams.

CONTENTS

This book is dedicated to the hundreds of volunteers,
many unseen and unsung,
who have given gifts of themselves to the poor
through Dan Allen's Neighbor for Neighbor.

"NFN has no guidelines.
We can't exclude any applicant for
any reason of income, location
or employment because we
have no guidelines.
Christ didn't give us any."

—Dan Allen

FOREWORD

I wonder what Father Dan Allen would say about the idea of a book with his name on the cover? Maybe we would hear raucous laughter, perhaps followed by a profane muttered growl.

He might be outraged that we would be focusing on him instead of the poor. We do know that just before Dan died, in November 1995, his niece Judy Allen Hess mentioned the idea of a book to him. Dan could hardly speak at the time, but he communicated back to her—in a few words and hand gestures—that such a book should focus on the poor, not himself. He wanted her to write the story of a broken family and the cruelty of poverty.

This book, in fact, focuses less on Dan and more on the poor and a remarkable constellation of people he inspired to fight poverty beginning in the 1960s in Tulsa, Oklahoma. Whether he would admit it or not, the center of that constellation was Dan Allen, a Catholic priest who could not, would not compromise in his fight for social justice. He became the conscience of his community and, in the process, inspired people to make significant differences in the lives of others. Dan changed hearts and lives and, in so doing, changed the community.

If I believed in reincarnation, I would have to suspect that James, the author of the Epistle, came back as Dan Allen. James, like Dan (and of course like Jesus), based his teaching of justice upon the fundamental distinction between the rich and the poor. God's love comes close to the poor and lowly. To draw close to the poor by coming to their aid is equivalent, in James's and Dan's view, to drawing close to God. It is the heart of faith and religious love.

When Dan died, a splendid *Tulsa World* editorial said, "To those who don't know him, the gruff and plain-spoken Allen may have seemed an unlikely candidate to be the chief advocate for local poor people. But to those who knew him well, those traits and others made him the lovable and unforgettable character he was. The people who Allen brought on board and trained in poverty-fighting techniques no doubt will try to carry out the vision that the once-dubbed 'radical priest' strived for his entire adult life. They will succeed, because his dedication, enthusiasm and timelessness were infectious. But they will never replace him. Dan Allen was one of a kind."[1]

Dan did not practice what he preached; he preached what he practiced. He was what he practiced. It came from his very being, and that is why he appeared so authentic—because he was.

I was privileged to call Dan Allen my friend. His mission, his interpretation of the gospel as unconditional service of the needy, and his tireless quest for social justice inspired many of us then and even now. Although he is no longer living among us, he lives on in those whose lives he changed.

This story of Dan Allen's War on Poverty—and of those who fought with him for justice for the least of these[2]—has the power to inspire us still, today and tomorrow, for now and for future generations. To that end—to continue Dan Allen's mission, his war on poverty—I commend this book to you.

—Father Bill Skeehan

PREFACE

Writing a book about Dan Allen is a challenge.

But writing about Father Dan's work and the people and institutions he changed is easier—delightful, in fact.

That's because Dan operated in a transparent way, passing through life like a mischievous wind that can hardly be tracked except through the evidence of change it leaves behind. Thus, writing about the person Dan Allen is like trying to capture the wind. The writing becomes, instead, an exercise in describing the people and causes he touched and rearranged, thereby creating an outline of his likeness, a mosaic of one man who made a difference, of a ghost who lingers still.

Dan Allen's story is worth telling. His War on Poverty blossomed from his remarkable view of the world, grounded in his certainty that the way to live the gospel was through unstinting service to the needy. His work focused on a specific place, but his work has universal lessons for us all.

Like most of the United States in the 1960s, Tulsa was sharply divided between the haves and have-nots. It was a two-city place where an affluent Southside could largely ignore the festering Northside poverty. Blacks were still kept separate in North Tulsa, and whites were quietly fleeing south. It fell to Dan Allen, an erstwhile Catholic priest turned renegade social activist, to find a way to bridge the divide. Many helped, but Dan was the catalyst who made the difference.

A social action committee of Dan's St. Jude Catholic Church began by turning the church vestibule, then the educational wing, then the parking lots into a gathering place for donated goods for the poor. Eventually it all spilled over into a nearby farm. It was ramshackle, untidy, and endlessly creative. As their efforts to provide help mushroomed, so did their understanding. From this beginning in 1967 was born Neighbor for Neighbor, a unique social service movement. (Dan refused to call it an agency.) In time, NFN would consume the lives of Father Allen and his followers, transforming both the lives of needy folk and those who sought to help them.

Dan's genius lay in creating a model of reciprocal help that empowered poor and rich alike. The important word was the humble preposition—for, as in Neighbor for Neighbor. He intentionally set neighbor to helping neighbor in reciprocal encounters. The idea was that one day a person needs help, the next day that person is helping his benefactor or others in need. From that mutual service comes self-respect that can lead to self-sufficiency. If you came to help, you were required to understand and respect human needs or risk being dispatched unceremoniously to a rejected-helper pile. The basis for Neighbor for Neighbor, Allen said, "is unconditional affirmation for that person on their own terms, period"—unconditional love—so that those who came for help could walk away with pride and dignity, helping others.

For Dan Allen, Neighbor for Neighbor was, first of all, a University of Poverty, an exercise in adult religious education that he used to teach the gospel and understanding of the poor. It wasn't mere charity. His end goal was social justice. "It is not charity the poor need, but justice," he declared.[1]

Many of today's mainstream assistance programs were birthed at NFN, such as the food bank, credit counseling, voluntary school desegregation program, and free medical and legal clinics. Similar "neighbor" agencies popped up around the region. But most important, Dan's NFN became, in the words of one supporter, "the social conscience of this city."[2]

The power of Neighbor for Neighbor arose in part from Dan Allen's own complex intensity. Like those he sought to serve, Dan was no stranger to anguish. Haunted by his own torments, Allen redirected his private pain into an uncompromising passion for service to what the Bible calls "the least of these."[3]

He railed against social injustice. He had no patience with bureaucracy. "The wealthiest nation in the world has lost its war on poverty," he fumed.[4] "Everyone who knew him knew he had a rage inside of him," said a volunteer.[5] "He was God's angry man," wrote one reporter.[6] "Give a damn," shouted a banner on his office wall, rising from the clutter of a hundred priorities attacked simultaneously.

Dan was never afraid of an unconventional, sometimes outrageously funny, scrap. He once staged a mock "parade of homes" to showcase poverty housing. He turned the table on auto thieves and converted them into entrepreneurs serving the poor. He relentlessly pointed out emperors who wore no clothes and routinely turned powerful institutions on their heads.

A newspaper reporter (me) who came to interview Dan at NFN was interrupted when volunteers carted off Allen's office sofa to give to a burned-out family; before the morning was over, the reporter found herself sacking Thanksgiving canned goods for the poor. I was never quite the same after that first (but not the last) encounter with Dan and the NFN family. From detached observer to committed activist in less than an hour: so it went, day by day, in Dan Allen's world.

Dan Allen and Neighbor for Neighbor changed Tulsa in profound ways. Their story line traces the evolution of a social revolution in an American city.

As he would have ordered, this book focuses less on Dan and more on the people who sought help and those who came to help. I wish it would be possible to recognize all those countless NFN volunteers and their tremendous work over many years. For sheer simplicity, this book focuses on a dozen of his followers whose lives were rearranged permanently by Dan Allen, but they merely stand for many others whose stories would be equally compelling.

You could call them living stones—these people who were changed for all time and spent their new lives building a better society. The phrase comes from 1 Peter 2:5: "Ye also, as living stones, are built up a spiritual house, an holy priesthood, to offer up spiritual sacrifices, acceptable to God by Jesus Christ." It is important to tell their stories, because they have lessons to teach us all. Theirs is a story of the transformative power of love, of rage against injustice, and of common service on behalf of the common good.

Dan died in 1995, but his legacy continues in a quest for social justice by a flock of true believers and institutions still carrying his torch. His light still shines through the faces of those who loved him.

He left us a model of community betterment that can change the world. Dan Allen is gone, and now it is up to the rest of us.

—Ann Patton

Dan Allen's Neighbor for Neighbor

In the following words, Father Dan Allen summed up his life's work, philosophy,
and spiritual vision brought to life through his Neighbor for Neighbor program.

"Neighbor for Neighbor doesn't ask why, it asks how. NFN believes that people change people by using their human and material resources to help one another acquire their basic needs: food, shelter, clothing, jobs.

"It isn't a matter of programs, guidelines, plans and objectives. People change only when their sense of themselves changes. The way a person feels about himself determines the way he acts.

"We attempt to change the attitude of the poor by making them aware of their potential, not just their needs.

"And frankly, we're trying to alter the attitudes of many among the affluent. Their contact with the poor helps them become aware that we are all creators of the conditions of poverty; and therefore we can recreate both, in the society of the poor, and in other environments.

"We seek to substitute a recognition of one's personal worth, regardless of position, for the feeling of shame for being poor.

"How do you start? Find some people who care, are not afraid of failure and have the capacity to learn through listening.

"There are two groups of people who care: those who will become personally involved in the lives of families and those who will help provide the resources to match the needs.

"This requires establishment of credit resources, transportation, housing and informing ourselves about local agencies, public relations and press contacts, legal aid, medical assistance and other services.

"Our number one concern is bringing people into contact with people. NFN acts as a resource center to create action and as a referral center. If there is no local source to fill a need, we strive to provide the service ourselves.

"Neighbor for Neighbor is a non-profit community corporation run by a Board of Directors elected from those concerned with the problems of the poor. Our finances come mostly from private funds.

"If you're looking for an easy solution to poverty, forget it. There is none. But this one can succeed, in part, because it involves people with one another: Neighbor for Neighbor.

— Dan Allen

Chapter 1

The Seekers

"Don't ask what you can do,
ask what you can become."

— Dan Allen

LORD KNOWS, DAN ALLEN WAS AN UNLIKELY CANDIDATE FOR SAINTHOOD.

"He swears like a sailor, doing the work of a saint," wrote one reporter. "He left the priesthood to fight poverty under the motto, 'Give a Damn.' He so hates bureaucracy that he doesn't want his Neighbor for Neighbor organization called an 'agency.' Dan Allen doesn't mince words about rich people who don't help the poor. He doesn't worry about being popular." [1]

"Dan Allen's bearded face is a mosaic of the sadness of poverty," wrote another, "the joy in plain people being 'for' others, anger provoked by damaging greed, and an articulate sense of humor, which bubbles up from a deep well of hope in the reign of God.

"Allen's base of operations is his jumbled, smoky office on Tulsa's down-at-the-heels north side. It's the headquarters of Neighbor for Neighbor, an antipoverty organization he founded.... Over the years, Dan Allen has become the voice of the poor in Tulsa. When he cries foul, people—even the high and mighty—listen because they realize he tells the truth." [2]

How would you describe Neighbor for Neighbor? another reporter once asked Dan.

"There is this man," Dan replied. He leaned back in his chair, locked his hands behind his head, and fixed his sad, tired eyes on some unidentified place. Smoke drifted up from his cigarette, circling around clusters of yellowed clippings and curling snapshots posted long ago, and long forgotten, behind his cluttered desk.[3]

"A good example of what Neighbor for Neighbor is about is a young mother who came here about four years ago. She had two children and, because of extreme difficulties, was in a state of despair."

NFN worked out a loan that allowed her to keep her house, and she was working off the loan by running the NFN used-clothing shed when Dan learned she just needed a few credits to complete her degree as a dental hygienist.

"So I told her, 'We'll help you complete your education. While you're doing that . . . I want you to volunteer in the dental clinic.' Her whole attitude, her whole life changed. She is an amazingly gifted lady. She now is a full-time staff person in our dental clinic and is so good that various dentists have tried to hire her."

Dan shifted uneasily in his chair. He was already weary of explaining.

"And then, there is this man: he and his five children live in a shack a few miles north of here. Leotis McHenry. He was half blind, and his teeth were rotted." NFN needed some renovation work. "I'll work for nothing if you'll just give me a chance," Leotis said.

"I told him, 'We don't practice injustice, so you aren't going to work for nothing—but first . . . we've got a dental clinic over here and the whole health schmeer. You need to get your body together because you look like death warmed over.' The health improvement and the job changed his whole concept of himself.

"Now he's heading our housing program. That's Neighbor for Neighbor."[4]

Years earlier and several states away from Tulsa, Oklahoma, where Dan Allen would create the singular institution called Neighbor for Neighbor, a young engineer named Don McCarthy was looking for justice in an unjust world. It was the 1950s, and Don was running a mining crew in Alabama.

"A bunch of these white fellows came up to me—I thought they were insurance salesmen, that's how naïve I was," Don said later. "I was helping my black carpenter set forms. His name was Eddie.

"They said, 'Nigger, are you square with the Lord?' I saw one of the men pick up a shovel to hit my carpenter. I was about twenty feet away. I took the shovel away.

"They said Eddie had to be gone or they were coming back Monday to clear out the place."

In those days, Don looked a bit like a fair-haired Abe Lincoln—tall, lanky, angular, with a long back, bony shoulders, knobby knees. He was always in motion, curious as a child, agile and persistent as a squirrel, interested in pretty much everything, and cursed with a perennially sunny disposition that sometimes misled people to underestimate his quick brain and iron will.

Don knew their gripe. They saw a black man working as a carpenter— proof he didn't know his place. And even worse, the carpenter was making $100 a week—when they were used to paying $10. "They knew he could buy beer with the best of them," McCarthy said. "He was making a good wage and taking money from some white carpenter, to their mind."

It was hot, and there was no breeze, as Don remembers it. The heat was like opening the door of a blast furnace, blazing down, boiling up, cooking the gritty rock surface and all that was on it, above the underground cavern.

"They said they'd bring reinforcements to destroy all our work. They said, 'Either he's gone or we will level this place, come Monday.'"

"I said, 'You fellows just come on back whenever you want.'

"These fellows didn't know I had ninety workers underground. They thought it was just me and my carpenter," Don said.

Now, what to do? "Eddie was a good man," McCarthy said. "I had to stand up for him. I was so naïve then, it never occurred to me I could have called the FBI. I figured we had to settle it ourselves.

"I made a decision to hold court right next to a state senator's office. I thought if they were going to demolish anything, it might as well be his place. He was one of the most powerful Alabama senators. I believed he was involved anyway, or at least knew about it. I picked his location and gave all my workers four-foot pieces of drill steel, and we were ready to do service right there.

"Then about 10:00 a.m., I got a call that they weren't coming right then—I guess they got wind that we were ready—but I had better get rid of this guy or they would be back. Well, I refused."

A week later, the carpenter came into McCarthy's office. "He said, 'Mr. Mac, one of these days you will have your back turned or this job will be over and you will be gone—and Eddie they will find in a ditch.'

"Well, I wouldn't doubt it, Ed," McCarthy said. "These guys are no good, and I will only be here so long."

"So I will take my money and go," Eddie said.

But it would never quite be over for McCarthy. Not even when he went back home to his family in Tulsa, Oklahoma, where things were better but not much.

Don went to church—"We were what I would call Sunday Catholics then"—and there was one black family in his church. They were endlessly wary. When they would take communion, the family would go up one at a time to keep watch for each other. "I would walk in and out with them when I could, and they would pass the little one to me sometimes. They sat in a back pew, and I sat behind them. They would walk backwards until they passed me in the aisle, to be sure there was nobody behind them."

It all chewed on McCarthy, grinding on him beneath his affable facade. McCarthy wasn't used to being cornered long by a problem. He was a problem solver—an engineer. Give him a puzzle and he would solve it. It just wasn't right. But what could he do?[5]

Elsewhere in Tulsa, at about the same time, a young Bill Skeehan was quite the man about town. He was a graphic artist, the staff artist for the National Junior Chamber of Commerce, doing corporate annual reports. He had spent his formative years in the affluence of Beverly Hills. Bill was a hearty fellow, apple cheeked, with a full head of dark hair, a glint in his eye, a ready smile and booming laugh—a charmer. Now he was enjoying the good life in Tulsa, certain of his entitlement to it all.

And then suddenly it hit him, without warning.

"My cousin's girlfriend told me at a party that I was the most selfish person she had ever known in her life," an elderly Skeehan recalled years later. "Me—selfish? No way. It could not be possible. But the more I thought about it, the more I saw that she was absolutely right."

That party was in May. By September, Bill was in seminary.

"Now, how can you explain something like that, a bolt that just comes from nowhere and suddenly changes the entire direction of your life?" Bill asked. "I think there is no explaining it. I think it is a mystery, one of the great mysteries in life. There are many mysteries in life. I think it was the Holy Spirit. I was moved by the Holy Spirit to become a priest—I sure as heck wouldn't have done it myself—and I cannot explain it."[6]

As the decade of the 1960s opened, Bill Skeehan was graduated from St. Thomas Seminary in Denver and ordained in the Oklahoma Diocese, ready to prove that he was not too selfish to do some good in the world.

"My cousin's girlfriend told me at a party that I was the most selfish person she had ever known in her life," an elderly Skeehan recalled years later.

Those were the days of Vatican II, the 1960s liberalization revolution within the Catholic Church. The civil rights struggle was in full flower in the United States. A wave of social reform was spreading around the world. It was reasonable that a boy reared in the milieu of Catholic mysticism would think of the church as his antidote to selfishness. But he railed against the structure. "For the present," Skeehan wrote at the time, "we must live with the stupidities of the Church [but] we hear the death rattle of the clerical, judicial, and triumphalistic Church, . . . the authoritarian structure. . . . The mission of the church is . . . bringing about freely a right relationship between a man and his neighbor." As he flailed about, he kept looking for a better way.[7]

Sometime in the early 1960s, Maynard Ungerman got a call from the wife of Oklahoma senator Fred Harris. Ungerman was a well-known Tulsa attorney from a prominent Jewish family, a liberal by political persuasion, and a member of the Congress on Racial Equality, spending a lot of his time on civil rights cases with CORE and other groups.

"I was a strong supporter of the civil rights movement," Ungerman said. "CORE would have demonstrations, and I would get kids out of jail. So Fred's wife asked me to help with two priests who had gotten arrested in Lawton for leading picketers at an amusement park. The park was excluding Native Americans from the city pool. So I went down and got them out of jail."

Shortly thereafter Ungerman got another call, this time from an assistant for Oklahoma's Catholic bishop Victor J. Reed. "The bishop had heard about what happened in Lawton," Ungerman said, "and he wanted me to help with a number of priests who were working in the civil rights movement. All four were quite active in North Tulsa, and could I help them?

"Those priests were Babe O'Brien, Lee O'Neil, James McGlinchey, and Dan Allen," Ungerman said. "I met with them, and I have to say, I just got caught up in Dan's philosophy. He had a social action committee, at that point, at St. Jude Catholic Church."

Maynard urged the social action committee to become formalized, incorporated, with a real board of directors.

"So that's how it started. And it has never ended. I have made a commitment to keep on it for all the rest of my life."[8]

In those days, Wilbert Collins was a young father, living in a part of North Tulsa named Reservoir Hill. Collins was looking for self confidence and fighting for a foothold in life, trying to find a way to make a decent living for his family.[9] He had married in 1961, had a first son in 1962 and another shortly thereafter.

His Reservoir Hill neighborhood was in the throes of change then, as black families like the Collinses edged farther and farther beyond the old Greenwood ghetto.

"Like everybody I knew then, we were fighting an uphill battle against bad credit and poverty," Wilbert remembered later. "No matter how hard we tried, there didn't seem to be any way to get ahead.

"I had a neighbor named Dan Allen," Collins remembered. "He moved into our neighborhood, right around the corner. Dan and I talked all the time. When I had problems, I could talk them over with Dan. I could just walk around the corner in my neighborhood, and Dan would help me figure things out and give me good advice. He was one true friend."

Collins was a Baptist—"Mt. Zion Baptist Church, all my life"—and Dan was a Catholic, a priest at St. Jude church a couple of miles north on 46th Street North.

"Dan and I were always doing something. We would get a hammer and

nails and keep things fixed at St. Jude. I would go visit him, and he would
tell me how he wanted to create a board to help serve people, and he wanted
me to be on that board. He made me feel like I had something to offer."[10]

Pat Flanagan was a young mother in the 1960s, with "three little stair-step
kids." Like Skeehan, Pat had been reared in wealth; her father owned Gaso
Pumps, manu-
facturing oil field   *Her life spread out before her, like looking down at*
equipment. Pat   *a patchwork quilt, and her late grandfather guided*
had grown into   *her through it. "He said, 'Everything that is alive*
a fetching young   *is connected with every other living thing. You can't*
woman with   *do damage to anything without damaging the*
dark searching   *others.' I had never heard of such a thing."*
eyes, a wicked
wit, and a quick
tongue. She did
not bear fools
well.

"I was one of those very conservative Catholics, very involved in church
life, one of those women of privilege destined to play bridge at the country
club," Pat said.

And then it happened—her epiphany.

Pat came down with pneumonia and some kind of rare blood infection.
She was hospitalized for weeks. One day things around her began to grow
distant. "I felt like I was melting," Pat remembered later. "And then I realized I was looking down at the bed, with this skinny woman lying on it, and
I was up here watching it all happen. I had never heard about near-death
experiences. I was a staunch Catholic. My idea of death was very baroque,
with fat cherubs and God on a throne. But it was all happening to me—
the tunnel thing, music that sounded as if it were under water, colors I had
never seen before, and a bright light."

Her life spread out before her, like looking down at a patchwork quilt,
and her late grandfather guided her through it. "He said, 'Everything that
is alive is connected with every other living thing. You can't do damage to
anything without damaging the others.' I had never heard of such a thing."

Her grandfather offered her the chance to return to life and said, 'You
will have peace some day, but first you have to work for justice for others.' I
never heard that kind of idea. To me, justice was the courts. I was not sure
what he meant, but I agreed. And so I went back."

It was a long convalescence. "I never told anybody about the death experi-

ence," Pat said. "It was private. I began to read, heavy stuff. I figured out
what justice meant. My friends thought I was crazy. Church didn't mean
anything to me any more; it had nothing to do with anything that mattered.
I couldn't speak the language any more. Of course, I knew about Vatican
II, and I kept searching and questioning—asking whether what I had been
thinking was really true for me."

Friends told her about a new organization that was trying to help poor
people, run by a renegade priest named Dan Allen. Maybe she should visit
the outfit, which went by the name of Neighbor for Neighbor.

She didn't like the sound of the place, but it seemed inevitable that she
would go there.[11]

Like others, Carol Falletti came to NFN after what she, too, described as a
kind of epiphany.

Carol was born in Edna, Kansas, in the middle of somewhere, out in the
country west of Coffeyville. Her father was not educated or employable,
and her mother took in ironing, ten cents per piece. The family had almost
nothing except trouble. They moved around a lot. One time they threw
everything they owned into a creek before they moved; she never knew why.

Carol wanted to go to college, but it seemed hopeless until her sister gave
her the $86 for tuition. She got into a pre-med program. Then she heard
about a program in Kansas City. If accepted, she could go to St. Mary's
Hospital, including a one-year internship working in a hospital laboratory.

"There were only eight interns accepted—I was lucky to get in. White
hose, white shoes. Learning medical ethics and how to handle things and
how to conduct myself as a professional. This was a way out for me—I
would do whatever it took to be educated enough to get a job." In 1959
Carol graduated and passed the national board registry as a Certified
American Society of Clinical Medical Technologist.

She married another young professional, Donald Falletti. He had
engineering jobs in the aerospace industry and the military. They worked
in Virginia, Wichita, and Tulsa. They started a family, five babies in six
years, but nothing could hold them back. She was clawing her way out of
poverty—such a triumph!

About 1970, Carol went to a workshop sponsored by her Resurrection
Catholic Church. "It was a poverty workshop," she remembered, "at Fulton
Family Y, with a lot of people sitting at round tables, and somebody named
Dan Allen running the program. Dan had a poor person at each table, talk-
ing about his or her life problems. The people at the table were supposed to
try to solve the problems. They were very involved problems, one thing after

another. None of us could solve anything. It was an eye-opener for most people. It made me realize, finally, what poverty I had grown up in.

"Dan talked about the gospel and justice. He was handsome and charming, and his words just stopped me short. I didn't want to do it, to make that commitment. I thought, 'Oh, no, I can't go back into the world of poverty again.'

"Don and I had said we would never look back. Nothing could ever drag me back to poverty again."[12]

Dan's exact words at the poverty workshop have been lost, but he repeated the thrust of them later, in responding to a newspaper article:

"Dan talked about the gospel and justice. He was handsome and charming, and his words just stopped me short."
—Carol Falletti

"Last August, in the Tulsa World, Tom Kertscher wrote a full-page article on NFN in which he began by saying, 'There is a small town for little people in North Tulsa, an oasis from suffering that the poor can call home . . . people would probably live there if it just had a church and maybe a tavern or two.'

"After reading the article, Father Skeehan commented: "An excellent article, but he missed a major point: the town IS the church."

"In 1965 when I returned to the area where I grew up, to pastor St. Jude's Church, that is exactly what I envisioned a parish church to be, in fact should be. Thanks to that period of time, people of all persuasions and backgrounds began "to pitch their tents together," and a credit union, filling station, legal aid, food store, etc., gave visible evidence that Luke's 'good news to the poor' was taking place—not, however, with just charity or just liberation into material abundance, but demonstrating a solidarity with the poor . . . in a protest against poverty [injustice]. In the midst of all this and the struggle over issues, the 'town' dwellers gave birth to NFN.

"A couple of years later, this small oasis lost its dwelling place and was given a lease to a small, old farm house next door. The fiber of this "small town" was put to the test severely, but new life through new people kept coming to town, and now . . . we old tent dwellers are deeply proud of our 'church town.'

"All, of course, do not see NFN this way. I, for one, knowing we have a long way to go, sense, in this 'small town for little people' a feeling of joy and hope . . . that here, in the best sense of our Judaic-Christian ethic, we find that the 'glory of God is man fully alive' . . . Because, true to our beginnings, we remain a 'town' . . . where justice separates the sheep from the goats and removes the

oppressor from the oppressed; where justice lies deep in people's personhood, moves convictions, changes values, shapes the tone and tenor of dialogue, celebrates the first-time victory, sets the climate for a parade, calls for a march!

"Where justice is the soil for soul songs, the fiber that weaves flags, . . . where justice senses a God in need of nothing, . . . we find a sense that we are we, God is God, with common sense the unwritten but living law.

"And who knows, someday our 'town' may have a 'tavern or two.'" [13]

As with Don McCarthy, Bill Skeehan, Maynard Ungerman, Wilbert Collins, Pat Flanagan, and Carol Falletti, others in that era were also thrust, often against their wills, into seeking something they could not resist or quite define. Sometimes the trigger seemed minor, and the destination elusive, but for each, something snapped the arc of their lives toward a new direction.

For these seekers, these were moments that made all the difference.

Sooner or later, their paths would converge, and all would become students in Dan Allen's University of Poverty.

They could not have known they were enrolling for life.

Chapter 2

A Good-Looking Guy,
Very Driven, Very Tough

ETEOR BACK PREPS FOR OPENER
Dan Allen (above), Marquette wingback, polishes up his punting
r the Catholic schools' All-City game tonight at Webster stadium.
len, who is slated to do most of the Meteors' booting this season,
ime through with an exceptionally vigorous kick for the World
otographer and succeeded in obscuring part of his face with his

"The dignity of a person in the Gospel is not the same as defined
in our economic order. Christ's 'good news' is that
a person has dignity because he is a person."

—Dan Allen

Tulsa Daily World, September 19, 1946.

WHAT CREATES A FORCE LIKE DAN ALLEN?
PERHAPS HIS CHILDHOOD HOLDS CLUES.

"Despite two sprained ankles and a broken nose," the yearbook caption begins, on a page titled "Lettermen." The caption accompanies a picture of an intense boy with dark wavy hair, eyes intently focused on the camera, without a hint of a smile. He is lean and lithe, leaping to throw a football. His entire being is focused on delivery of that ball. The caption speaks of blocking, driving, sparking, and an 85-yard kickoff run. His jersey says he is Number 55. The year is 1949, and he is 18, a senior at Marquette Catholic High School in Tulsa.

Later in the yearbook, Number 55 shows up again, looking a bit discomfited in a scuffed-up football uniform. On his arm, in full regalia, is Donna Hunt, being crowned queen of the football squad. Number 55 is team captain, the caption says. Facing page: Ms. Hunt again, bearing a trailing bouquet of giant chrysanthemums and wrapped in a velvet cloak. She is clutching the arm of Number 55, who has been transformed into a shining knight in black tuxedo and formal black bow tie, with gleaming patent leather shoes and regal bearing.

And again on other pages: Here the royal couple is preparing for the grand ball. There, Number 55 is accepting the 1948 conference championship trophy. Again elsewhere, Number 55 is graduating, with a mortarboard flat across his brow, tassel carefully under control; senior vice president and treasurer, yearbook cover designer, "A friend received with thumps on the back."

But always his face is the same: handsome and intense, unsmiling, someone to be reckoned with. Somehow Number 55 appears to be solitary, even in the midst of revelry. His clear eyes appear fixed on some distant reality known only to him. In every picture, young Dan Allen stares directly into the unblinking eye of the camera as if living his life in perpetual challenge.[1]

The story of Daniel Richard Allen began in central Oklahoma, on a farm near Deer Creek, west of Edmond. The date was April 19, 1930.[2] The world was in the throes of the Great Depression, and Oklahoma was entering its horrific Dust Bowl era.

Dan was the seventh of eight children born to Arthur Lowe Allen and Mary Ellen McAuliffe. The seven boys were Jim, Art, J. D., Jack, Ted, Dan, and Duke. The lone daughter was Mary Frances Allen, whose married name became Pankey.

"No!" Frances Pankey said years later. "We were NOT poor, even though Dan used to say we were. I heard him say once in a speech that we were poor, and I thought, Dan, you are an idiot. There's poor and poor. We weren't rich, and the Depression was really bad, but we never went hungry. Mother was a great cook."

Their mother was a lifelong Catholic, born to an Irish mother. Mary Ellen's family had come from Plattsburg, Missouri, to Oklahoma in a covered wagon during a land run. "She learned to cook so well because, when she was growing up, if you let your daughters go to work, you were no good," Frances said, "but Mother wanted to get off the farm so she went to work for a wealthy family in Oklahoma City, and that's where she learned to cook. As a young woman, she worked a little as a telephone operator.

"She was always busy, busy, busy. She was a great mother, but she was never one to chit-chat. She said, If you don't have something nice to say, don't say anything. She was a good neighbor; all the neighbors loved her. She belonged to the Altar Society and took care of the linens. Christmas was wonderful. She was always sewing and made dolls and stocking monkeys for all the children. Once she caught her hand in the needle—she had a treadle machine."

Frances contended they were not poor because they were always clean.

Frances contended they were not poor because they were always clean. As the only daughter, Frances was in charge of the endless washing and ironing.

Frances's daughter Kathie Jackson remembered Dan's parents were devout. "Grandmother had a devotion to the Sacred Heart of Jesus. I still remember in the living room—this was later, after they moved to Tulsa—it was just a little white frame house, but it had all the signatures of the family. Over Grandma's chair was the Immaculate Heart of Mary, and over Grandpa's chair was the Sacred Heart of Jesus. Next to Grandpa's chair was the radio, and later a little TV. He could read the newspaper, listen to the radio, watch TV, and still carry on a conversation with you. If you have eight kids, you have to have those skills. It takes a lot of multitasking, a lot of focus."

"Grandpa and Grandma were a darling couple," remembered Dan's niece Judy Allen Hess. "He was always in love with her. In every photograph, there he is with his arm around her. He loved her dearly and treated her very special."

Dan's father, Arthur Lowe Allen, lost his mother when he was very young. After she died in childbirth, Arthur was reared by his maternal grandparents. But despite early hardships, his family remembers Arthur as upbeat and witty. "He was a kidder," said Dan's niece Kathie said. "You could never tell when he was kidding and when it was for real."

Unlike his wife, Arthur was not reared a Catholic. After he quietly took Catholic instruction from a priest, "Mother was surprised when he took his first communion at midnight mass. She had no idea he was taking instruction," Frances said.

In Dan's early years, his father worked as an electrician. When rural electricity came to the farm, Arthur had them take it to the barn, not the house. He had a light bulb put in the barn because the boys had to get up early to do their chores there, before they went to school.

Tragedy struck when a team of horses ran away with Arthur. "The buggy flipped over and broke Dad's collarbone," Frances remembered. "The doctor came—they came out to the house then—and we had to put him to bed. He was really bummed up. Mother was expecting Duke [her eighth child]. I thought she was gonna—

"Our oldest brother Jim had to quit school and take care of the farm and the family then. That's when Jim took over. He never got to go back to school."

Dan was still an infant when Duke was born. "Mother told me, 'We're gonna have another baby.' I said, 'No! If it's another one of those boys, we're sending it back.' But when he got there, she had him at the house, and she said, 'Well, Frances, it's another one of those boys.' She gave him to me, and I was rocking him, and she said, 'Are you going to send him back?' And I said, 'No.'"

Dan was a very happy child, as his sister remembered it. He and his youngest brother Duke were like twins, Frances recalled. "They were always out playing. I didn't pay much attention to them; I was working all the time. We all had chores—that was how it was. You had your place in life and you didn't question it. We were happy kids. We had a lot of love, a lot of laughter."

Frances had a doll buggy, a metal one that had been retrieved from a dump. "One day the boys tied it to a billy goat and chased it around," Frances said. "That was so much fun, they tied one of the boys to the goat. They cracked the boy's head open."

An aunt gave their mother some baby chickens. "Well, Dan and Duke decided the chicks ought to swim. We got our bath and cleaning water from a cistern then. Mother was pretty upset when she found them in the cistern— she had a mind to raise those chicks for Sunday dinners. She saved some of them by putting them in the oven and warming them up."

Frances remembers nothing remarkable about the young Dan Allen. "We were just too busy to pay a lot of attention. When he was real little, his only real chore was to set the table. He did a lousy job. I said, 'Dan, I'm going to show you how to do it, and I want it done that way,' He still didn't do it. He said, 'Well, I figure if I don't do a good job, you won't make me do it any more.'"

The Depression didn't lift. Arthur went to work with the WPA (Works Progress Administration), and the family moved to Tulsa. "We lived with Aunt Jenny until we could find a place," Frances remembered. "With all those boys, we couldn't rent easily. Finally we found a house on 4th Place."

On the farm, the family always said the rosary together. In town, it was not so easy to get the family together and keep the old traditions going. "But we always had prayers at meals and we always did the nine first Fridays," said Frances. "With Daddy being a convert—it was funny because, no matter who was there, when it was bedtime, he knelt down in front of that chair and said his prayers. He prayed to himself, not out loud. There he was, every night, with the Sacred Heart of Jesus over his chair."

Dan and Duke were not yet in school when they moved. "One day they were out playing and we didn't know they had set a fire out back, but they did," Frances said. "Dan made Duke go to Momma for a glass of water and said they were watering the garden. He kept coming back for glasses of water. They poured and poured the water and finally got it out."

The Allens were always angling for ways to improve their family's lives. Arthur found a bigger house on North Atlanta Avenue. "Then Dad found a house across the street that was vacant. Kids were vandalizing it. He went to court to find the owner so he could fix it up, rent it out, and take care of it. The owner was out of state, in California. The court clerk said to Dan, 'Well, if it was me, I would be glad if somebody moved in and took care of it.' So we moved into it, because it was a bigger house than the one we were living in. I don't remember what happened with the owner, but that's how we moved into 1801 North Atlanta."

The little boys were steeped in religion, Frances remembered. "They were all altar boys and were always at church. They served and everything, and then when they came home, they would play church."

There was another crisis: while working for the WPA, Arthur got a splinter in the palm of his hand that became infected—a very dangerous problem in the days before antibiotics. The doctor had to operate. "He told the doctor, he said, 'I have eight children to raise, so do your very best.' And he did, he put in draining tubes through his hand, and eventually Daddy could use his hand again. He was an electrician and he had to have his hands," Frances said.

During World War II, Arthur worked as a metal spinner in the bomber plant, making nose cones. After the war, Arthur met Frank Zeigler, a jeweler who had a little lathe and metal shop in his garage. Zeigler hired Arthur as a gold spinner, and they developed a specialty of making religious articles. "A lot of priests have his chalices," Frances said.[3]

"Maybe we'll get our heads beat in. But it's worth a try."
—Dan Allen

The children went to nearby St. Francis Xavier Catholic School from kindergarten to eighth grade, then on to Marquette Catholic School. It was only a few miles south; but Marquette was a world apart, drawing students from wealthy families, highlighting the contrast with those from poor Northside neighborhoods.

The boys had cars that they were always working on, recalled Dan's sister-in-law Anne Allen, so they could roam. "They had an old Cadillac that was a funeral hearse. It had three rows of seats and looked like those mobster cars. One time a neighbor boy got a mannequin, and they would stick her legs outside the car and kick her legs as they drove."[4]

How Dan fared through adolescence is a matter of conjecture. His family remembers him as a cheery altar boy playing church at home. When he was a teenager, he was a church deacon and helped the poor in a nearby community of Turley, Oklahoma; it made a big impression on him, his sister recalled.[5]

Others say Dan remembered a difficult childhood and turbulent adolescence, recalling that he dropped into a social cesspool in the streets. "He talked about stealing food as a kid. He used to brag to me that he had been as rough as they come, a member of that infamous local gang named the Dirty Dozen. I heard they killed people," one friend recalled.[6] Maybe; maybe not. Certainly Dan came up with an uncommon knack for profane speech that would have shamed a sailor.

If Dan said he belonged to the Dirty Dozen, he was probably just bragging, said his sister-in-law Anne Allen. "They had a pretty strict upbringing, as far as where they went and what they did. And they definitely did not fight among themselves; they would have been in big trouble with their father. Dan wasn't necessarily one of the guys then—he was so handsome, his looks made him special. He definitely had ideas of his own about what people should and shouldn't do, and he was able to articulate them, but he didn't make a big deal of it. When Dan left home and got into college, he was shocked—mortified—at the immorality he saw," she recalled.[7]

"Dan was very driven, very tough," recalled his high school best friend, Tim Dennehy. "He and two of his brothers, Jack and Ted, were the ones with the tempers. Dan was quick to spark.

"We used to go to ball games at TU [University of Tulsa], and one night some guys—maybe from Will Rogers [High School]—there was one big guy looking for a fight. He was a foot taller than Dan. Somebody said something to Dan, and Dan lit into him and creamed him. The guy was just whimpering. We never had any trouble from them after that."

Poverty? "Well, sure, we were all, or at least most of us, poor," Dennehy said. "My mother died when I was fourteen. I was with her when she died. But we had some good times, Dan and me."

One big thing that saved Dan Allen from the courts was his family. "They were wonderful people," said Dennehy. "Those eight kids adored their parents. They were just plain old blue-collar people. I enjoyed them so much. His dad was a goldsmith, made chalices at Zeigler's. They were wonderful people.

"We all had a very Catholic upbringing. Dan's family was like mine, and we grew up in it—Mom and Dad, his brothers, the Benedictine nuns at St. Francis and Marquette, the priests. It was what we were—it was not a hard trip from the Northside."

But then, nothing much was hard for Dennehy, letterman in football and basketball, senior class treasurer, whose motto in the '49 yearbook was "Keep cool, and you command everyone."

"I knew Dan from the ninth grade," Dennehy said. "I would say we were best friends from 1940 to 1950, when our lives went different ways for a while. He was an average student in school, except he was very good at physics. He and the guys from the Northside were really good mechanics. Dan could fix anything. He was amazing.

"Where he really stood out was in sports, football and fast-pitch softball. He was a hell of

"He was an average student in school, except he was very good at physics. Dan could fix anything." — Tim Dennehy

a ball pitcher, and we had some good teams. He was an excellent football player; he was just ferocious, with that hair-trigger temper. He was a great running back; he lettered three years. He was the football captain, and our senior year we were 8 and 0 to win the Catholic championship. He was a good-looking guy, too, and sometimes that made things pretty complicated."

The girls were always after him; that is how the family remembers it.

"Well," said Dennehy. "We were seniors in 1949, that's when we graduated. And Dan was—he was in a quandary. He had two girl friends, the prettiest girls in the school. He didn't know what the hell to do. Then a guy from Holy Family High School came to Dan and begged him to back off one of them, because he said he was going to marry her. So that got Dan off that hook."

"I went up there with him, and I sat there for an hour and a half and never said one word. And at the end of it, Father Sullivan said, 'I will get you both in seminary in January.' I said, 'Jesus, Father, I'm not going.'"—Tim Dennehy

In the fall of 1949, Dan Allen, Tim Dennehy, and classmate Tom Cody all went to what was then called Oklahoma A&M College in Stillwater. "Dan's parents took us down there," Dennehy recalled. "Dan was enrolled in dairy manufacturing. Why? Because this girlfriend of his, her dad ran a dairy manufacturing plant in Tulsa, and he got Dan a job at the dairy barn."

Dennehy said the boys lived on a thin margin. "We were at this crappy place six blocks from the campus at Stillwater, three of us in one room. It was an old Army shack with one table, two chairs—we had to buy a chair. It rained, it was cold all that September.

"Two other guys who graduated from high school with us were in a Catholic fraternity on campus, and after we had been there about a month, they came down and asked us to pledge a Catholic fraternity. Dan had a job, but the only way we could do it, Cody and I had to borrow the money. Tuition was $45 a semester at that time. I had to borrow $21 from my dad that year, and they let us work in the kitchen, serve meals and do the dishes. That was in September when we pledged the fraternity."

Who could predict what happened next? It was November when Dan said to Dennehy, "Father Sullivan is going to be at the parish at Stillwater Sunday, and I'd like to go up and talk to him about seminary."

"Well, I'll be damned, that's something," Dennehy said.

"Will you come with me?" Dan asked.

"I don't want to go up there," Dennehy said. "I don't want to be a priest. I am not the least bit interested."

"Well, just to be moral support?"

"So," Dennehy remembered, "I went up there with him, and I sat there for an hour and a half and never said one word. And at the end of it, Father Sullivan said, 'I will get you both in seminary in January.' I said, 'Jesus, Father, I'm not going.'

"So Dan finished the semester and went to seminary."

Why? As Dennehy remembers it, it came on Dan suddenly, without explanation. "I don't think anybody will ever know why. One time he told me he had been thinking about it for a year, but I think he made up his mind about seminary that one day.

"So I said to him, 'Our girlfriends are coming from Tulsa at noon. Are you going to tell your girlfriend?' And he knew he had to. Halfway through the movie, Dan and his girlfriend walked out. Jean and I went out there, and his girlfriend told Jean, 'We are going back to Tulsa.' She was really mad. But Dan—I swear, I think he was relieved and happy. That's all I know about it. I think he was being pushed by his girlfriend and her dad."

Had Dan been under religious pressure to become a priest? "Well," said Dennehy. "We got pressure in Catholic school from first grade on, the nuns on the girls and the priests on the guys. From one class, I think forty-nine of fifty people went to seminary. They all left eventually. Cody became a Trappist monk, a brother in a mission down in Chile. So yes, the nuns and priests were encouraging us all to go to seminary. And then, too, seminary was paid tuition."

Dan had the summer off, and he and Tim worked together. "All the people we knew from high school worked downtown, but we worked for Stubby's concessions. They had kiosks around town selling pop. We delivered soda pop and picked up their empties. Dan's brother Jim—the eldest, who had been wounded in the Pacific—did well with Coke. We worked rodeos, sold 15-cent beer. For Stubby's, we slept in the back of the truck."[8]

It was 1950—the beginning of a brave new decade that would bring sweeping change.

"I don't think anybody will ever know why. One time he told me he had been thinking about it for a year, but I think he made up his mind about seminary that one day."
—Tim Dennehy

Top: Tulsa's black community was burned in the 1921 race riot. (*The Nation*, June 29, 1921; Oklahoma Historical Society)

Middle: Farmer Arthur Coble and his sons walk into the face of a dust storm in Cimarron County, Oklahoma. (Arthur Rothstein, photographer, April 1936; Library of Congress)

Bottom: The dust storm on "Black Sunday," April 14, 1935, turned day into night.(www.weru.ksu.edu)

Chapter 3

As Long As Rivers Run

"It's absolutely ridiculous,
with the resources we have in Tulsa,
that we can't solve our problems."

-Dan Allen

Dan Allen's family, with Dan on lower right. Dan Allen family collection.

IT WASN'T AS IF THERE WAS NOT TROUBLE ENOUGH ALREADY IN OKLAHOMA.

In 1930, the year Dan Allen was born, the first black dust storm blew trouble across the middle of America, starting in southwestern Kansas and rolling into Oklahoma. It blocked out the sun, plunging the world into its swirling darkness.

It tumbled like a dark mountain, historians say, driving grit like sandpaper against cheeks and jowls, sneaking into the sheets and cupboards of sod and dugout homes, heaping like a shifting desert over barns and barbed wire. The grinding friction created a storm cloud of static electricity, enough to short out a car, if you should be fortunate enough to own one. In time, repeated storms would choke lungs, clog empty stomachs, and suffocate cattle, children, and old people with deadly dust pneumonia. Even more broadly, the rampaging dust would strip all life from the broken land, wreck entire towns, snuff out entire economies, and ruin lives.

Before, in the time of the buffalo and Native America, the land was anchored by a sea of grass waving in the wind. Some grass, such as the little bluestem, was tall enough to brush horse bellies as white settlers ventured across the treeless plains. When homesteading families brought the plow that broke the plains, they set the stage for the very ground to crumble beneath their feet. Add an extended drought with merciless heat, plus the unending plains winds, and the land took flight.

Over the next decade, the Great American Dust Bowl would cover more than a hundred million acres in six states. It put at least a third of the population of the Great Plains in flight like the soil, more than a quarter-million people on the road hunting a place where they could draw a breath. Despite New Deal transformations in farming practices, the dust storms left wounds that will never be healed. The dust bowl degradation could well be called America's worst natural disaster. [1]

To understand Dan Allen's story, it's important to understand the state where Dan and his family lived.

Dan Allen's story rose against a backdrop of misery, greed, and exploitation of man and nature—and occasional heroic triumph. Poverty and injustice were intimately intertwined throughout the history of this land. And it was not necessarily accidental.

Before white settlers, Native American bands roamed across what became known as Indian Territory. By the late 1830s, they were joined by tribes displaced and reassembled, forcibly, in the great removals and the Trail of Tears. The lands of Indian Territory were promised to Native Americans as long as rivers run.[2]

But westward expansion was unabated. By lottery and land run, section after section was opened to land-hungry settlers who came by the tens of thousands, lured by the promise of free land.[3] Most were white. Early black settlers came, too, often fleeing the oppression of the Deep South.[4] They had this in common: they were chasing the dream of a promised land.

In the early years of the twentieth century, oil was discovered beneath the crust of Indian Territory. Now the story sped up: the land rush became the frenzy of boomtowns, wildcatters and daredevils, Sooners and cutthroat competitors awash in gushers and instant wealth. The rough frontier had only fragments of governance.

Even in the best of times, living could be hard on the cusp of the frontier, where the Allen family would make their home.

It's impossible to understand Dan Allen's home state without knowing about "Alfalfa Bill" Murray. A lawyer who hailed from Toadsuck, Texas, William H. Murray had married a Chickasaw woman and slithered his way into state leadership at the ill-fated 1905 Sequoyah Convention, which tried to establish a State of Sequoyah in Indian Territory. At the Oklahoma Constitutional Convention at Guthrie in 1907, Alfalfa Bill Murray was elected president and etched his angry populist philosophy for all time into the Oklahoma Constitution.[5]

Murray hated banks, big business, Jews, and blacks, but not necessarily in that order. Each state should set aside a reservation county where blacks could live separately but unequally, Murray wrote in a diatribe called *The Negro's Place in the Call of Race*. [6] "If the Creator of races of men had intended them to be equal, he had [sic] not made them so unequal in intellect, in morals, in physical strength, et cetera." [7] Murray was merely echoing the view of many in Oklahoma and the United States.

There were more nuances to the story of Oklahoma. After oil was discovered, promises eroded that were to last as long as water flowed. When Indian Territory became the state of Oklahoma in 1907, a first task was to wrest the land and oil from Native hands, by intermarriage, by legal maneuvers, by trickery, even by murder, if necessary. [8]

"The orgy of exploitation that resulted is almost beyond belief," wrote historian Angie Debo. "Within a generation these Indians, who had owned and governed a region greater in area and potential wealth than many an American state, were almost stripped of their holdings and were rescued from starvation only by public charity." [9]

The dramas of westward expansion played out memorably in Tulsa, where Dan Allen was later to come of age. In many ways, the northeastern Oklahoma town was a mirror of the state and nation.

A nub on the tracks when the 1882 railroad came south, by statehood Tulsa had grown almost overnight to 7,000 souls and was well on its way to becoming the self-proclaimed Oil Capital of the World. [10]

There was a concept called "the Tulsa spirit." Nursed by the Commercial Club and, later, the Chamber of Commerce, town boosters and roustabouts took on audacious challenges. Some amassed tremendous wealth. Need a bridge across the Arkansas River to link the east-side upper crust with the west-side oil fields? No problem, although engineers predicted the bridge would sink into the river sand. "You said we couldn't do it, but we did," bragged a sign when the bridge opened. That pretty much summed up the Tulsa attitude of the early 1900s. [11] "Tulsa, Oklahoma, which would have been a real town, even if its people weren't greasy rich with oil, for it is founded on the spirit of its people," wrote Oklahoma humorist Will Rogers.[12]

But there was a shadowed side, not just in Tulsa but in the rest of the United States.

By the 1920s, Tulsans were spending a million dollars a month on downtown construction. Oil barons were erecting luxurious businesses, churches, and mansions, landscaped and decorated by the finest designers. Indian beads and prairie sod gave way to limestone building blocks, stained glass windows, and polished marble stairways, with fittings of shining brass and gold. Prized art, luxuriant furniture and tapestries, gourmet dining, and fine wines were the order of the day. High-stakes negotiations and unrestrained deal-making were day-to-day occurrences in sumptuous hotels and private clubs. Tulsans created top-quality schools and playgrounds for their children, lovely shops for their wives, and one of the best water systems in the world—and all of it almost overnight, as a city rose that was far above the days when cattle ran loose through the town and horse droppings and sewage mingled in the knee-deep mud of frontier streets.[13] "Indian and white man, Jew and Gentile, Catholic and Protestant, we worked side by side, shoulder to shoulder, and under these conditions the Tulsa spirit was born and has lived, and God grant that it never dies," said booster Tate Brady. [14]

But there was a shadowed side, not just in Tulsa but in the rest of the United States. This remarkable town also had a deep well of high-class, well-heeled racism and greed. There were even people who believed that

Tulsa's wealth was built on the broken backs of exploited under classes. West of the river was reserved for oil-field workers' tar-paper shacks; the Greenwood district north of the railroad tracks, for people of color. These segregated living patterns would haunt Tulsa for all its history, causing incalculable harm; in time, they might well spell the city's doom.

Of course, Jim Crow was alive and well in Tulsa, as elsewhere. Intricate maneuvers effectively disenfranchised the black population in 1910. [15] Non-white Tulsans were not welcomed into hotels or restaurants south of the railroad tracks. "Whites only" signs on drinking fountains and rest-rooms were the way of life. Separated by law, restrictive covenant[16] and exclusionary custom, black Tulsans created a second city, with their own schools (separated by state constitution), [17] churches, neighborhoods, and business districts.

If law and custom could not keep down unruly classes, perhaps vigilante justice could do the job. The Knights of Liberty rose during World War I, garbed in black masks and robes, to enforce patriotism with lash and tar. [18] The lash was supplemented by the noose: In 1921, fifty-nine blacks were lynched in southern or border states. [19] It was not a long stretch from black robes to white, with the rise of the Ku Klux Klan.

It took only a nudge, a shot, and a torch to spark Tulsa's infamous 1921 race riot. In a wink of time, white mobs were burning and looting "Little Africa." Within hours, the Greenwood district was a burned-out shell. "Overnight, over one thousand homes occupied by blacks had been de-stroyed in Tulsa," wrote historian Scott Ellsworth. "The Greenwood district had been put to the torch. The city had been placed under martial law. Many, both black and white, had died or were wounded." [20] The number of black deaths is uncertain, and estimates range from scores to hundreds. Some historians believe the Tulsa race riot was the worst in American history.

The riot was used effectively to build membership in the Ku Klux Klan, fat in its Twenties' resurgence around the nation and in the throes of its multipurpose war against immigrants, Catholics, Jews, and persons of color or questionable moral character. The KKK fraternity was the place to be in 1922, '23, '24, and '25. At its zenith, 10 percent of Oklahoma's eligible population joined the KKK, including many (maybe most) of Tulsa's establishment who believed cleaning up lawless towns required extra-legal extremes. [21]

It is important to know that the post-riot rebuilding of North Tulsa set the stage for long-term living conditions of squalor. People rebuilt with what they could gather, wherever and however they could. [22] Some see a darker cause and effect for the black ghetto. "The chamber's plan was to fill Greenwood with 'cheap shacks ... because when the proper time comes to condemn it [for industrial use], it will be possible to finance the proceedings," wrote historian Danney Goble, citing chamber minutes of the day. "For the same reason, the city thereafter ignored its own housing and sanitary codes in Greenwood." [23] Tulsa's oil-baron era in the Roaring Twenties brought one city unimaginable wealth and lavish excess. In her shadows, in that second city, hardship was the rule.

In October 1929, the stock market crashed, eventually plunging the world into economic chaos. [24] The bubble had been swelled by years of boom and binge. "We spent six years of wild buying on credit (everything under the sun, whether we needed it or not) and now we are having to pay for 'em under Mr. Hoover," wrote Will Rogers in 1930. [25]

The Dust Bowl and the Great Depression compounded misery for the poor in Oklahoma. German immigrants had come to No Man's Land with turkey red wheat (and some incidental thistle) sewn into their vest pockets. Soon water wells punched far beneath the surface to tap the vast underground lake named Ogallala, and then wheat ruled the plains. [26]

When the stock market crashed, the wheat and oil markets were not far behind. [27] What was left was that incidental thistle, which had grown and spread to become omnipresent tumbleweed. That was fortunate for the dusters who stayed put, since they discovered they could can thistles in brine. When they ran out of jackrabbit and rattlesnake, and when the only alternative was starvation, it was possible—although not pleasant—to eat tumbleweed. [28]

In Tulsa, the poor bore the brunt of it.

For some in Tulsa, things improved with some combination of time, the New Deal, and World War II. By the late1940s, builders were hastily framing up cheap, mass-produced neighborhoods that fanned out across the countryside—especially in far north, northeast, and west Tulsa—to serve wartime workers, returning veterans, and the predicted post-war nirvana. [29]

The 1950s would be comfortable years for that first Tulsa —white, south and east. They called it "America's most beautiful city."

Chapter 4

Let Justice Roll

"Basically, the civil rights movement of the 1960s was an effort
to restore the original sense of justice and at-one-ment . . .
In the original sense, justice and caritas (love and charity) were one
and the same action. Gradually people began to separate the two.
Justice became more and more a matter of codes (laws),
and hence people had rights only if they were protected by law.
Justice got lost in the shuffle. Charity came to mean what they 'who have'
give to the 'have nots' (which) fosters paternalism
and the separation of people in a society. . . .
Justice and charity are one and the same action."

—Dan Allen

Dan Allen holding ordination chalice, with his parents. Dan Allen family collection.

THE RECORDS OF DAN'S TWO DECADES AFTER HIGH SCHOOL ARE SCATTERED.

Here and there—from among his papers—can be found shards that, pieced together, create a rickety framework of the years that shaped a boy into a man.

Imagine memorabilia of a life thrown into an old trunk. Drag things out, one at a time—old yellowed news clippings, brittle and shattering with age; faded mimeographed documents; a bit of ribbon encircling letters and cards; postcards; some coins; dog-eared photographs.

Ah! The photos. The images best tell the tale. Here is the star football player—Number 55—kicking so high, his knee hits his nose. The suave young man dancing with a girl; then posing like a debonair model on campus, one hand jauntily in a pocket, wearing a patterned argyle sweater and sly grin. And then—

Standing, the earnest young man is leaning over an elevated desk, reading intently. He is slender, with close-cropped black hair. He is wearing a floor-length black cassock with a white clerical collar. Another image taken at the same time shows him staring boldly into the camera, chin high, hands behind his black-garbed back.

Even more remarkable—here is a choir of fifteen young men, dressed all in white. Each has a satin scarf draped over his arm, wearing embroidered trim and crosses, tassels, clerical collars, and white floor-length robes edged in various lacey designs. Each has his hands folded upward in prayer, and each is staring solemnly toward the camera, in holy contemplation—except for one. Middle of the front row: a good looking Irishman with a devilish grin.

Here's another of that Irishman and his parents. The picture is dim, but their pride shines through. And more— rows of white men in black with white collars; then a pyramid of fifteen young graduates in black robes and mortar boards.

A flash of time—the remnants of a life, told in shades of black and white.[1]

It was January 1950 when Dan Allen entered St. John's Catholic Seminary in Little Rock, Arkansas, beginning what would be more than eight years of theological study.[2]

Once he got to seminary, Allen became an excellent student, said his friend Tim Dennehy. "He was very well read. . . . Dan kept up on all the Martin Luther King stuff. He really knew it well. I think that's when he got the social justice part of his beliefs—in seminary, in his reading about the civil rights movement. He decided he wanted to walk with Martin Luther King."[3]

Dan's religious education occurred during years of revolutionary change in the United States. As the nation convulsed, the dramas touched a young Dan Allen.

> *1953: Dan received his B.A. shortly before the landmark Brown versus Board of Education decision ordered desegregation of America's schools.*

> *1955: As Dan was branching out in his studies, a seamstress named Rosa Parks refused to move to the back "colored section" of a Montgomery bus, triggering a bus boycott that lasted for more than a year until buses were desegregated at the end of 1956. A leader in that boycott was a Baptist minister, the Reverend Martin Luther King.*

> *1957: As Dan prepared for the priesthood, the civil rights movement was heating to a boil. Arkansas governor Orval Faubus blocked black students from entering Little Rock High School until President Eisenhower sent in federal troops. Martin Luther King and others established the Southern Christian Leadership Conference, which spearheaded a civil rights move-ment based on principles of nonviolence and civil disobedience. "We must forever conduct our struggle on the high plane of dignity and discipline," King said.[4]*

On May 25, 1957, Dan Allen was ordained as a Roman Catholic priest at Our Lady's Cathedral in Oklahoma City. Eugene J. McGuinness, bishop for the Oklahoma City–Tulsa diocese, officiated. At 9:00 a.m. Sunday, the next day, Father Dan's first mass was sung at St. Francis Xavier Catholic Church in Tulsa, where he had attended grammar school.[5] Among his papers, Dan saved an avalanche of congratulatory cards and letters.

His official portrait looks spiritual, a dark-eyed young priest staring toward some distant truth, this time with only a hint of a smile. His family gathered for the service. When he celebrated his first mass, he used a golden chalice made by his father, the gold spinner. Embedded into its base, at the point where Dan's fingers grasped it, was his mother's gold wedding band.[6]

Later that year, Father Dan officiated at his first wedding ceremony for his good friend Tim Dennehy.[7]

An important change occurred in March of 1958, when Victor J. Reed was installed as bishop of the Oklahoma diocese. Reed was destined to have a dramatic influence on Dan Allen's life—all the more so because Reed's service years included those of major upheaval and change in the church, when Pope John XXIII convened the Second Ecumenical Council known as Vatican II, October 1962–November 1965.[8]

"John XXIII was this little pope with a big nose, a funny little dumpy guy," remembered Father Bill Skeehan. "They voted him in thinking he would not live very long. But they didn't understand what they voted in. He moved quickly to revamp the entire church. And the people who went to the council were educated and changed. Bishop Reed was one of those at Vatican II, and he began to revolutionize the Oklahoma diocese. Tulsa was unique because Reed set up a Little Council that was modeled after the one in Rome, and every parish sent participants a couple of times a year. Bishop Reed was the greatest bishop we ever had. And he liked Dan Allen."[9]

> *1960: Four black college students began a sit-in at a Greensboro, North Carolina, Woolworth's lunch counter that refused service to non-whites. The idea of sit-ins soon spread to other communities.*

Skeehan was ordained in 1960. He and Dan were both assigned to Sacred Heart Catholic Church in Oklahoma City, where they served as associate pastors for three years. The priest was Msgr. S. F. Luecke. "The monsignor would send us off; he didn't really know what to do with us," Skeehan said.

"We went everywhere, all around Oklahoma and around the country," Father Skeehan said. "They sent us to Catholic girls schools in Philadelphia and Chicago and elsewhere, recruiting girls who would give a year of their time to education and service, kind of like a domestic Catholic Peace Corps. It was the first time lay women had that kind of voice in the church."

Skeehan remembered a visit to a prominent East Coast girls' school with an Order of the Holy Child when, in the midst of a formal social discussion, Dan piped up: "Sister, there isn't one." What? "There isn't a Holy Child. He grew up and died." Skeehan said the nuns were shocked speechless until Dan's grin showed them he was teasing. He charmed the sisters, and the priests were invited back again.[10]

> *1961: The Southern Christian Leadership Conference (SCLC), the Student Nonviolent Coordinating Committee (SNCC, pronounced "Snick"), and the Congress of Racial Equality (CORE)*

*sponsored more than 1,000 Freedom Riders, black and white
volunteers, who tested public accommodation laws throughout the
South. In Washington, D.C., a Catholic boy from a large family was
sworn in as president of the United States.*

John Kennedy became a magnet for Dan, pulling him out of a past where
Catholics were stigmatized in Oklahoma, thrusting him forward to future
endeavors beyond what he could have dreamed.[11]

Dan sent a postcard to his parents, postmarked 1961, showing an aerial
view of Notre Dame University. "Cold here," he wrote in hasty printing.
"All is going okay. Will be anxious to get back on the job, though." Dan
had been honored by being selected to study at Notre Dame to further his
education, a friend remembered.[12]

> *1962: In Tulsa, police were dragging protestors from sit ins at
> Piccadilly and Borden's restaurants.[13]*

Father Dan became a teacher, the calling he would follow the rest of his life
in one fashion or another. He was on the faculty of Mount St. Mary's High
School in Oklahoma City. A yellowed clipping shows a handsome, smiling
Irish boy in clerical collar, identified as the diocesan director of youth, a
position Dan held for a number of years.[14] Another postcard, postmarked
in 1963, says he was making the rounds from Canon City, Colorado, to
Colorado Springs, to Chicago.[15]

> *1963: The civil rights cauldron was boiling. Dr. King was jailed
> in Birmingham, where Sheriff Bull Conner used fire hoses and
> police dogs on black demonstrators. Those images of brutality
> produced worldwide sympathy for the civil rights movement, and the
> nation was lulled by the thought that nonviolence was an effective
> way to bring about change. Then, in June, Mississippi's NAACP
> field secretary, Medgar Evers, was murdered. In August, 200,000
> people heard Dr. King deliver his "I have a dream" speech in
> Washington. In September four young girls were killed in a
> Birmingham church bombing. Before the year ended, President
> Kennedy would be dead.*

"Dan was active in a lot of things in those days," remembered Father
James McGlinchey. "Religious education, different things. Dan was at

Sacred Heart and then Mount St. Mary's high school, where he was a counselor. Even in those days, Dan had his own gifts. He was a gifted man who
could talk to people in very plain language. He could do things with
teachers, religious educators. Dan had a way of reducing theological con-
cepts into everyday language, in a very colloquial way. He was good at it."

The young priests were strongly influenced by one of their group, Bob
McDole, McGlinchey said. "He was a true pioneer in the civil rights movement in Oklahoma City and was participating in the demonstrations and
sit-ins. He changed us. Bishop Reed was a very forward-looking man, and he
encouraged us to be involved and was very permissive and understanding."[16]

> *1964: Malcolm X was assassinated February 21. Dr. King focused
> on Alabama, where blacks had long been denied voting rights and
> were subjected to particularly cruel intimidation, even death. In early
> March, six hundred set out to march the 54 miles from Selma to
> Montgomery to petition Alabama governor George Wallace to
> protect blacks who sought to register to vote.*

> *On March 7 — "Bloody Sunday" —the Selma marchers were
> assaulted on the Edmund Pettus Bridge by troopers on horseback who
> charged the crowd with whips, nightsticks, and tear gas. The
> horrifying images of bloodied protestors flashed around the world.
> King issued a call for clergy and citizens to come to Selma and join
> him in a second march.*

> *On March 9, King led a symbolic march of 2,500 back to Edmund
> Pettus Bridge but obeyed a court injunction and did not cross. He
> began planning a third march when the injunction could be lifted.
> That night, three white ministers from the march were attacked and
> beaten; one died.*

"We were on spring break, so we decided to head on down to Selma,"
remembered McGlinchey.

In a rare moment of concern for protocol, Skeehan suggested that the trip
might be a bad idea. "I told Dan, 'I'm not sure how the church will react.'
And Dan said, 'If I do it on my vacation, they can't say anything.'"

"There were five of us," McGlinchey said. "Dan Allen, Bill Rath, Paul
Donovan, Paul Gallatin, and me—and we drove nonstop, I think about
seventeen hours. When we stopped for gasoline, we would jockey to see
who would get stuck in the middle seat in the back. We were young and

idealistic, and we knew a bit about the church documents, Vatican II, and some of our social teachings that I think motivated us in a sense. Of course, Bob McDole was already down there and he influenced us, too. In a clumsy way, we all had a vision about what was going on in the society. We saw the discrimination and injustice of it, and Bishop Reed didn't have any objections. Somehow we just knew it was the right thing to do."

They had no idea what they would find. Images were fresh of Bull Conner's dogs and Bloody Sunday. But they found it peaceful. They stayed in a Catholic hospital in the black ghetto with its dirt streets and shanties. "We met people from all walks of life, and there was a wonderful communality; everybody was there for all the right reasons," McGlinchey said. "We were insignificant, but we were able to see that the people who were running things were very smart. They had a lot of things going on, court injunctions, negotiations that stretched to Washington, lots of delays. It was very important that it be a peaceful march, but it could have exploded into something disastrous.

"We saw Martin Luther King at a distance. He was such an orator. We were part of some gatherings."

Then spring break was over, and they had to return to Oklahoma, again driving nonstop. They were five tired priests, changed forever.

"This experience was, for all of us, like nothing else in our lives, before or since," McGlinchey said. "It was a conversion experience—a conversion to justice. We could sense that there was something going on here that would change our lives. But most of all, it was an awakening for Dan. He really lit up. It opened up a bigger world for him than just the church and teaching. Even as we were driving home, we could feel it working on him—like yeast, like leaven. It was the turning point in his life."[17]

> *March 15, 1965: Dr. King called for revolutionary change, quoting the Prophet Amos: "Let Justice roll down like waters in a mighty stream."*[18]

> *March 21, 1965: King led a third march from Selma that made it to Montgomery. President Johnson had nationalized the state troopers and proposed the landmark Voting Rights Act. It was the watershed point of the civil rights movement. On March 25, King mounted the steps of the Alabama Capitol to declare: "The end we seek is a society at peace with itself, a society that can live with its conscience. . . .I know you are asking today, how long will it take? I come to say to you this afternoon, however difficult the moment,*

however frustrating the hour, it will not be long, because the arc of the moral universe is long, but it bends toward justice."[19] *Within three years, Dr. King would be dead.*

Back in Oklahoma, Dan and Skeehan were assigned to Bishop Reed's experimental program to provide religious education for church members—a direct outgrowth of the Vatican II sharing of leadership with lay Catholics. The Extension Lay Volunteer program was revolutionary, for its time.

Allen was assigned to work with Mary Christie, and Skeehan was assigned to work with Elizabeth McMahan. The young women were religious educators assigned to Oklahoma from the East Coast, part of an amazing lurch forward of women's roles in the church. The bishop assigned the extension teams to offer lay religious education.[20]

The girls were very attractive, Don McCarthy remembered. Their photos show young women, in their early twenties, with dark hair and clear eyes, strikingly beautiful.[21]

Both women are included in a photo, found among Dan's papers, that shows a gathering of handsome young people on a summer evening by a campfire. It is titled "The camp-fire counselors of '66." Five young women, three young men. Most are laughing and teasing. But to the far left is a suntanned Irishman with black curly hair, mid-thirties, in plaid shorts and dark tee shirt with a strip of white collar. He is perched on his tennis-shoed toes, with cupped hands outstretched. A guess would be that he is teaching, with an urgent message to share. He is smiling but remarkable for his intensity. One thing is clear: the boy had become a man.[22]

"The bishop sent teams out to educate us poor Catholics," Don McCarthy said. "They saw there was a shortage of priests and nuns coming, so they wanted to educate us to take the place of priests and sisters on Sundays when needed. I think Dan and Mary had the northern half of the state, and Skeehan and Liz had the southern half."

An undated *Tulsa World* article describes one activity: "the first adult education program in the history of Catholic churches in the Tulsa area." The Tulsa classes started on Monday nights in January, probably somewhere in 1965 or 1966. Dan and Mary were teaching "Salvation and how best to teach it." Father Dan was cited as diocese youth director and a teacher at St. Mary's High School, Mary as a member of the Apostolate of Diocesan Catechists.[23]

"My wife Carmen and I attended the classes," McCarthy said. "The first night, we thought Mary was very attractive but that she didn't know anything. She was about twenty-five. Well, she set us straight that first week.

She taught us how to develop classes and teach kids, and Dan taught about what the gospels really meant—not just going to church on Sunday but more of a liberation theology, more of helping people pay their bills and keep a stable family. I think there were more than a hundred people taking the class. We could all feel the same vibrations going through the class, getting more and more enthused. As we took it, we could feel Dan's view changing. We finished the first year and enrolled right then for the second year."

Dan was working out his philosophy and vision, class by class, as he spoke, McCarthy said. "We could see Neighbor for Neighbor just about as well as he could after that second semester. He had built up a clientele of enriched volunteers who would gladly work at NFN. That's how we got involved, the whole bunch of us."[24]

There are several versions of Dan's next move, with most accounts saying he was assigned to Tulsa's St. Jude Catholic Church in 1966. On January 28 of that year, *The Oklahoma Courier* reported he was training teachers through the Diocesan Office of Religious Education.[25] A September 9, 1966, article from the state Catholic newspaper shows him still pastor of St. Camillus Church at Marshall, Oklahoma; he and Mary were helping move the religious education office.[26]

Despite many accounts that he moved in 1966, Dan sometimes placed the move in the spring of 1967, sometimes earlier. (He was not much interested in time-date precision.) The assignment was part of Bishop Reed's ambitious social action agenda, which included creating a Little Council in Oklahoma in June 1967, to mirror Vatican II. Council members were working to re-create the Catholic Church as a servant church, focused on breaking the cycle of poverty: "Suggestions . . . are to get involved with minority group people and poor people as individuals . . . and to continuously speak to the white middle-class population to help cure their hatred and prejudice."[27]

Here is the way Dan remembered it in one newsletter article he wrote a decade later:

> The *Tulsa World*, dated June of 1967 in an article entitled "One Church, 4 Stations," describes an experimental effort on the part of the Diocese of Oklahoma to engage four Catholic parishes, two black and two white, to form one entity for the welfare of the total community. The following is an excerpt from the same article:

"With other groups and churches the parishes have been active in the establishment of a credit union, cooperative buying clubs, restoration of cars for transportation, all of which allows consumers to purchase at lower prices. Out of this they think may come cooperative stores among the indigent. . . . St. Jude has spearheaded a 'Neighbor for Neighbor' program."[28]

The endeavor started modestly, by aiding two needy families[29] but grew rapidly. Poor people began to flow in the door of St. Jude church like a mighty river of needs. It was perhaps providential that St. Jude is the patron saint for desperate cases and lost causes.

Chapter 5

Neighbor *for* Neighbor

"The key word in the concept of Neighbor for Neighbor is *for*.
It's what love is in the New Testament:
to become one for the many, for their sake, without any conditions.

In the NFN logo, the F is represented by a symbol of the Eucharist (a chalice).

I believe that taking our faith seriously means that we have to make damn sure
that society's "rejects" become part of and experience the Good News."

—Dan Allen

Checking the fit at NFN. Les McClelland photo, *Tulsa Magazine*, November 1977.

THE ONLY ROLE OF THE BELIEVER WAS TO PUT THEMSELVES BETWEEN THE OPPRESSED AND THE OPPRESSOR. PERIOD.

"I had been down to Selma," Dan remembered later, "and I knew before I went that I was going to return to Tulsa. And I had really settled in my own mind that it was time for me to do what I was telling the students to do, . . . what I'd been teaching for years at the college level."

Dan shifted in his chair and lit another cigarette. Beneath his rumpled plaid flannel shirt, he looked a bit tight through the shoulders, not so much at ease now talking to the CBS cameras for yet another documentary—this one for the Ford Foundation—but his old friend Al Cox was interviewing, and Dan's words were strong.

"So when I came here, I had long ago intellectually realized that the fundamental and only role of the believer was to put themselves between the oppressed and the oppressor. Period."

Well, fine—but how to do that?

Always the educator, Dan seized the tools of unity, justice, and caritas (love and charity) and wielded them simultaneously for a kind of open-heart surgery on individuals and institutions.

"During those days of John XXIII, you know, conformity was out the window and people were treated like, thank God, they might have brains. . . . You know, can make up their own minds. We knew that we'd been out of it for years just playing the ritual game. And so we came here, two black churches, two white churches, and the whole concept was to bring those entities into one union in order to serve the greater community of north Tulsa. . . .

"With that in mind, in those days ecumenism was very strong, . . . Protestants, Catholics, Unitarians, the whole smear, and all the diverse races," he remembered. With the goal of intervening between oppressed and oppressors, he began speaking out while also uniting churches and volunteers to launch direct services to the poor.

"We simply started taking on the issues and coupled [them] with the services so that you wouldn't have charity over here and legalism for the sense of justice. But you'd have justice and caritas, or charity, into one single action, you know, not separate.

"And that's what we've been trying to do." [1]

With Neighbor for Neighbor, everything was experimental and unconventional, as precarious as the lives of the poor, salvaged from chaos only by a mesmerizing vision and relentless dark humor. Dare to try this. If it doesn't work, learn and discard. If it works, build on it and spin it off for others to manage and claim the credit. The management was jazz-band at best; the methods were fluid; but the mission was clear, fixed, and fierce. Rising from the serendipity and untidiness of it all, what evolved, then, was a series of bold, clean, elegant swipes at poverty and injustice.

NFN dated its beginning back to around Thanksgiving 1967, although Dan sometimes cited varying dates for its inception.

"In 1966, when I was assigned pastor at St. Jude's," Dan recalled later, "I came here as part of a team for two black and two white churches. Our team tried to bring these four parishes into a unit to jointly address the problems of social injustice and the tremendous racial tensions in this area of Tulsa.

"Since the 1930s, blacks had been restricted to an area about three miles south [of NFN]. But following legislation that opened things up, the black community in the 1960s was migrating north into this area. This led to white flight with horrendous negative effects."

Bishop Reed was challenging convention to pair the four churches across a wide racial divide. Even as late as the 1960s, Tulsans spoke of race only in backroom whispers. Open discussion of the 1921 riot, in particular, was embargoed, for fear open discussion might spark another "colored" riot. In 1967, a newspaper reporter tried to cite the riot's destruction as one cause of Northside housing problems, but editors changed riot to "a big fire."[2]

The team of fathers, Lee O'Neil, Babe O'Brien, Jim McGlinchey, and Dan Allen, tried to address poverty, Dan said, "but we also spent a lot of energy building an ecumenical base. We got together with 24 area churches and congregations from probably 15 denominations—Protestants and Jews."[3]

The first NFN organizational meeting was chaired by Jack Helton, a stalwart volunteer who later became director of Tulsa County Social Services and spearheaded the credit counseling service. Another charter member was Wilbert Collins.[4]

The group initially focused on providing food and basic services to the poor. "But from the beginning, the idea was not to run simply a charity, but to integrate charity and justice into one," Dan said. "If you separate them, you end up with paternalism or legalism.

"We formed a group of 15 people to lay the foundations for a more focused program that would address both the injustices at the political level and the physical needs of people who are poor. That's what led to the founding of Neighbor for Neighbor."[5]

Within a year, the caseload had grown to 450 families. By New Year's 1969, NFN had aided 900 families, for a total cost of under $17,000—all donated. "Run more on faith than good business principles," wrote the *Tulsa Tribune*, NFN's estimated expenses averaged 23 cents per man, woman, and child. The tally for its first year: Food given to 476 families, utility help for 53, housing for 62. Jobs found for 64, medical help for 96, furniture for 215, clothing for 365, loans for 316, legal aid for 252. And volunteers repaired and gave away 132 donated automobiles.[6]

"NFN doesn't ask why, it asks how," Allen said. "We change the attitude of the poor by making them aware of their potential. And we're changing the attitude of the affluent. Their contact with the poor makes them aware they have created these people; therefore, they can recreate justice in the society for the poor and in their own environment."[7]

"In those early days, we matched up with a family," Pat Flanagan recalled.[8] "One family unit to another family unit," as Dan said at the time, "the idea being there isn't anybody who doesn't have something someone else needs, be it talents or skills—no matter how poor they are. The basic concept is that one family becomes the agency for another. Each family is the assisting agency and resource."[9]

"When I went out to Neighbor for Neighbor, he looked me over and said I was not fitted for the work and to go home." — Pat Flanagan

In Dan's curious way, he challenged Pat. "Now, I was intellectually a liberal but had never gotten my hands dirty and I had never seen poverty up close," Pat said. "Dan changed all that.

"When I went out to Neighbor for Neighbor, he looked me over and said I was not fitted for the work and to go home. He was really rude to me. And I said, 'I will do this.' So he gave me a family's name and told me two things. 'Remember that the need determines the response.' I forget the other one."

Pat went to meet the family. There was no visible father. The woman was only twenty-four but had seven children, including two sets of twins. They were sleeping on a mattress on the floor.

"The mattress was horrible," Pat said. "All she wanted was a new mattress. You could see they needed everything. Her name was Eileen—I did a painting of her face later on. I was determined to get that mattress, period, so I could go back and tell that damned Dan Allen that I did it."

Pat found somebody to donate a mattress, and NFN told her to connect with a guy named Charles to haul it. "Charles said, 'New mattress? Sure.' So I gave him Eileen's address. But damned if Charles didn't rip off the mattress.

"So I found where he lived and went over there and read him the riot act. He thought I was funny at first; why should he care what I thought? I said I was not going to end it there. I would go to the police, whatever it took. Well, finally he agreed and gave the mattress back.

"That was my introduction."

Pat stayed to work with families for years, later taking on a number of projects for NFN, too. She was the first woman on the NFN board, in the early 1970s.

"Dan didn't upend my life the way my death experience did, but he taught me the way to go. I don't think he ever really changed much; I'm not sure he was much different from the beginning to the end. He was still being rude and telling people they were full of it when they came in. I think it was a teaching tool, really; a test. Some people never came back, but he made sure the strong ones were worth having around.

"Dan was an educator. 'That's my job, to educate people,' he always said. He wanted to foster understanding to facilitate systematic change. It doesn't help to give somebody gas money if the people running the gas company are evil. Unless you are changing the system, nothing is ever going to change. It's a lofty goal.

"He did a lot of odd things. That was part of his charm."[10]

Pat Flanagan and Sandra Downie came together when they were cochairs of the Social Action Committee of Christ the King, which was Tulsa's elite Catholic church in those days.

Sandra was a matron with three young children, married to an attorney at the time. She had a soft face framed by brown waves of hair, a keen intuitive intellect, and a good heart. Her mind moved so fast that sometimes she talked in a kind of code, and her voice sometimes dropped below hearing level as she struggled for confidence, but she had a natural flair for organization and fierce determination. Sandra was searching earnestly for ways to improve the world. She and Pat Flanagan were a good team.

Christmas was coming; this would have been probably 1968 or '69. What could the Christ the King social action committee do to help those in need? They knew there were mothers who needed food for their families, fathers who needed warm gloves, little children who needed Christmas toys.

Sandra took the lead in raising money for Christmas baskets filled to the brim with food, toys, and other goodies. They were beautiful, tastefully outfitted, a labor of love. Just before Christmas, she loaded her car with the baskets and called Neighbor for Neighbor. Could she bring Christmas baskets there to be distributed?

The man who answered was brief. No, hell no. Don't you understand, he yelled. These people are poor all year, not just at Christmas! He slammed down the phone.

"It was the beginning of my religious education," Sandra said.[11]

Dan's brand of religious education was not easy. When Gloria Caldwell, a member of the Tulsa League of Women Voters, first heard Dan in the late 1960s, she was a Methodist, head of her church's education committee. Gloria, a tall handsome woman, had a liberal heart burning beneath her quiet, conservative façade.

"There was a lot of ecumenical fervor in those days," Gloria recalled. "I said to my education committee, we need to join together with other churches and put on community forums for this area of town—essentially, the near Northside.

"We put on four forums on issues of the day such as poverty. I have forgotten three of them. At the fourth one, Dan Allen came to speak. He talked about the new group named Neighbor for Neighbor, and he talked about their mission," Gloria said.

As she listened, Gloria thought, "That is a church. That is more of a church than my own."

Thus inspired, Gloria tried to raise some money from her church for Neighbor for Neighbor. "I begged and I pleaded, without success. No one was interested, but I wouldn't give up. Finally I wore them down to give me $100 for NFN. It was a great triumph.

"But the next thing I knew, my church decided to spend $3000 on new pew cushions. There was no debate, no begging, no question about the priorities. And at that point, I left the Methodist Church."[12]

What kind of people were coming to NFN for help?
A mother, forty-two, with terminal cancer and seven children ages fourteen to two. The kids couldn't start school because they had no shoes. When NFN learned of the situation, the children were in rags and there was no food in the house. The mother was in a hospital and might not leave it alive, Dan reported. Where was the father? Who knows? The kids were being cared for by an aunt who was penniless and had small children of her own. "The proper government agencies have been notified," Allen said, "but

they often get snarled up in red tape. These kids need help now."

Neighbor for Neighbor was depending entirely on "the kindness, generosity, and consciences of people in the Tulsa area," wrote a *Tulsa World* reporter. "If you'd like to help, contact Father Allen. You'll get more out of it than you put in."[13]

A family of eight with an injured, unemployed father, living in a two-room house. After the *Tulsa World* wrote about the family, the community response was swift. "There were 80 calls in the first two days," Allen reported. "They received food, beds, a refrigerator, clothing, and $550 in donations." NFN helped the father get a job. Many people drove to NFN with donated goods, and a dozen people volunteered to help NFN. "This could develop into something big with the help of the entire community," Dan said. "There is no danger of oversubscription. We have many families listed in need, and we can use almost anything someone else doesn't want."[14]

People trying to get on their feet. NFN volunteers created classes for poor women in grooming, home management, physical fitness, sewing, and cooking. Their children were cared for in a learning center, too. "In other programs," said a pretty young mother named Ruth, "you get the feeling they don't want you to better yourself. If you get a job, they don't want you to make too much. If you get ahead, they punish you for it. But here, they understand. They'll help you as long as you need it, no questions asked. Somehow, they find a way. They believe in you."[15]

People who were hungry. When there was enough food, NFN established a free grocery store. Donated food came from everywhere. For example, Don McCarthy drove by a Wonder Bread bakery every week and came to Neighbor for Neighbor with a station wagon full of day-old bread.[16]

Families with disabilities. One young family of five lived in a condemned shack, barely 300 square feet, so open to the wind that it was nearly impossible to keep a match lighted to start the unvented gas stove. The father was unemployed, unschooled, untrained for anything except menial jobs, and handicapped by a speech impediment that made communication almost impossible. NFN took up paying their $65-a-month rent while searching for longer-term help for them.[17]

People who were cold. "Our most pressing problem," Dan said, "is that there are more poor people seeking help than there are people volunteering to help. We need people to man our truck, to drive people to doctors, to work in our warehouses. Winter is approaching, and we need heavy coats, blankets, and shoes—especially for children. People need help with heating bills."

Callers sometimes asked whether applicants were white or black. Neighbor for Neighbor is color-blind, Allen said. "The majority of poor persons in Tulsa are white. But we're only concerned with poor people and how to help them—nothing else."[18]

Many families who came to NFN for help were caught in a squeeze by unexpected illness or other financial crises, Allen said. "We've been able to keep a lot of people off welfare. . . . "We don't accept an impoverished family for help until we have a counseling volunteer family to relate to them."[19]

He estimated that there were 16,000 Tulsa families with incomes below the federal poverty guideline of $3,000 a year. Eighty percent of them were white, he said. Many of those helped by NFN were earning just over $1 an hour for menial work.[20]

NFN worked, wrote a *Tulsa World* reporter, because volunteers were matched well with jobs such as repairing old cars, tutoring students, repairing houses, delivering furniture, and helping distribute donated food.

The rolls of volunteers were growing and included housewives, professionals, teachers, and church members from across the city. Students at the University of Tulsa were spending Saturday afternoons tutoring youngsters at St. Jude church. "We have firemen who spend their days off working out here," Allen said. "They find housing for those who need it. They locate furniture that someone might need. They try to find jobs for kids in the Neighborhood Youth Corps. All kind of things."

Churches were asking their congregations to contribute food regularly to a "living basket" that stocked a commissary. The demand for food was a constant struggle, consistent across all spectrums of need.

"People get hungry more than at Thanksgiving and Christmas," Allen said. "We keep the food here at the church and let them come in and pick out what they need. We let them at least have the dignity of planning their own meals."

In a trailer parked out on the back lot, Wilbert Collins was operating a little credit union, offering short-term emergency loans at a low interest rate. It was a branch office of the anti-poverty credit union that went by the unwieldy name of TEOTF—the Tulsa Economic Opportunity Task Force, part of Lyndon Johnson's Great Society program.[21]

The unconventional approach of Dan Allen to his Neighbor for Neighbor mission captured the fancy of the local news media. It could be argued that the news media made NFN; certainly Dan knew intuitively that his success hinged on public education through the mass media. Reporters generally loved him, and he spared no effort to keep them intrigued.

In addition to countless local media accounts, Dan also won some national and international notice. CBS, for example, did at least three broadcasts about NFN. "CBS was looking for how to deal with poverty at the local level," recalled Clayton Vaughn, the dean anchor of Tulsa's CBS affiliate KOTV. "They selected Dan because NFN was unique—and I use unique in its exact definition, one of a kind—in America. His essential idea was to help anybody and in return that person helps others. Here was a man who didn't have a lot of resources [or] material worth, all he had was the power of persuasion and conviction that if we work together and care about each other, everybody will benefit. His primary contribution was the firm belief that if one person helps another, both will benefit."[22]

"His essential idea was to help anybody and in return that person helps others."

Of the many reporters and editors who wrote or spoke about NFN over the years, none was more influential than Beth Macklin, the venerable church editor at the *Tulsa World*. A local icon in her own right, Beth quickly grasped the importance of the NFN philosophy, and she led the first wave of reporters who, story by story, educated the public about poverty and prejudice. Few knew that Beth, who famously worked far into the nights and often slept at her *World* desk, was driven by her own epiphany: Her husband died when she was young, and Beth saw no reason to live. "I was going to kill myself," she once told a friend, "but decided, instead, to spend the rest of my life giving myself away." In days of creative turmoil and community change, hers was an invaluable gift.[23]

In part because of people of goodwill like Beth Macklin and Dan Allen, in part because of Vatican II, the War on Poverty, and a worldwide upsurge for change—who can identify all the many contributing factors?—a small cluster of Tulsans coalesced over their dedication to social justice. Like a cluster of microscopic cells, a counterculture progressive movement began to multiply and collide with tradition. These idealists pursued, singly and together, a more just society. They worked with religious zeal, as local editor Larry Silvey said, "reflecting Dan Allen's conflicting rage and compassion, a city's conflicting humanity and dismissal, and a spiritual determination that conflicted with much religious stance of the day."[24]

It was, recalled one of the group, Dr. Nancy Feldman, "a time of dreaming the great dreams, when we really believed we could solve these problems."[25] In time, these progressives would produce results far beyond their numbers.

In the spring of 1968, NFN organized as a 501(c)(3) nonprofit corporation, enabling the organization to accept tax-deductible donations and to work with other programs more effectively. "We will go on as long as needed," Allen said. "That's why we formed a corporation."[26]

Jim Hess, a young employee of American Airlines, became president of the corporation. "I've got bags under my eyes and a slightly thinner pocketbook to show for what I've done, but for me, Neighbor for Neighbor provides the answer to a question I heard in the sermon last Sunday morning: 'Will the real Jesus Christ stand up?'"[27]

From the beginning, NFN had a multiracial, ecumenical board, with members from Catholic, Jewish, and Protestant faiths. NFN was destined to become the most successful of the Oklahoma Catholic social action projects of the era, according to one Catholic historian.[28]

Board meetings developed a rollercoaster tradition, with intense debates over how to attack poverty, black tirades against insensitive power structures, shared camaraderie, and unforgettable MASH humor. Always Dan was smoking. "The board once challenged him to stop smoking," a friend remembered. "He made it for thirty minutes."[29]

"I don't remember board meetings being contentious," said Jeff Nix, a member of early NFN boards. "But this was no ordinary adventure. I figured out right away that whatever this Dan Allen wants to do, I'm in. The first time I met Dan, I thought he was from another planet. I never met anybody more convinced they were absolutely right than Dan.

"He didn't spout, he didn't preach. I never heard him say anything inspirational. All he wanted was, he wanted you to do 100 percent of what you could do, 100 percent of the time. He had a way of sticking out his jaw, literally and figuratively, and he would just say, 'What are you going to do about it?' Dan knew how to motivate people on every level.

"I swear, the first time I saw him, it was like one of those religious paintings of an ordinary scene, and somebody has an aura. Listen, if anybody ever had an aura, it was Dan. I thought, I want to hang around and help him because he is better than anybody I have ever known. If I had said that to him, he would have just said, 'Ah, bullshit.' He saw his mission so clearly—never said anything of philosophical import, it was all just, 'How are we going to help these people?'"[30]

Some people loved Dan, some did not, but one thing was becoming clear: The scope of NFN was growing to the point where Dan had to struggle to keep it from becoming a bureaucratic agency. "We want to keep broadening our base, to avoid being specialists in one thing," he said. "But we want to keep the grassroots spirit—to keep this movement alive and effective."[31]

Chapter 6

What Is A Church?

"The poor should be welcome guests in our churches.
They should know our prayers are effective in making a difference
in their home life, physical needs, the realities of existence,
and being a part of our society.

Instead, they are forced to appeal to government agencies,
prove their worth and eligibility, and grow hungry and desperate
waiting for processing of their applications."

—Dan Allen

Car repair in NFN transportation project. *Tulsa World* photo, April 14, 1968.

WE'RE FIXING CARS,
AND THAT IS RELIGIOUS WORK.

"When the city sued NFN over the transportation project, I was a young lawyer helping Maynard Ungerman defend Neighbor for Neighbor. My role was to sit outside the courtroom and interview out-of-town witnesses who came pouring in to defend Dan Allen's work.

"Here they came, one after another—here came the cassocks. I think they must have come from Rome. 'Hello, I'm Father So and So,' or Monsignor, or Bishop, or Pope, or whatever, it all was the same to me. Here came one in a purple robe, and then another in blue, or crimson, or gold. They were a rainbow.

"This thing was way below their grade level, and sometimes they were just bemused about what they were going to say. I tried to explain: 'We're fixing cars, and that is religious work.' And then it would click, and then they would go into court and talk about Christ and what he would have done if people's mules were broken.

"It was hilarious, and so very smooth."—Jeff Nix[1]

It was not tidy. By 1969, St. Jude church was overflowing with a tidal wave of donated food, old clothes, and odds and ends of furniture that recycled continually into needy hands and homes. To get through it all, you had to circle around towers of canned goods and boxes overwhelmed with dry goods, then edge by racks of shirts and blouses, beside tables of folded pants and threadbare towels.

Equally important (perhaps even more important because they were means, not ends) were the resources in the back lot that stretched behind the church. Automobiles provide lifelines for the poor and perfect metaphors for poverty: rattletrap castoff cars (financed through loan sharks), with flapping crushed fenders, flaccid tires, and cardboard-covered broken windows, lurching forward, then sputtering and dying. And what is she to do, the single mom, trying to get the children to school and herself to a job on time, when the car is always broken down and the nearest bus is miles away?

So it came to pass that St. Jude's grounds became the visual equivalent of a salvage yard.

Driving along 46th Street North in the spring of 1969, you would have seen St. Jude Catholic Church, red brick iced with concrete details and an oddly undersized square steeple. Jonquils and the first spears of irises were peering up near brambled rosy burning bushes, the early miracles of spring. White blossoms were exploding like popcorn on knobby limbs of old pear trees. An expanse of lawn, greening up after a hard winter, stretched back to a line of trees—and, incongruously, a tumbled collection of dusty old cars. On any given day, there might be 450 cars there, in various stages of decay and reincarnation.[2]

"That's our garage," Father Dan Allen said proudly. "Ninety percent of these people work on the south side. They have to get there and back somehow every day."[3]

The years since he graduated from seminary had not been easy for Father Dan. The weight of his calling pressed him down like double gravity. His black curls were ragged around his temples, and fatigue drew lines around his eyes. Meticulous grooming was increasingly a luxury he did not afford. There might have been times you would see him spic-and-span in his midnight-black coat and stiff white clerical collar, but more often than not you would have seen Dan in bulky earth-colored overalls and a plaid flannel shirt. He was in his element when he joined the volunteers on the car lot, leaning far into the engine or snaking under the car—revealing, to those who cared about such niceties, mismatched socks.

"We need mechanics and repair men," Dan said, "but we don't have them, and we sure don't have the money to hire them."[4]

So he mobilized volunteers, starting with VISTAS, young people working through Volunteers in Service to America. Some folks came to donate time like Mack Polk, one of Tulsa's few black policemen; others were volunteers working to repay NFN help.

Then there were people like Booker: "I was volunteering on the front desk at Neighbor for Neighbor when I heard what sounded like two trains colliding out on 46th Street North," Pat Flanagan remembered later. "We all went running to the street. There stood Booker, thoroughly dejected, next to the scattered remains of his truck which, without benefit of collision, had fallen in on itself. When somebody asked Booker what had happened, he said, 'They don't make coat hangers like they used to.'"[5]

Here's how it worked: If Sally and Willie needed a car or food, and if Willie had a knack for motors, he could work off their debt by repairing an old donated car for Booker. Meanwhile Booker, who was a genius with coat hanger engineering but not so good at engines, might help strip out a third vehicle of its parts, to be used on a fourth one to repair for Leroy—who was, let's face it, really crazy but could help sweep out the place on his good days.

Father Dan gave away the cars, or offered them at the price of the repairs, through loans from a nonprofit credit union Wilbert was operating from a trailer in the church parking lot. Down the street, they leased a service station to set up a nonprofit outlet for cheap or free gas, auto supplies, and tires—for folks like the guy who abandoned his car in the church parking lot because he didn't have money to replace the tires.[6]

Dan was recycling cars, parts, donations, debts, people, and redemption. The words "debt" and "loan" were said with tongue in cheek. There was no real collection process. "You've got to get taken now and then," Dan said with a wink. His operation ran on honor and hope. Get a handout when you're down and then help others who are down—one neighbor working for another.[7]

"Neighbor for Neighbor is making transportation available to families who cannot afford it," reported the *Tulsa World* on April 14, 1969, in a laudatory Sunday story with a photo of Mack Polk and others repairing a car.[8] Within a year came the next article: the city had issued an order giving NFN thirty days to shut down its car repair operation. Two neighbors had complained. Using residentially zoned property for nonresidential purposes, such as a salvage yard, was a violation of the city's zoning code, the building inspector said.

"This is no salvage yard," Dan said. "Sure, we have cars there, but the property is clean and neat and we have been operating it for 18 months. We have 40 to 50 cars on the property right now, and we have given cars to about 80 families so far, to give them a way to get to work."

Mayor Jim Hewgley, a jovial Republican with a genius for a light touch in a crisis, admired Neighbor for Neighbor and the idea of a privately financed war on poverty. "I'm sure this can be resolved easily," he said.[9]

Some weeks later, a *Tulsa World* reporter found Father Allen at the kitchen table that served as his desk stacked with clutter of notes, articles, and letters, and a phone that rang incessantly. An unending line of people maneuvered to get his attention. Two young boys, finished with one project, asked what they could do next. He told them to mow the lawn. When they came back later, hot and sweaty, he gave them $10 from his pocket.

"Go to the store and get some soda," Allen said. "You've been working hard. Get yourself a whole carton. You can drink that much."

He lit a cigarette and looked out the window. "The Bishop called me and said we'll have an injunction filed against us for running a salvage yard that's against zoning laws. I haven't been told it won't go to court, so I guess it will.

"We're doing a lot out here. We're teaching Aid to Dependent Children about personality development. Things like how to dress better, how to apply for a job, what to say. We're trying to teach mothers how to raise their children so they'll be psychologically balanced. We're trying to teach women who have to live on commodities how to make the meals imaginative and nutritional."

As he spoke, young people were building a playground from cast-off materials on St. Jude's lawn. These were street urchins who didn't have much themselves, but "they are helping people, a whole lot," Dan said.

A product of the process was self-respect. "How can you measure the person's opinion of himself? You have to wait for that. It is his opinion of himself that dictates his behavior. And people change, you know. . . .

"When people need a car, we let them have one after they work so many hours to help other people. . . ."

"Father Allen stopped," the reporter wrote. "He didn't know what else to say. He wants to be allowed to continue what he feels is the most necessary project of Neighbor for Neighbor. He's afraid he won't be. And that worries him."[10]

There was more to it than zoning; that's how it looked to Dan and civil rights attorney Maynard Ungerman, a charter member of the NFN board of directors.

"We were getting old cars and giving them to women on food stamps so they could hold jobs; that was the primary idea," Maynard remembered. "We were picking up abandoned cars from highways—don't know that we should have been doing that, but we were. Storey Wrecker got really hacked about that, because they had some kind of contract with the city, although I don't know that the city had that authority either. Rather than going after us on the question of the cars, the city went after us on zoning—sued us to restrain us from using that area for cars, on grounds that we were actually a salvage yard and not using the land for a church."

So what could be done? Dan and the board debated the options.

"Ultimately we agreed," Ungerman said. "This really was a religious activity—we were actually doing the work of the gospel by repairing cars for those in need and giving cars to those in need. In fact, it wasn't a salvage yard, it was a church."

Could they win that argument? "We'll see how good a lawyer you really are," Dan told Maynard.[11]

A year earlier, CBS had done a thirty-minute television documentary on Neighbor for Neighbor, at the same time that NFN received an award from a program called Oklahomans for Individual Opportunity. Ninety days later CBS came back to do an hour program. "We decided to come back," said CBS News's Chalmers Dale, "because we felt this was the most singular approach to the poverty problem we had found anywhere in the country."[12]

But now, in 1969, just after Halloween, lawyers for the City of Tulsa marched into the courthouse to challenge Neighbor for Neighbor's operation. At the city's table, unsmiling, were city engineer Bob Forth, metro planner Bob Gardner, and Tulsa City Attorney Waldo Bales. Neighbor for Neighbor's team included Maynard Ungerman, Jeff Nix, and an impressive lineup of local and national religious leaders.

"If a church is directed only on a religious basis, then the modern church cannot hope to survive."
—*Reverend Frank Manning*

Keeping junk cars at St. Jude was a violation of city zoning ordinances, Bales said. Two neighbors said the operation was unsightly and noisy.

Ungerman did not disagree, although witnesses later said the cars had been placed behind a wooden fence. But the activity was, in fact, "Christ's original principle," Maynard said. "To live as a holy man, one must work for his neighbor."

"Does Neighbor for Neighbor hold prayer services or any other formal church operation such as praying or Bible lessons?" Bales asked.

"Not aside from St. Jude, which is one and the same," said NFN Board Chairman James Hess. Car repair was only one aspect of NFN's programs, which included such activities as distributing bread that the group bought for two cents a loaf, as well as other food items donated by other churches, he said.

"(This case) goes to the heart of what a church is," Maynard said. "Is it a building where people gather and read from books; is it a place where they listen to an address; or is it a center where people are inspired to go out and help their fellow man?"

Maynard's string of witnesses backed his argument, including national and state leaders in Catholic and Episcopal churches and the National Council of Churches, best-selling religious authors, and respected religious journalists including Al Cox, consultant on the CBS News documentaries.

"Combating poverty is not a matter of dealing with people in isolation," said Cox. "You don't just feed them and figure their problems are solved. The genius of Neighbor for Neighbor in my opinion is the organization's ability to deal with the whole person and the broad spectrum of his problems, whether it is hunger or getting to his job."

"If a church is directed only on a religious basis, then the modern church cannot hope to survive," said the Reverend Frank Manning, a Catholic priest and religious scholar from Oklahoma City. "Christ did not present himself as a founder of a religion but as a way of life. Worship without works has no real meaning or significance in this day and age."

The most confrontational testimony came from the Reverend Dean M. Kelley of New York, representing the National Council of Churches. "Churches sometimes are troublesome neighbors," he said. "The church has a history of serving as a catalyst and of fulfilling responsibilities where there are palpable needs no one else is filling," such as soup kitchens. No national or religious authority can tell a church what to do, Kelley said.

"For each church, who do you think should decide what is 'conventional' and what is 'unconventional?'" Bales asked.

"The Christian," Kelley said, "must be obedient to his conscience, in his understanding of the will of God. If this entails violation of the state law, then he must disregard the state law. This has been a characteristic of Christian teaching throughout the centuries."

"It's your position," Bales asked, "that if this court told you to do something, you would have the right to refuse?"

"If it were against his conscience, then most Christians would follow their conscience and expect to take the penalty of the law," Kelley said.[13]

Meanwhile, back at NFN, there were other challenges aplenty.

The board had reluctantly decided to close the service station because it was an unsustainable drain on funds. "We feel the dedicated people who have worked long hours can be used better by aiding the hundreds of poor people of Tulsa who have no where else to turn," the board president said. Several members of NFN who donated station start-up money accepted the loss without complaint, he said.[14]

It was hard to find volunteers who could tear down and repair the cars. Even more disheartening for Dan, somebody was stealing from his car lot.

"There were three guys stealing us blind every night," Pat Flanagan remembered. "One night Dan hid in the salvage yard and watched. He said he's never seen guys drop an engine so fast. He made his presence known and struck a deal with them—for every three cars they broke down for NFN, they could have the parts from the fourth car for free. And they could name their own hours. It was our first economic development project."[15]

After two days of testimony, Associate District Judge Bill Means issued his ruling on November 6, 1969. Neighbor for Neighbor's transportation department had used property belonging to St. Jude parish that had not been properly zoned for church use, the judge said.

The judge carefully sidestepped the question, "What is a church?" Under American law, he said, the freedom to believe is absolute, but governments can regulate the time, place, and manner of practice. In essence, the city had the right to require a church to obtain proper zoning to operate, and only the tract containing St. Jude's church building had the right zoning. The churchmen had failed to change from residential zoning on two of the three church tracts, he said.

The judge issued an injunction prohibiting Father Dan Allen, Maynard Ungerman, or Neighbor for Neighbor from operating a salvage yard on the St. Jude property in question, one of three tracts.[16]

"No one was more disappointed at our loss than the three auto thieves turned entrepreneurs," Pat Flanagan said.[17]

"We appealed, but the net result was, the injunction stayed in place," Maynard said. "It was a permanent, personal injunction. Forever, Dan and I are prohibited from operating the car repair program on that land."

Well, now, what to do?

"Let's think about this," Dan said, taking a long draw on a cigarette.

"It was all becoming a big publicity problem for the city," Maynard said. "And a major public relations coup for NFN, because we had all these people rallying around to help us. I think that was the start of NFN being ultimately accepted in the community, across the entire city."[18]

Perhaps NFN had managed to win by losing.

"The city got their ass kicked in the court of public opinion," said Jeff Nix. "Now most people would have said, 'Well, maybe we'd better lie low for a while,' but not Dan. The great thing about Dan was: 'Which one is the accelerator? Full speed ahead!' He didn't have a compromising bone in his body. He was a street fighter, and the last punch wins."[19]

"One of us—maybe Dan, maybe me—came up with the solution," Ungerman said. "The prohibition was forever, but it was narrowly defined on only one of the three tracts of land. Perhaps we could move the operation to the third tract, by the old rock house that had been the church rectory? The zoning was the same, still residential, but to challenge us again, the city would have had to come back and sue us all over and go through the whole thing again.

"So we just moved the operation next door and got on with the business— the church work—of Neighbor for Neighbor."[20]

Chapter 7

I Don't Understand What You're Doing.
Go Do It!

"Our main job is interesting churches in responding
to the needs of the poor.

They must recognize the fact that
Christ identified with the needy as well as with worship."

—Dan Allen

Dan Allen at Neighbor for Neighbor. *Tulsa Magazine* photo.

WITH TIN CUPS RAISED, WE TOASTED JOE LOUIS AND BABY JESUS. IT WAS A FINE CHRISTMAS.

"Back then, we gave out all the food and money until it was gone. By Friday afternoon, there was seldom anything left. It was such a Friday afternoon in 1971 that Leroy came in, wearing a trench coat and a face rearranged by better boxers than he. He'd been to every welfare agency in town for food. He hadn't eaten in two days.

"When I told him we had no food or money, Leroy took out a gun and told me that I was either going to come across with some food or he was going to blow my head off.

"I told him I guessed he'd just have to shoot me because we really didn't have any food or money. Leroy pondered that and finally said that he might reconsider if I would let him talk to my supervisor.

"The truth was that there were no supervisors. The crazy place was totally organic, and some days no one was really in charge. But . . . I found myself saying, 'Hey Leroy, meet my supervisor, Wilbert Collins.' . . . And Leroy put away his gun.

"For at least a year, Leroy singlehandedly provided enough pro bono work for all of our volunteer attorneys. . . . Dan finally decided that Leroy was a dangerous lunatic whose presence threatened the safety of everybody at NFN. Leroy was no longer welcome.

"Still Leroy would call me. 'Sister,' he would say. (. . . for some reason Leroy thought I was a nun.) 'Sister, I'm hungry.'

"So unbeknownst to the others at NFN, I would take food to Leroy in his room on the top floor of the Eldorado Hotel. . . . One Christmas, when I took him groceries, Leroy served me strong tea in a tin cup and talked about his dreams. He was going to become a boxer again, only this time he was going to win a fight or two. . . . Then, with tin cups raised, we toasted Joe Louis and Baby Jesus. It was a fine Christmas."—Pat Flanagan.[1]

After a couple of years, Father Dan left St. Jude Catholic Church to become full-time director of Neighbor for Neighbor—but not by choice.

"The Rev. Daniel R. Allen, former pastor of St. Jude Catholic Parish, has been appointed the full-time director of the Neighbor for Neighbor program to aid poverty-stricken families," the *Tulsa Tribune* reported on May 7, 1970. "He will also oversee Neighbor for Neighbor offices in Oklahoma

City, Broken Arrow, and Sand Springs. His headquarters will be at 1506 E. 46th St. N. [in Tulsa]."[2]

There are several versions of what happened. Some said Dan had given his heart and soul to NFN, and that Bishop Reed agreed to relieve Dan of the burden of managing the parish. There is some evidence to support that view. Certainly, NFN demands were taking their toll on Dan, whose supporters were fiercely loyal—including some exceptionally rich and powerful local Catholics. It didn't hurt that reporters loved him and lavished publicity on him and NFN.

Others said the bishop jettisoned Dan because of concern about his rising radicalism.

"I always had the feeling that Dan was always sort of in hot water with the church—with a Capital C—and that Skeehan was a sort of buffer for him."—Jeff Nix

Certainly Dan was a subject of controversy in the Catholic Church and elsewhere. He took literally the charge to defend the poor, and he didn't curb his tongue on subjects of poverty and injustice.

One Catholic historian, Jeremy Bonner, tells of the time that a Tulsa Catholic layman, Doug Fox, took Fathers Dan Allen, Forrest (Babe) O'Brien, and Lee O'Neil out to dinner, hoping to develop a better rapport among the three Northside priests. Instead of a pleasant dinner, Fox recalled that the priests denounced South Tulsans in general and Fox in particular for "indifference to human suffering and the poor." Bonner wrote that Allen said, "Some of you will at least write checks, but that's all you ever want to do. You don't want to be involved in [our work] because it's very distasteful and unpleasant."[3]

Later, Bonner reported: "When one well-to-do Tulsan told Reed that if the Tulsa trio worked for him he would fire them, . . . the bishop replied: 'They don't work for me. They work for the church.'"

"I always had the feeling," said Jeff Nix," that Dan was always sort of in hot water with the church—with a Capital C—and that Skeehan was a sort of buffer for him. It was apparent that Dan was not running a church in any traditional sense."[4]

Only Bishop Reed knew his real reasons for sending Dan Allen from St. Jude. In any event, Dan didn't go far. Next to St. Jude, also on church land, was a small farm with the little rock house and relocated NFN car lot (aka, a church). The bishop assigned the house and land for NFN use,[5] but apparently no salary or expense account came with the assignment.

He gave Dan his blessing. "I don't understand what you're doing," said

Bishop Reed, a wise and patient man. "Go do it."[6]

"When I was at St. Jude's," Father Dan recalled, "somebody left the parish some property. That's where we started the credit union and financial counseling. . . .

"Because we based the direct services in our parish, daily the poor were in the parish hall. . . . I saw my role as pastor not as bringing more people into the church but bringing the church to the people. But many of St. Jude's white parishioners disapproved of what we were trying to do. They didn't like being challenged about their racial prejudices, and in fact many became part of the white flight."

"I don't understand what you're doing," said Bishop Reed, a wise and patient man. "Go do it."

When he was appointed pastor in 1966, St. Jude had four or five masses every Sunday. By the time he left, four years later, they were down to two that were only half full, Dan said.

"Eventually, the opposing parishioners succeeded in having me removed and reverting their parish to the old style. We moved Neighbor for Neighbor to its new location here, and the bishop appointed me diocesan director of Neighbor for Neighbor. The only problem was, we had no funds or income. I had a title, but that was about it."

Then came the challenge for Dan and the NFN family: to rebuild. "The Eucharist was central to our rebirth," Dan said. "I understand the Eucharist to be for the sake of those present so they will become God's love *for the many*. When we say in the Eucharist, 'This is my body, my blood for you and for the many,' . . . they are the many of 'I was hungry, I was naked, etc.'

"So we had our own Sunday community and liturgy. There were about 25 to 35 just plain old folks. We'd start with the Liturgy of the Word in the morning, then we'd go out to work on housing or do other work in the community. At the end of the day, we'd come back, talk about our experiences, and then celebrate the Eucharist. That's the core that we began with, and we remain faithful to it."[7]

If life was tenuous for the poor, it was not a lot better at NFN. Armed with nothing but a title, Dan refused to give up. He hit the road, talking to churches, working the news media, soliciting donations and volunteers, serving those in need.

Twice Dan was offered federal funding to sustain NFN. Twice he declined. NFN would not accept guidelines on the poor and wouldn't ask people whether they were qualified or "deserving." Welfare programs were run from above, he contended, with no voice from the people who know the most about poverty, those who live it.[8]

"He followed Christ out into the poor," said his niece Judy Allen Hess. He had a way of setting his jaw, she recalled, "as in the scripture, when Isaiah 'set his face like flint' and Jesus 'steadfastly set his face to go to Jerusalem,'" she said.[9] "Creating something new became his focus. He could have done anything, but he chose poverty—for himself, too. He lived poor and he died poor. He relished the work. I remember in one letter he wrote about greeting the poor every morning at Neighbor for Neighbor with joy—opening the door and welcoming Jesus. He wrote: 'My life is what I know and believe to be Christ's basic message to meet him daily, as under the guise [of the poor] he comes to us at the door of NFN, and respond as we would in the days we were more prepared to receive Communion.'"[10]

Dan refused to stockpile anything and took no note of any need to create an NFN-supporting backlog of funds. It wasn't about creating the institution. A donation might linger at NFN no longer than moments. His business rule was that if it was needed, he gave it away immediately—"100 percent in, 100 percent out." He routinely gave away more than they took in, and the agency was always tottering on the brink. "Why not?" Dan said. That was how the poor lived; why should NFN be any different?

"He could have done anything, but he chose poverty—for himself, too. He lived poor and he died poor."

Dedicated donors and volunteers kept NFN afloat. A case in point: Ken's Pizza entrepreneur Ken Selby, later to run Midwestern chains of popular restaurants including Mazzio's, printed the NFN newsletter as a donation in the early years.[11]

The early 1970s were years of exceptional idealism in the life of the Tulsa community. Tulsa Mayor Bob LaFortune would have described himself as a moderate conservative Republican, but progressive programs thrived during his administration. Lyndon Johnson's War on Poverty and the landmark Model Cities program were setting the stage for sweeping social change—"opening doors that will never be closed again," in the words of Tulsa Model Cities Director Ken Bolton.[12] It focused on the traditional black community, a boomerang-shaped area covering thirty-three square miles north of downtown, which contained nearly all of Tulsa's black citizens in that day when segregation was still the de facto law of the town. Model Cities' idealistic goal was to raise the standard of living in the ghetto to that of the community as a whole, and it helped set in motion a wave of self-determination as a community-development activity.[13]

LaFortune routinely went to meetings anywhere in town, unaccompanied and unassuming, just to listen; "We're all learning together," he said.

Whites shivered at the raised fist of black power, but most local leaders ruled with a light hand. Tulsa had its small share of militants: the Black Panthers had a tiny den of friendly, lavishly armed fellows in black leather; and the Black Muslims had Theodore G. X. and a little storefront mosque on Greenwood.[14] The leading local militant, Homer Johnson, was a city employee who drove a street washing truck. (Former Mayor James J. Hewgley used to laugh that Homer would drive the big street flusher to public meetings, yell at the mayor, and then go back to work washing down streets.) NFN old timers recall that Mayor Bob LaFortune attended NFN's annual meeting picnics. LaFortune routinely went to meetings anywhere in town, unaccompanied and unassuming, just to listen; "We're all learning together," he said.[15]

Dan Allen had little patience with the bureaucratic machinations of government programs. He did make use of two antipoverty endeavors, outgrowths of the federal Office of Economic Opportunity: the antipoverty credit union, managed by Wilbert Collins under the guidance of a consultant named Charles Harrington, and a credit counseling service run by Bob Gunn and Jack Helton. Both Collins and Helton were originators of NFN and were dedicating their lives to helping people climb out of the hole of poverty. The credit union and counseling service operated a branch from a trailer on the NFN back lot.

"This is a sincere effort for indigent people to become involved in the mainstream of our American society," Collins said.

Churches and other idealists invested capital to start the credit union, which offered small short-term loans to the poor. Debtors were required to repay 1 percent a month on any unpaid balance, and credit union consultant Harrington said the delinquency rate was about 15 percent, which he called amazingly low. By mid-1969, about 3,000 people were credit union members, and a number of organizations and individuals— including Dan Allen—had placed their savings and faith there. Investments were said to be some $78,000. The credit union was "very firm and stable," Allen said, and was helping change the economic status of poor people.[16]

In those days, credit unions were not guaranteed by the Federal Deposit Insurance Corporation. Trusting a credit union was a high-risk endeavor, and there was, in essence, no safety net.

It all operated on faith, which faltered.

In mid-1970, the *Tulsa World* ran a picture of one Mrs. Nettie Carrie, a seventy-three-year-old widow sitting in her rocking chair with pursed lips and folded arms—waiting. After a run on investments, the credit union had frozen its assets.

People like Nettie Carrie wanted their deposits back. "That was years of hard labor I put in there," Mrs. Carrie said, "from working in the south end at 35 and 50 cents an hour. They convinced me it was all right, and the federal government was behind it." While she tried to get her money back, her husband grew ill. She called the credit union every day. He was hospitalized, and she kept calling. He died, and she was still waiting.

A federal audit blamed the consultant, Charles Harrington, for mismanagement.

"Certainly the lawyers involved knew that it was not guaranteed, in the sense that bank deposits are guaranteed by the FDIC," said NFN's Maynard Ungerman. "At the same time, we were told that the loans were guaranteed in the sense that they were under a league of credit unions. If one got into trouble, there was a larger pooled account that would pick up the deficit. They were rather vague about where the pool was."[17]

It was a bitter pill for Allen, who had always said with a grin and a wink that it was important to get taken once in a while. Dan had put up his own savings plus about $10,000 in NFN funds and $2,000 from St. Jude. Worse, he had encouraged others to invest on the assurances that their funds were secured by the Oklahoma Credit Union League. "We weren't experts, and we knew it," he said, "but we placed our money and our faith in the hands of the experts. And now, where do we go for answers?"[18]

Some years later, federal law was changed to provide insured protection to federal credit union deposits, but it was too late to help Nettie Carrie and the Tulsa Economic Opportunity Task Force Credit Union.

It was a hard time. Father Dan's health was suffering, and he had bouts of heavy drinking. He was forced to take pastoral leave to a Catholic Guest House to regain his health and balance.[19]

Dan's niece Janet Allen spent summers volunteering at NFN. "I was very attached to my 1954 Chevy I had been driving to and from Washington University in St. Louis," Janet remembered. "I worked in the NFN service station, and one of the guys there helped me rebuild the engine. But one morning, I awakened to find an empty place where I had left my car the night before. Dan had given it to a migrant family sometime during the night. My brow went up a bit at this

Before the winter was over, NFN was destitute. "We are out of food and clothing. We especially need beds and clothing for children."
— Marilynn McDaniel

news, and Dan hastily promised me my pick of the next vehicles that came through."

Fresh from college, Janet moved into the little rock house next to St. Jude, where she and Dan's secretary Marilynn McDaniel spent a winter while Dan was away. "The back room of the rock house became my bedroom and sitting room. Marilynn and I shared her VISTA stipend and donated food, heating it over the floor furnace because the kitchen had no range. We distributed what came through as best we could, knocking on doors when the money wouldn't cover the utilities."

Before the winter was over, NFN was destitute. "We are out of food and clothing," Marilynn reported. "We especially need beds and clothing for children."

"After Dan came back from Guest House," Janet said, "I went to live in the mountains of Guatemala for three months to assist in a well baby clinic. Near the end of my time there, I received a brown envelope in the mail with several pieces of broken bark. Taping them back together to decipher the words, I learned that Dan had plucked this piece of bark from a track of land that we both loved, and that he had landed an emergency food and medical grant. He wanted my help to spend it. I cried leaving Guatemala, but also mused over the intrigues I would enter with Dan, one of which would in time bring a medical clinic and the transformation of my back room into a medical dispensary. Not too shoddy."[20]

Wilbert Collins came back to NFN to manage the emergency food and medical services grant. Meanwhile, Dan and NFN got into another scrap. The Northside had been ringed by large public housing complexes, populated by poor people including large numbers that had been displaced by urban renewal and expressway construction. Problems were festering at Apache Manor, Comanche Park, Seminole Village, and Mohawk Manor.

Neighbor for Neighbor was finding that the tenants needed it all—food, clothing, rent assistance, utility help, transportation, job training, medical care, child care, school crossing guards, police protection. But when NFN appealed to the Tulsa Housing Authority to help meet tenants economic and social challenges, they were met with a cold shoulder.

THA was in the business, in those days, of building units, full speed ahead. The goal was to warehouse the poor in huge projects, apparently based on a theory that there was some kind of economy of scale—never mind what would happen when large numbers of people with difficult lives were jammed into people-warehouses and then blamed for any ensuing problems.

It all took place through a federal maneuver that encouraged construction by funding large sole-source construction contractors to provide turnkey projects. This system had the advantage of speeding up construction but opened the contractors and housing authorities to charges of kickbacks and sweetheart deals. Allegations were that some contractors over-bid the jobs, cut corners, provided shoddy materials and construction, and pocketed the difference—sharing the take with friendly inspectors and administrators. The overseeing authorities were typically peopled by development interests who argued their jobs were to build, as quickly and economically as possible.

NFN believed THA should help meet the social needs of tenants, not just provide units. They also believed that THA purposely discriminated in the assignment of units. Was it just an accident that Northside projects contained all the black people? What some white neighbors viewed as an invasion helped create panic and flight, which escalated further when crime (surprise!) broke out in the units.

NFN believed Tula Housing Authority should help meet the social needs of tenants, not just provide units. They also believed that THA purposely discriminated in assignment of units.

In October 1970, State Senator Gene Howard convened hearings into the problems of Tulsa housing projects. All day the legislative subcommittee heard charges of racial discrimination, mismanagement, unresponsiveness, and conflict of interest against THA and its director Jim Clouse.

Maynard Ungerman, representing Neighbor for Neighbor, presented seven affidavits from tenants and a former THA employee. "Neighbor for Neighbor is in no way opposed to public housing," Ungerman said. But NFN volunteers were encountering problems "which must be solved." He urged that the legislature enact strict criminal penalties for racial discrimination, and presented the affidavit of a THA employee who said "there is a very clever form of discrimination against blacks" in assignment of units.

The employee said Clouse had instructed her to send no more than one-third black residents to a high-rise for elderly tenants. He told her, "I don't want that many colored people." Ungerman said the committee should change the composition of housing authorities to include people with experience in working with the poor; and should support tenants associations. Clouse said there was no discrimination. Nonetheless, THA practices were changed to avoid discrimination, and laws were later changed to require competitive bidding on housing authority projects, rather than the turn-key method.[21]

But Neighbor for Neighbor's fights over public housing were far from over.

Chapter 8

Rules?
There Are No Rules.
We're Trying To Get Something Done!

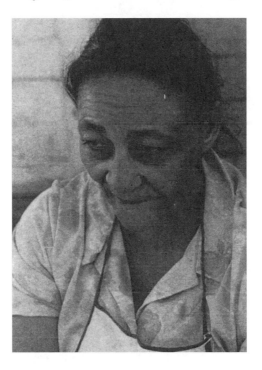

The priority is finding enough people really concerned about humanity;
when that happens, the money will naturally flow."

— Dan Allen

Liller Waller. Stephen Crane photo, *Tulsa World*, March 29, 1971.

LOOK AT HER FACE:
IT IS THE FACE OF POVERTY.

Mrs. Liller Waller has a heart-shaped face, narrow at the jaw and chin because she has lived much of her life without her jawbones, which were removed for cancer. Widowed; mother of thirteen in a day before the Pill; now rearing grandchildren, too. Her dark hair is tucked into an unruly bun. She always wears a bib apron and an accommodating half smile, with lips closed to try to hide the fact that she has no teeth. She has the wrinkled brow of an old lady, with dark circles under her eyes. Those sad eyes are as gentle as her voice, and she is too shy to look directly at you when she speaks.

"I don't want to start any trouble," she says from the front porch of her home, a shabby yellow frame with white trim and a couple of broken windows. "I just got a bad deal. I didn't have a lawyer. The man kept coming to my house, and I signed papers that didn't have nothing on it."

Just beyond the yard hydrant, her "bad deal" sits next door, slowly decaying into the dust. For eight years Liller has been paying $55 a month for a house she bought from a door-to-door salesman, but she can't afford to move in. The salesman told her that her house was about to be condemned and she had to pay $4,000 to get the "new" house moved in from another lot.

She knew she would have to add wiring and sheetrock and a foundation. She didn't know that she mortgaged her home and lot, that the new house had no kitchen or bathroom, and that she would end up owing an out-of-state mortgage company nearly $8,000. Or that over the years, month by month, she could never stretch her dead husband's social security enough to move in.

She and the children finished the foundation and are trying to sheetrock it, she says. It's hard; she has no car, lives in an area without bus service, and has to depend on friends for transportation. She tends a big garden and keeps neighbor children, but the money never quite stretches. Every year she pays $217 on a $900 bill for new neighborhood sewer services, but she can't afford to hook into the line. "If water or paving comes in, we'll have to pay our part of that, too," she says, without resentment. "Those things just happen.

"My trouble is, when I feed these children and pay all my bills and the medical bills— there's nothing left.[1]

By the spring of 1971, Father Dan Allen had become focused, some might say obsessed, with the problems of Liller Waller's neighborhood, where some forty poor families lived. They were taxpayers dwelling inside the city; living for a generation, they said, on the "outskirts and scrapings of Tulsa," but missing some basic city services.

Dan was determined to create a University of Poverty, to help people understand. The dilemmas these families faced were instructive on the interlocking problems facing the poor. Those who understood sometimes turned fiercely radical, and Dan was well on his way there. When he talked about the plight of these families, he didn't spare the profanity. He ground out cigarettes, one after another, with a vengeance, and his eyes burned with an almost frightening fire.

> *"There isn't enough water out here for a decent baptism."*

The neighborhood was named Mohawk Heights, cut in half by Harvard Avenue. On one side, twenty-seven families got their water from a single yard hydrant by one of the houses. The area around the hydrant was blackened from fires set all winter to try to keep it thawed. It was about the same in a next-door neighborhood across Harvard.

Neither neighborhood had working sewers, of course, and most people didn't have indoor plumbing. So even as late as the 1970s, in a prosperous city of 350,000, the area was dotted by ubiquitous little wooden sheds with swinging doors and one or two holes. Stray cats chased rats around the outdoor priveys. On hot summer days, a bit of an odor lingered over the scruffy terrain, and strange stains cropped up in standing puddles after a rain.

Dirt ruts served as roads, sometimes spread with a little chat. There were a few broken trees, a scattering of zinnias and rosebushes, some vegetable gardens with straight rows of okra and corn, and plots of high weeds. Mowing was not much of a problem. Over many years, hundreds of little feet—of children and hounds and sometimes chickens—had taken care of the grass. Dust and scattered trash piles offered the children playground materials for their beloved games such as Kick the Can.

Here was the city's rule: If you didn't have indoor plumbing, the only water service you could have was from a yard hydrant, which was about the height of a small child and had to be at least fifteen feet from the house. Mrs. Olivia Reed managed the "master meter" contract for twenty-seven families. Their billing was peculiarly high—didn't make sense—and they were billed at a master-meter rate double what other Tulsans paid. But the water pressure was often frustratingly low. Turns out they were all being served by a two-inch main, little bigger than a garden hose. Send little Johnny to the hydrant to carry back a pail of water, and he might wait a long time to fill it. Sometime people had to wait until the middle of the night to get water, Mrs. Reed said.

"There isn't enough water out here for a decent baptism," Dan Allen said in disgust.

Every month, regular as rain, the city sent the families utility bills for sewer and refuse service, although nobody had either.

You had to pay for trash service even if nobody came to take it away.

Not everybody got their water from group yard hydrants. Some had well water—"from God, not the city," one said. Others carried water, as did Mrs. Olivia Scott Gatewood, a seventy-three-year-old widow who cleaned houses five miles south. A friend drove her to work; Mrs. Gatewood had no other transportation. You could see her every week, rain or shine, dressed fit for Sunday church, heading out and heading back, toting as many plastic jugs as she could carry home for her ten-gallon weekly water supply. She still hoped the city would provide water someday, but hope was dimming. "It seems like the city just wadded us up and threw us away," Mrs. Gatewood said.

You couldn't have water 'lessen you had indoor plumbing and sewer or septic, because the city was determined to protect the health of the neighborhood. You had to pay for trash service even if nobody came to take it away. So it went.

Someday the city would bring water and sewer to the area. City fathers promised it. The city had voted money to build a half-million-dollar sewer "outfall line" and a $3.3 million "interceptor" sewer. The city also planned to spend $200,000 to send water mains toward the families. But when the lines snaked to their area, in that great time ahead named someday, there would be another truckload of problems.

If city mains were laid, the families would become eligible to tap in. The key word was eligible. If the sewer was available, the families had to—by law—hook up, which meant they would have to pay $500 each, get licensed plumbers to build the lines into their houses, and build indoor plumbing. Same with water: $90 each to tap in, plus a plumber to bring lines into the house and some sort of indoor plumbing to use water.

For people like Mrs. Liller Waller and Mrs. Olivia Reed, water might as well have been on the moon. In the worst of cases, they might even lose their homes.[2]

Maybe they could accomplish more in a group, so they started meeting and talking. Father Dan Allen and NFN volunteer lawyer Jeff Nix met with them, in the home of Mrs. Priscilla Jones over on 30th Street North.

With Dan's help, they began to pool their money, hoping against hope that they could raise enough when the opportunity came.

Well, maybe more could be done. Dan Allen dragged in NFN volunteer Don McCarthy who brought NFN volunteer Don Falletti out to visit the neighborhoods.

"I didn't believe that there could be an area like that in Tulsa, with people in that kind of condition," Falletti remembered.

McCarthy and Falletti were both problem solvers, engineers who could not stop picking at a problem knot to save their lives. The two Dons were well on their way to being radicalized by Dan's University of Poverty. What was this? These families had no water, no sewer, and nothing could be done? Don't believe it. Of course they could FIX it—somehow.

"It looked pretty clear to me," Falletti said. "They should have water. Why not? No water lines. How come? Didn't have the money. No voice was a big thing. I don't think we ever had a strategy. It wasn't that big of a project. Dig some trenches, lay some plastic pipe. It didn't seem like that much of a challenge. Once we got water to their houses, they could drill a hole in an outside wall, run a pipe inside with a faucet—no more than $10, maybe $20—and they would have water and inside plumbing. It didn't seem like a big challenge, just something that needed to be done."

First stop was the city, at the desk of The Commissioner—the City of Tulsa Commissioner of Waterworks and Sewerage. The commissioner was a patrician old man, from a long-line, well-regarded family. He prided himself on keeping a tidy desk; on a sunny day, you could see his face reflected in the polished mahogany. When he was angry, which was fairly often, his neck turned bright turkey red.

Too bad. But nothing could be done. There were rules; the city had to follow them.

The commissioner listened politely as Falletti outlined the problem. Too bad. But nothing could be done. There were rules; the city had to follow them; he had no authority to go beyond them; it was all about health, safety, welfare; the bond funds were being spent in accordance with law and proper procedure; in time, there would be city service for that area. Then people would have pay for the lines on their own property and have to hook up or there would be liens. Those were the rules.

"We really didn't get any help from the commissioner," Falletti remembered later. Perhaps it was not surprising. The commissioner was not particularly fond of people who broke rules of decorum. At about that same time, after a heated hearing when an impassioned audience challenged city policies toward the Northside, the commissioner's neck was red when he confided to a reporter that the audience was nothing more than "jungle savages."[3]

Back to the neighborhoods. What now? "We had a couple of meetings at one of these homes, and it took us thirty minutes to get enough water for eight cups of coffee," remembered NFN volunteer Don McCarthy. "It turned out that these master yard hydrants were not exactly legal, either, but the city didn't want to push it because then there would be all these families with no water at all. They had nothing really, just a shack or old house with no facilities, no water.

"Dan Allen knew I had a background in construction and said would I handle the construction? I said sure," McCarthy said. "I had no idea what we were constructing. Jeff Nix took care of the city part, and Don and I took care of the field part, the construction. We just headed out like we knew what we were doing."

> *The commissioner's neck was red when he confided to a reporter that the audience was nothing more than "jungle savages."*

"You have to learn what people are vulnerable to," Don Falletti remembered. "That was the first time I understood that bad press was the issue for City Hall. The mayor was really nice to me, but he said he couldn't do anything because there were rules. So I said to the city, 'Well, we got this project going and we'll have photographers there and the city won't look very good. But can you have your water guy come out and tell us where he wants the city lines? Then we will meet them there.'"

Don Falletti quit asking permission. He drew up plans, based on a lot of guesswork. The houses were scattered without much pattern, with occasional hints of dirt chat roads. The two Dons asked all the homeowners where they wanted their kitchens, if they could ever have kitchens. Then Falletti drew imaginary roads, based on sheer logic, pretending they were actual paved roads. He laid out where the water lines would stretch along the pretend roads, from imaginary kitchens to imaginary city connections. He went to his company, Rockwell International, and got their Good Neighbor Fund (Falletti was fund chair) to put up $1000, enough to pay for materials. Falletti also got NFN board members to serve as volunteer laborers.

"I have a crew," Dan Allen told Falletti. "I have a friend who owns a ditching company, and they are going to come here from Perry, Oklahoma, with their people and equipment. They will pay all their own expenses and food. They will come two weekends."

The Dons each took a neighborhood and gathered up volunteers, mostly from Rockwell. It was summer. "It was in the days when psychedelic stuff was in," Falletti remembered. "We worked in shorts. I had one of those god-awful shirts and tie-dye shorts, yellows, blues, greens. I didn't care. I was sporting a beard. I am not that short, but in some places there were weeds taller than I was. We had to knock them down. Can't tell you what the chiggers were like.

"The city kind of took a back seat, like they didn't know anything was going on—which was great."

"We bought PVC pipe, the best you could get at that time," Falletti remembered. "Jatasco Plumbing Supply gave it to us at cost. We laid it out, and the Al Admiston Excavating people dug wherever we told them to dig. They were great. And we glued the pipe together and laid the homeowners' lines from where their kitchens would be to where the city connections would be. Then we covered them all by hand.

"But then the city balked on putting in their city mains in their easements along streets in the neighborhood. Well, we didn't want to give the city any chance to weasel out, so we just put in the city mains, too. The excavating people got a big kick out of that. And NFN paid for the meters, too."

Don McCarthy brought his sons John and Lawrence, ages twelve and thirteen at the time, to help with the work. "It was an excellent project for them to see how the others get by in life. There was another fellow with a Polish name who lent us heavy equipment backhoes and front-end loaders without charge. The city kind of took a back seat, like they didn't know anything was going on—which was great. We had a licensed plumber who put the meters in, and we took it from the meter to the house. I think we got forty to sixty families hooked up, all with volunteers and just the $1000 donation. You couldn't even get one meter in for that. The whole thing was done in two weeks, maybe three. The credibility of Neighbor for Neighbor just jumped right up."

But . . . what about insurance protection, liability, getting right-of-entry forms from the citizens, getting city approval for the project, getting engineering seals, and—?

"I remember what somebody famous once said," Falletti said. "Rules? There are no rules. We're trying to get something done."

"These people had been promised and promised and promised, all their lives," McCarthy said. "Right at that time, Tulsa won the All America City award, but here were these families. And—how can I tell you? —they were just so grateful.

"The people couldn't believe it," Falletti said. "There was one guy who didn't want to cooperate with us. His was the last home, and he watched us work through his neighborhood but wouldn't talk with us. When we were almost done, I knocked on his door and said, 'You are the last house in the area that needs water service. Where would you like to have your line?'

"He said, 'I can afford to do it myself.' Well, just look around, you could see what he had, more than the rest. We could tell he didn't think he deserved help. I said, 'We would like to do it.' He looked at me for a long time and then he said, 'Right over here.'

"When we were putting in his line, here he came in his little camper pickup, and here was all this sandwich food and pop.

"We had quite a feast," Falletti said. "The fellow had tears of gratitude in his eyes. And so did we.

"We knew we had done something real."[4]

Chapter 9

Health Care: From Dreadful To Deplorable

"Why should we—an organization that works with and for the poor—
be any more financially secure than our clients. . . .
NFN has never organized a fund-raising campaign.
If an agency stresses fund-raising,
you end up doing what it takes to raise money
rather than doing what it takes to get the job done."

—Dan Allen

Dan Allen. Photo courtesy Dewey Bartlett.

"Hush," whispers the mother. "It's almost our turn."

It is dusk when Father Dan Allen opens the door. It's late December, cold, with a steady drizzle that will freeze before the night is over. The wind is sharp. A long line of walking wounded shuffles through rivulets of mud, shifting uneasily, edging back and forth, hoping to wedge ahead and get a chance inside that door, where a warm light beckons. Some have umbrellas. A young man's shoulders are wrapped in a black garbage bag.

A young woman in a headscarf asks an old man to hold her place in line. She crosses the driveway filled with junker cars and retrieves two toddlers from a parked car. She carries one child, flushed and feverish, wrapped in a frayed quilt, snuffling and grabbing at his ears. The other, a girl of maybe four, begins to cry. "Hush," whispers the mother. "It's almost our turn."

Some have waited outside all afternoon. At the first chance, a dozen people push their way through the open door and seize places in rows of uneven metal folding chairs. A dozen more edge in behind them and line up against the rugged stone walls of a reception room, crushed against metal filing cabinets and a dog-eared reception desk. The air is heavy with the odor of wet wool. Children giggle while they play with chipped blocks and stuffed toys on a worn oval rug.[1] A baby begins to howl, and an old woman coughs and gags without letup.

"Dan," calls Carol Falletti, and Father Allen looks in from a rear door. "The phone," Carol says. "A woman dying with cancer, and nobody can help her because she doesn't fit anybody's guidelines. She can't get here."

"Get her phone number and address. We'll try to get somebody to go help her," says Allen.

"I can't," says Carol. "She doesn't have a phone and doesn't have a dime to call us back."[2]

So it went, night in and night out, at the Neighbor for Neighbor free clinic, established in 1971 to address a gaping wound in the body politic of health care for the poor.

Why did Father Allen need to establish a free medical clinic? For openers, Tulsa was the only city of its size in the country without a charity hospital, Dan said. That was just the beginning of problems caused by ignorance of Northside needs and prejudice against the poor in general, Allen said.[3]

The history of Tulsa's poverty health care runs from dreadful to deplorable and is as sorry a story as Oklahoma has to tell. The roots of bad health and medical care for the poor are deep and long. Consider this word painting by Socialist Oscar Ameringer when he first visited Oklahoma in 1907:

> *I found toothless old women with sucking infants on their withered breasts. I found a hospitable old hostess, around thirty or less, her hands covered with rags and eczema, offering me a biscuit with those hands, apologizing that her biscuits were not as good as she used to make because with her sore hands she could no longer knead the dough as it ought to be.*
>
> *I saw youngsters emaciated by hookworms, malnutrition, and pellagra, who had lost their second teeth before they were twenty years old. I saw tottering old male wrecks with the infants of their fourteen-year-old wives on their laps. I saw a white man begging a Choctaw squaw man who owned the only remaining spring in that neighborhood to let him have credit for a few buckets of water for his thirsty family. I saw humanity at its lowest possible level of degradation and decay.*
>
> *I saw smug, well dressed, overly fed hypocrites march to church on Sabbath day, Bibles under their arms, praying for God's kingdom on earth while fattening like latter-day cannibals on the share croppers. I saw wind-jamming, hot-air-spouting politicians geysering Jeffersonian platitudes about equal rights to all and special privileges to none; about all men born equal with the rights to life, liberty and the pursuit of happiness without even knowing, much less caring, that they were addressing as wretched a set of abject slaves as ever walked the face of the earth, anywhere or at any time.*
>
> *The things I saw on that trip are the things you never forget.[4]*

It could be argued that the world Ameringer found was one in which almost everybody was poor and suffering. Not so as time went on in Tulsa, where the contrast between rich and poor would become stark and shocking after the discovery of oil around the time of statehood. In fact, Tulsa's impacted traditions of deplorable health and insanitary living conditions for the poor in North and West Tulsa were largely unrecognized, and aggravated, because other community sectors had such splendid care.

Consider the case of West Tulsa, where refinery workers were living in marginal clusters of despair as late as the 1970s. The roots of these wretched neighborhoods stretched back at least to the Depression, when the oil market had foundered on its own excess.[5] In 1933 Tulsa Methodists went door to door in West Tulsa oil-patch housing and reported on the deplorable living conditions. Nearly all homes were in a "bad" category; some were just tents. Large clusters of families shared common, open privies. Few had employed breadwinners. Some children could not attend school because they had no clothes. Seventy-five percent of preschool children had contagious diseases. The area's morbidity and mortality rate was worse than Calcutta. To be poor in Tulsa was dire, indeed.[6]

That West Tulsa population was almost exclusively white, since there were no black refinery workers then. For blacks, packed into a North Tulsa ghetto, the Depression was also perennial. Bad as the record was for poor whites, it was even worse for blacks because dreadful living conditions had been created after the race riot, then institutionalized by custom and even law that isolated black Tulsa.

A snapshot of those conditions was contained in an application that was submitted in 1967 by Mayor Jim Hewgley, seeking federal money for the landmark Tulsa Model Cities program. On the issue of health, the application said the Model Cities area had infant mortality rates of 46.3 deaths per 1,000 live births (compared to below 10 in higher income areas.) "Essentially all maternal deaths and the majority of preventive prenatal complications are occurring in the . . . indigent population," applicants wrote. The area reported 61 percent of Tulsa's tuberculosis and 86 percent of its syphilis cases. Mental health needs were similarly demanding.

The on-the-ground reality, the application said, was one of neglect by absentee landlords and nonexistent public services. Many crowded, decaying buildings were infested with rats and served by community outhouses.[7]

Tulsa health systems, "on the whole, are geared for the general community with little attention to specialized approaches needed in obtaining results in lower-income areas . . . in which health problems are greater," the report said.[8]

In 1967, South Tulsa had five hospitals and a mental health complex. North Tulsa had one marginal health center; West Tulsa had none. The basic cause, the application said, was that the poor did not attract private doctors or medical facilities that depended on income or private donations. Indigents did not have health insurance, of course. Ambulance service was another case in point: ambulances were provided on a rotating basis by private funeral homes, which had little incentive to make runs into areas where there was little chance they would ever be paid.[9]

The sorry record of health care for blacks was described by Tulsa's Dr. Charles Bate, a distinguished black physician who served North Tulsa for many years.[10]

Bate wrote that Oklahoma was settled in the 1800s by an amalgamation of removed Indians, fleeing slaves and freedmen, homesteaders, and post–Civil War drifters. After Indian Territory became a state in 1907, an important first task was to disenfranchise blacks by invoking a grandfather clause: Blacks could not vote unless they could prove a lineage of property owners who qualified to vote before 1866 or 1867, before Emancipation.[11]

The universally marginal health care picture changed for some after oil created an upper class that could afford the finest in medical care for its own. Formerly poor whites, newly rich, were often extremely racist, Bate said. Now, and for decades to come, Tulsa health care was a tale of two cities separated between rich and poor.

Tulsa health care was a tale of two cities separated between rich and poor.

Until late in the twentieth century, a typical black doctor operated from his home, practicing medicine, pharmacy, or dentistry in a segregated community. He could receive only basic education in Oklahoma.[12] Self-trained midwives presided over most births at home. After the 1921 race riot and during the Depression and WWII, a public health nurse served the black community, then confined within about four square miles. She operated from a house next to a chicken house.

"The health conditions in north Tulsa were more than deplorable," Bate said. "Many streets were unpaved, little sewage [service], junk heaps within the city, rodents were uncontrolled, outdoor privies were prevalent, and many times five and six homes used one toilet facility. . . . In many places three and four shacks were lined up one behind the other on 25-foot lots with hardly passing room between them, and many times the only way to get from one house to another was thru another one in front or behind."[13]

"Although the medical facilities and societies were separate and segregated, diseases were not," Bate said. Tuberculosis and venereal diseases did not respect Tulsa's hard lines of segregation between black and white, rich and poor.[14]

Even the American Red Cross blood bank was segregated. For a time, one small black health center and poorly equipped hospital offered "separate but equal" care and "colored clinics." The public hospital was named Municipal and later Moton.[15]

Most white doctors did not allow black patients to sit in their waiting rooms, and there was no contact between white doctors and what they called "nigger doctors," Bate said. The Tulsa County Medical Society was organized in 1907 with a "whites only" clause that was repeated in every monthly bulletin. The society gave $25 and medical instruments to each of the black doctors who lost everything in the riot, but for much of its history, black Tulsa had no surgeons and no X-ray equipment.[16]

Thus, blacks sometimes had to seek care in white institutions, where they were rigidly segregated, if accepted at all. Even linens and instruments were segregated, Bate said. If a black doctor referred a patient there, he was not allowed to witness the operation. "Regardless of financial status, educational or otherwise, black patients had to be admitted to squalid and poor conditions in the local white hospitals if admitted at all," he said. One hospital treated blacks only in the basement. In another, the occasional black patients were housed in the furnace room, which had a patient capacity of two. Black babies could not be delivered in white hospitals; a premature infant with rare complications was relegated to the janitor's supply closet.[17]

The Tulsa County Medical Society was desegregated at 1952 with admission of Dr. Bate, who was instructed not to socialize with white members. St. John's Hospital maintained a "colored ward" and didn't begin integrating patients until 1962, Bate said.[18]

Moton Hospital struggled for many years. The community donated window air conditioners after five babies died there in a 1954 heat wave. Bate contended that white hospitals blocked federal funding for Moton, which closed in 1967, leaving Tulsa effectively without a charity hospital and 140,000 people in North Tulsa without an accessible hospital.[19]

For all those reasons, Dan Allen made the decision in 1970 to start a charity clinic at Neighbor for Neighbor. He must have known that the job was probably the most difficult in NFN's history of impossible windmill challenges.

Chapter 10

The Free Clinic:
Let Him Come In, He Might Be Jesus

"It's the unconditional, positive regard for that person,
under their terms, period!
...They don't have to perform, they don't have to pray,
they don't have to look the way,
you know, white people need to have people
act to be accepted. . . .
All the rest of this—the dental, the medical, the legal,
whatever—is . . . so that they can walk away from here feeling
like they are themselves, and they're always welcome in that way."

—Dan Allen

Carol Falletti bandages child. Tom Gilbert photo, *Tulsa World*, August 10, 1987.

WHERE ARE THE HOLY MOMENTS?

The folks . . . at Neighbor for Neighbor meet the Word of God when they are creating a kinder, gentler environment for the sick.

This is a holy moment, across the desk from the volunteer during intake. "Intake"—one of those funny clinical words we use—is "taking in" that person, at that moment, with unconditional personal regard for the whole person sitting there, flesh and blood and spirit . . . the interviewer.

People meet the Word of God through the nurse's loving touch, the nurse who makes no judgment about the patient's clothes or smell or lice in the scalp. That is a holy moment.

People meet the Word of God through the competence, sense of humor, and serious care of those filling prescriptions . . . words on paper taking flesh in healing medicine.
That is a holy moment.

People meet the Word of God through the doctors whose skilled hands, intelligent mind and gentle heart listen well and respond with compassion. That is a holy moment.

People meet the Word of God through the medical technicians who patiently and carefully test the body fluids.
That is a holy moment.

—Father Bill Skeehan
To Dance with a Cross on Our Back

If Carol Falletti thought she was getting away from the world of poverty, she could not have been more wrong. Once she agreed to volunteer at NFN, the rest of her life—for Carol, her husband Don, and their five children—was to be consumed by volunteer service to the poor.

Father Dan had picked Carol Falletti—an unassuming young housewife, Church of the Resurrection parish member, mother of five little children—to develop and run the NFN free clinic. Some may have thought Carol was a peculiar choice: she was a Registered Clinical Medical Technologist but lacked any training or experience in developing or managing a poverty medical clinic. Pictures of the day show her looking young, idealistic, thoughtful, and a little wistful. She could well have been described as a mere slip of a girl—but only by those who did not know her well.

What photos did not show was Carol's 360-degree vision, oversized heart, unyielding commitment, stern professionalism, and iron backbone. She turned out to be one of those irrational, intuitive, home-run decisions that were becoming a Dan Allen trademark. Dan trusted her completely.

"We threw Dan out of his office and moved his office into the garage..."

Dan saw clearly that a most pervasive and persistent problem facing the poor, including the working poor, was chronic health and medical crisis. By the fall of 1970, Allen was willing to accept a federal grant to bring in seed money. "I heard about this Emergency Food and Medical Services grant," Dan Allen remembered. He found Wilbert Collins, then running a butcher shop, and convinced him to come back to NFN to help secure and manage the grant. "Never before or since have we pursued federal monies . . . but I knew the future of NFN depended on this venture," Dan said.[1]

In a program spearheaded by Carol and Don Falletti, Resurrection volunteers donated materials and labor to renovate the little rock house to create space for a walk-in clinic as well as for a food project next door.[2] "We threw Dan out of his office and moved his office into the garage—Dan was cussing, swearing never to move again," Carol Falletti said later.[3]

Dan gave Carol free rein to create the NFN free clinic, for which serious planning began in 1970. There was no rule book for how to create and run a clinic, so Carol created her own. "Maynard and Wilbert were telling me about big clinics being set up in other cities, but all I could see was starting up a little clinic and seeing how far we could go with it," she said.

Everything hinged, of course, on recruiting doctors and nurses who would work for free. To begin recruiting, Carol sought out the Tulsa County Medical Society and asked for help. "They told us they would not do anything to stop us, but that we should not practice quack medicine," she remembered.[4]

"When we first started out, we didn't realize the density of the problems out there. Some people didn't agree with the idea of a free clinic," Carol said.[5] By contrast, others offered invaluable help. For example, Dr. George Prothro, then director of the Tulsa City-County Health Department, worked step-by-step to help put the clinic together, Carol remembered.[6]

"When I came to the Health Department in 1968," Dr. Prothro recalled later, "health and medical care in South Tulsa was close to the top of the national charts, not far behind the Mayo Clinic. North Tulsa was close to the bottom." He worried about problems of tuberculosis, venereal disease, infant and maternal mortality, anemia or obesity from malnutrition in Tulsa's poor neighborhoods. To Prothro, the root causes were simple to see— prejudice, poverty, and lack of education—but the solutions were complex. Tulsa's fight for better health and medical care for the black community had been stirred by the civil rights movement and LBJ's War on Poverty, but institutional improvement proved elusive.

"In 1968, health and medical care in South Tulsa was not far behind the Mayo Clinic. North Tulsa was close to the bottom."

As Dan pointed out, Tulsa lacked a charity hospital or workable clinic solution for the poor. Before the NFN clinic, Tulsa's only indigent outpatient clinic was at one or another South Tulsa hospital, first Hillcrest, then St. John, but it was a financial drain for them. "People learned they might get cheap treatment on a certain day. People might wait all day to be seen for five minutes. It was not very satisfactory," Prothro said.

North Tulsans engaged in a spirited fight to get a Northside hospital, but their efforts ultimately proved futile. Prothro capitalized on Model Cities money to reopen Moton Health Center in North Tulsa, but Moton had severe financial problems and had to operate under federal guidelines that shut out many needy people. Also, Moton had a $30 "visitation fee" that some people couldn't pay. So Prothro threw his support behind the fledgling NFN Clinic that would not be hidebound by guidelines.

He wanted to send Health Department doctors to NFN, but he had only two and they were busy throughout the county. Instead, he became an advisor to Carol and the NFN Clinic, helping with problem solving and issues such as the management and disposal of drugs, and tapping community resources and assistance. He also helped mobilize visiting nurses to follow up in patients' homes after treatment.[7]

The doors opened July 27, 1971. The clinic was staffed by volunteer doctors and operated by volunteers. They dispensed donated medicine. It all started with two volunteer doctors: John Watson and Paul Park. Both were from Resurrection Parish.

"Dr. Watson and Dr. Park gave us the courage to go on," Carol remembered. "They were willing to work from 8:00 p.m. to 11:00 p.m. one night a week, Wednesday nights, and they would see as many people as they could see. Then we would go out and eat after the clinic. It was like the high point of our week.

"The rest of the week, our nurse and I would review the charts, call people to see how they were responding, follow up to solve problems such as how to pay for X-rays or antibiotics or how to beg donated equipment.

"Give me a good nurse anytime, and we had the best. Sally Turner was the first clinic nurse. She lived across the street from me, and she went to emergency rooms to learn more before coming to NFN. Sally was so perfect and ready for this thing," Carol said.

"I gave patients my home phone number. We were casual about everything but the treatment. We might be wearing jeans, but we were all completely professional, and nothing was left open-ended.

"People came from anywhere, some walking, some riding the bus, some begging a one-way ride with a friend and then we had to figure how to get them home. We began by providing acute care for anybody who walked in the door. Later our big problem was chronically ill poor: people with diabetes, thyroid, high blood pressure, heart, asthma, emphysema."

"I gave patients my home phone number. We were casual about everything but the treatment."

In the beginning, everything about the operation was experimental, trial and error. "I probably had the finest education possible on what to do and what not to do in terms of clinic management," Carol said. "I remember Dr. Stephen Adelson, who said, 'Don't ask your doctors to do "well baby" exams because those types of services are available elsewhere. I will see only sick children.' That was one of the best lessons I ever learned. From then on, I knew to learn what was available elsewhere in Tulsa for the poor, so when people came to us, I knew to refer people first. We focused on the services that only our clinic could provide."

They started by dispensing donated samples of medicines and bought other needed prescriptions for people. "We started in a little closet, and the docs brought their samples. We never called it a pharmacy; it was a dispensary. If we didn't have what a patient needed, we would find a way to buy it for them."

The clinic was in a house, so the lab was logically in the kitchen, because that's where the water was. "We had a sterilizer in the lab, where we cleaned, sterilized, and wrapped our medical instruments. It worked well.

"We had a little bathroom to collect specimens and drew blood in the lab. We had the most wonderful med techs who volunteered in that little lab; they came from St. John and adopted us as their personal project. We had this huge blood chemistry machine they had scrounged from their storage spot. We had microscopes and quite a lot from the beginning," she said.[8]

An amazing transformation occurred when a patient entered treatment stalls. From the chaos of the intake room—the living room of the little rock house—a patient would be admitted to the bedrooms for one of three examining "rooms" divided by sheets. "We wanted to create a sense of privacy for the patients, although of course you could hear whoever was talking in the next space," she said. "When you went into a patient room, it was like sacred ground. It was like a little friendly and personal and professional bubble behind those curtains."

"Good medicine is practiced here," Carol said at the time. "We're not just Band-Aid medicine. If we can get a doctor to come out once, they see how well-organized and smoothly run the clinic is, and they stay. We don't have that big a turn-over."[9]

In time, as the patient numbers grew, it became harder to ensure proper clinical conditions in the lab, and St. John Hospital started doing the lab work. "I can't say enough good things about St. John and their administration and their pathologists," Carol said.

"Sometimes people needed care we couldn't give. The doc would say, 'This person has to have an X-ray.' Well, where were they going to get an X-ray, for Pete's sake? Those things don't grow free on trees. Insurance? Ha! You've got to be kidding; nobody had insurance. The clients didn't have any money, and neither did we at Neighbor for Neighbor. We had to figure it out, negotiating it, convincing the hospital that we would pay $15 if they would pay the other $15. Sometimes people were too sick for us, and we had to find a way to get them into an emergency room or hospital when they didn't have any money," Carol said.

"We knew it wasn't fair to keep people waiting and waiting. That's part of being poor."

They didn't turn anyone away. "We didn't need guidelines. It was not easy or pleasant, standing outside for hours for a chance to see a volunteer doctor, waiting more long hours in a crowded room full of sick people. We learned the hard way that we had to wait to open the door until the volunteer docs got here after their regular office hours. People might wait a year for glasses or dental care. We knew it wasn't fair to keep people waiting and waiting. That's part of being poor, always waiting. We didn't think anyone would go through the hassle if they could help it, so we didn't play detective a whole lot."

Sometimes nothing worked. "I would call the teaching hospitals in Oklahoma City, and sometimes they could help; other times I would tell patients, just show up and tell them your plight," Carol said.[10]

What sort of people came to the NFN free clinic? People in crisis, like the fellow who had just enough gasoline to make it to NFN. The rambling collection of rock and metal buildings was the end of the line for him, in more than one way.

> *"We serve the people who fall through the cracks. Half of our clients have an income of less than $200 a month. Almost 90 percent have an income below $500 a month."*

"He was really troubled," a volunteer remembered. "And I could see why. One of his children had just been killed in an accident, and his wife had tried to commit suicide. He was trying to hold it together. But he couldn't find a job, and he was sick besides—in need of surgery and medicine—and there was no food in the house for his children. We helped him with the medicine, food, and some small bills, and gas money. He seemed overwhelmed to find somebody who cared enough to listen. He wanted to pay us back."

NFN served the working poor: the mother of four working as a waitress, the grandfather still trying to work as a mechanic on the days he was able, the day laborer with sick kids and no insurance.

"We serve the people who fall through the cracks," Father Allen said. "Half of our clients have an income of less than $200 a month. Almost 90 percent have an income below $500 a month—how the hell can you manage on that, much less pay a medical bill? Only one NFN client in four gets any public assistance, and that is usually just social security, not welfare.

"These people are trying to help themselves. They aren't grifters. I don't know where people get the idea that these folks have two cars and a color TV set. A lot of our people can't even get here because they have no transportation at all."[11]

An example that illustrates the way NFN worked was the story of a young woman named Cheryl whose meth addiction was destroying her teeth and her life, Dan said. All her money was spent on drugs and alcohol. "I want to save the teeth I have left," she said when she came to NFN, in desperation. Years later, Dan cited Cheryl's success: drug free, sober, with a healthy smile, she worked for years helping in the NFN dental clinic. "I got a second chance in life," Cheryl said.[12]

Before long, the free clinic was able to open several nights a week, with new equipment, more space (created by volunteers and donors), and 350 volunteers. All served without compensation. "We are rewarded with a smile, rather than something we can put in our pocketbook, and that really means more to me," said one volunteer doctor, Dr. James Wolfe.[13]

Jim Wolfe went on to become the clinic's longest-serving volunteer doctor, Carol recalled later. Among many other long-term volunteers was Dr. Tim Dennehy, Dan's high school chum, who grew up to become an MD. "Every time I came, I would get to visit with Dan a few minutes," Tim said. "He didn't meddle in the management; Carol ran the medical clinic and Lorraine ran the dental clinic. The problem was that other places wouldn't take people without insurance, so they would just get sicker and sicker until they came to us or the emergency room or just died. In the back, they had the little dispensary with donated medicine, all unopened, labeled and organized. I would write prescriptions, and Skeehan would take them to the patients—no pain medicine except ibuprofen, no sleeping pills, no antidepressants. If people needed surgery or were having critical problems, we helped them get referred, mostly to St. John and to doctors we knew would see them. They didn't have Medicaid then," Dennehy said.

"There were so many great doctors who worked with the NFN clinic— like my friends Don Pfeiffer and Vince Barranco. It was a very professional little operation and a great time for me. It was the people who made it worthwhile—it was a gift."[14]

In short order, the NFN free clinic expanded to include pediatric, dental, and optometric care for the poor.

The original dental clinic, founded by Dentists Jim Maxey and J. R. Wightman, was partitioned off by a shower curtain, but Maxey and Wightman hustled good equipment and surgical instruments.[15] "We had one dental chair and an X-ray machine, with really fine hygienists," said Lorraine Lowe, who became dental clinic director. "We had the cream of the crop in every way."

How did they field volunteer doctors and medical professionals? Most were volunteers, many fielded by Carol. Occasional voluntary institutional arrangements helped, too. In the 1980s, the Internal Medicine Department of the University of Oklahoma began assigning resident students to NFN, under the direction of Dr. William Yarborough, plus an attending physician who saw patients one day a week. Later Pranay Katuria, MD, began coming weekly to see patients, too.[16]

Another notable example of service came from Tulsa's prestigious downtown church, Boston Avenue Methodist. In the early 1980s, Dr. Duane Brothers and his wife Sue, NFN volunteers, convinced their Boston Avenue social concerns committee to adopt the NFN clinic. The committee had been looking for some kind of outreach activity to help medically indigent people. "It answered a prayer for us," Sue Brothers remembered later. She and Duane were coordinators.

"It worked perfectly," Carol Falletti said. The Boston Avenue group provided doctors, dentists, nurses, pharmacists, clerical workers, and other volunteers. "That's how the Monday night clinic was created, under the supervision of Lorraine Lowe, who also served as dental clinic director. Boston Avenue provided all the volunteers for the Monday night clinics. It was a wonderful relationship that lasted for twenty years."[17]

Dr. Duane Brothers and his wife Sue at the Boston Avenue social concerns committee adopted the clinic. "It answered a prayer for us, remembered Sue Brothers.

Lorraine Lowe was one of the NFN miracles, Carol said: "a beautiful person and one of the best I have ever known. She is so symbolic of NFN. Lorraine didn't have a medical background. She had been raised in Harlem by very strict parents and worked as an administrative assistant in the garment district. She worked for Dan and over time came to run the dental clinic, and it was just amazing." A dental hygienist, Jan Shurts, developed the dental clinic's sterile techniques and taught them to every volunteer.

"We practice preventive dentistry—the only kind the poor can afford," said Dan Allen. [18]

People crowded into the dental clinic four nights a week and sometimes on Saturday, too, Lorraine remembered. "We had lines from here to there. We tried requiring appointments, but they just kept coming. Dan taught us to treat everyone with dignity and respect, the way you would want to be treated, and we did that. We couldn't turn anybody away.

"We gave out numbers to manage the lines, and people started making up their own numbers to try to get relief from aching teeth. It was hard to close the door. I remember one night, late, we were all worn out, and here came another man in great pain begging to get a tooth pulled."

"'Let him come in,' said the volunteer dentist, Dr. Phil Marano, "he might be Jesus."[19]

"Neighbor for Neighbor was an on-going miracle every day, and so much fun among clinic volunteers and staff," Carol recalled. "These people were hilarious—a sense of humor goes a long way in a crisis. That was something I appreciated in Dan, and he in me. Dan's wit was one of a kind.

"I could never say no."
— Dr. Jim Wolfe

Dan and I used to go round and round over some of the decisions—he thought I was too legalistic, but I knew what we had to do to maintain quality care. But in the end he would always encourage me and he trusted me. 'Do what you think you have to do,' he would tell me. Outside of his chain smoking—six cigarettes at a time—he wasn't that hard to get along with. He hated the word 'charismatic' because he wanted very much to be just an ordinary person—but even with his crusty personality, charismatic is what he was."

Lunch hours became legend among the clinic flock. "Lunchtime became a sacred, celebratory sharing of food, ideas, and fun among clinic volunteers and staff. Anybody was welcome—there was always an extra place at the table," Carol remembered. "We would potluck every day, nothing planned except to share what was always a feast—we were top-heavy with amazing Southern cooks. As we ate, we had spirited debate over health care issues and intense shared education about social injustice. Then we had at least fifteen minutes of hilarity."

With birthday roasts, holiday celebrations, and shared jokes, "we would laugh until our faces hurt. Then were the drawings for incredible door prizes, ridiculous found treasures everybody would bring.

"We did good work," Carol said. "It was a special time of service to the poor. I had the med tech and pathology background, but mostly I was just the glue, the continuity to hold it all together; that was my one talent in the clinic—but the genius came from the tremendous community support we received."[20]

"I could never say no," said Dr. Jim Wolfe, who racked up the longest tenure, thirty-five years as a clinic volunteer doctor. "It was never convenient, and there was always something else to do, but—I just got hooked. When I would leave the clinic and drive south on Peoria, going home, I always had a great feeling.

"But I didn't have to drive very far south before I saw the difference. It was a different world. Within a few miles, there was no comparison in the health care people were getting. It never seemed fair to me. We never had enough resources at NFN to provide the care people needed, and they had no money for insurance or doctors. Sometimes I would tell them to come to see me in my hospital emergency room—just ask for me so you don't get charged, and that way we could follow up," Wolfe said.

"The thing that weighed on me was, I couldn't do enough out there. I was focused on blood pressure, but they had all these other problems, too. I never knew if I was really helping, but I couldn't help myself. I was addicted. I had to go back and get my fix."[21]

Sometimes NFN threw volunteers into their own kind of crisis, and Carol had to work with them carefully to get them through it. Father Allen warned newcomers that the facilities "are totally inadequate—but that's okay, the poor are comfortable then. The rooms are so cramped, you may get on each other's nerves. But at least you know you have nerves."[22]

"The most important thing Dan taught us was that every single person deserved unconditional positive regard. Dan would not accept anything less in terms of service. And I insisted that we do everything in our power to practice good medicine, put the patient first, use whatever resources we could scrounge up for chronically ill patients, and always operate in a totally professional, ethical manner," Carol said.

That system worked. Dr. Prothro was pleased to observe the progress and professionalism of the little clinic. In time, the NFN clinic developed its own excellent reputation. Doctors recruited doctors, and even the Medical Society, and the Tulsa County Dental Society as well, became strong partners.

In the first 15 years, the clinic provided over $1 million in medical services, serving 8,500 needy people a year.

The clinic evolved over the years, providing care for thousands and thousands of needy families and individuals. In the beginning, the clinic was open only Wednesday nights; by the time Carol retired in 2005, the various clinics were open four days a week from mornings to 6 or sometimes 10:00 p.m.[23]

To celebrate its first fifteen years, NFN assembled some statistics: clinic volunteers were providing more than $1 million annually in direct medical, dental, and optometric services to the poor, to help an estimated 8,500 needy people a year.[24]

It would take a book to cite all the people who worked to make the clinic a success. "What Carol Falletti meant then and means now to the poor, the staff and volunteers, is a book in itself," Allen said in 1991, on the clinic's twentieth anniversary. "The clinic is a living memorial to the hundreds of persons who portray people in their finest hours . . . the unconditional gift of themselves to others simply for the sake of these others.

"The volunteer presence did not require proper gratitude from the poor, their names in the papers and on the walls. In fact, this is the only time we have acknowledged them. Hence our esteem and gratitude is even more deeply felt. Their work is sacred and daily shared."[25]

Like Carol Falletti, most of the volunteers came through the experience with a lifetime commitment to social justice.

"The more we are able to educate the affluent to the problems of the poor, the quicker social change will take place," Carol said.

"Our work is our advocacy."[26]

Chapter 11

With All Deliberate Speed

Dan Allen in his office. Mike Wyke photo, *Tulsa Tribune*, November 21, 1986.

"Our whole concept has been
to bring the world of low-income people
into the ghetto of those with means.
Their work is sacred and daily shared."

—Dan Allen

FEW PEOPLE KNOW NFN'S ROLE IN
INTEGRATING TULSA PUBLIC SCHOOLS...

"Telling the truth would violate a fundamental tenet of Neighbor for Neighbor, never to pat itself on the back or take credit. . . .

"But I think it's in the interest of future historians to know that NFN was a key participant in Tulsa's voluntary desegregation of the schools. The community was drifting toward chaos, in need of a particularly creative kind of vision to draw us together. It arose, as a matter of fact, at Neighbor for Neighbor, starting on a windy spring evening in Pat Flanagan's living room."

—Gloria Caldwell [1]

You might say this chapter of the Dan Allen story started in 1896, when the U.S. Supreme Court ruled in *Plessy v. Ferguson* that separate was indeed equal and that segregation of the races was constitutional, and just fine, thank you.

Or perhaps it was after Tulsa's 1921 race riot, when blacks were jammed into a small finger of land north of downtown.[2]

It could have been in 1941, when the Oklahoma legislature made it illegal for an administrator to admit even one student of a different race to his or her school, or for a teacher to instruct even a single student of a different race, or for a student to share a classroom with even one student of another race.[3]

Maybe it began in 1945 when the National Urban League determined that Tulsa was the most segregated city in the nation. That news didn't make much stir. Tulsans, like many Americans, lived in two separate societies, where preferential distribution of resources and opportunities to white citizens was legal and accepted policy.[4]

It was in the years after World War II that life began to change. Returning veterans had seen different ways to live. Black soldiers hankered for equality. One of the early changes came in 1948, when President Truman issued an executive order outlawing segregation in the U.S. military. About the same time, the U.S. Supreme Court ruled against restrictive covenants that had segregated housing by race. But it was another decade before Tulsa banks began slowly lending to blacks, allowing them to begin to creep into areas formerly reserved for whites.[5]

A black (he called himself "Negro" or, proudly, "colored") attorney in

Tulsa, Amos T. Hall by name, began to bring court challenges to overturn discrimination in policing and other practices.[6] Amos had a way of speaking: gently but with great authority. "I am Amos Hall," he would say quietly, and you knew that meant something. He had earned his right to be heard.

Amos came to Tulsa from Mississippi a few months before the race riot. "We had no paved streets, no water," he remembered later. "We did have walls, gas lights, outdoor toilets—and a Baptist church on every corner. Our business district thrived on Greenwood, and Tulsa was considered at that time to have one of the best Negro districts in the country."

During the riot, "most homes in the Negro district, including my own, were burned by fire. . . . There was a move to rezone the whole area industrial (so homes would not be rebuilt there), but fair-minded white citizens stepped forward to help some of us rebuild. Others, wiped out and without 'riot insurance,' erected what shelter they could and rebuilt their lives as best they could."

Like most other black people, Amos had found only menial labor when he came to Tulsa. He worked as a janitor at First Methodist Church, where he found a discarded set of books: *Learn to be a Lawyer in Your Spare Time.* He began studying the law. In time, without benefit of formal schooling, he passed the bar (he was stunned that he passed and very grateful). Amos set up a law practice in the Greenwood area. He was elected justice of the peace, serving for six years. He joined the Prince Hall Masons—a separate black fraternity, since people of color could not join the white Masonic lodge. He moved up easily through its ranks, becoming the Grand Master, the number one global leader of the international Prince Hall Masons, which represented many of the world's most distinguished black leaders. He also became a leader of the NAACP, chairing the Tulsa chapter for many years.

What Amos saw in his hometown troubled him. "We were separate societies, by law," he said. He set about working to "erase the lines those laws drew between us—a color curtain through which we could only view each other with fear and suspicion." [7]

In 1945, Amos and NAACP attorney Thurgood Marshall sought a qualified black applicant to challenge segregation at the University of Oklahoma law school. They found a volunteer. On January 14, 1946, Ada Lois Sipuel, granddaughter of slaves, applied to the OU law school and was denied because of race. The legal fight took years. Hall and Marshall won their first round of argument before the U.S. Supreme Court, but then the Oklahoma Regents for Higher Education decided to set up a separate Langston University School of Law, just for Ada Lois. Back to the courts; up to the

Supreme Court and back; on and on.

Meanwhile, Amos was also fighting the case of George McLaurin, a black applicant to OU's graduate school. Citing precedents already set in the Sipuel case, the courts ordered OU to admit him or disband their school; OU complied but erected a barrier rail around his seat to separate him from the white students.

Finally, on June 18, 1949, Ada Lois Sipuel was allowed to enroll in the OU law school. A year later, the U.S. Supreme Court ruled that OU could not maintain the barrier around the seat of George McLaurin. Amos T. Hall's crusade was bearing important fruit.

In 1954, the U.S. Supreme Court, in *Brown v. Board of Education of Topeka, Kansas,* unanimously declared that school segregation was unconstitutional. Thurgood Marshall successfully argued that separate educational facilities are inherently unequal. The court ordered southern schools to dismantle their segregated school systems "with all deliberate speed."[8]

Over the subsequent years, some of the bravest little children in America marched resolutely through white mobs to slowly batter down the walls of segregation.

Tulsa's historical dual school systems, one black and one white, were merged in 1955, but little occurred in the way of classroom desegregation because the races still lived in separate worlds. At all costs, white parents wanted to preserve their neighborhood schools, and those neighborhoods were still segregated. Despite the landmark 1954 ruling, and despite a handful of radical programs around the U.S. that began busing children for racial balance, little changed in Tulsa public schools for a generation.[9]

To help maintain the racial status quo as fringe neighborhoods changed color, Tulsa Public Schools made frequent school boundary changes and established a system of allowing— perhaps encouraging—minority-to-majority transfers. If your white child was in a minority-white school, he or she could easily transfer to a school with a majority of whites, for example. Or vice versa, if your child was black. It led to some strange machinations.

Consider the case of Burroughs Elementary, a tidy red brick school in a quiet middle-class (read: white) neighborhood of North Tulsa. In 1959 as black families drifted into the area, and as white families quietly fled, all-white Burroughs changed almost overnight into a school with 30.9 percent black enrollment. By the end of that school year, Burroughs became a majority-black school with 62 percent black students. In addition to black migration and white flight, the change was caused by the school board's policies that encouraged whites to transfer out to majority-white schools.[10]

Concern mounted after the 1964 Civil Rights Law gave the federal government power to enforce desegregation, giving new urgency to Tulsa's schools question.[11]

Years of confusion followed, with the schools presenting timid plans that were alternately accepted by hometown judges and overruled at the higher federal bench. The school board was hesitant to go beyond the minimum requirements forced upon them by the courts. Among the few white voices raised on behalf of desegregation was a local reporter who accused the school board of "making major decisions in secrecy and failing to grapple with problems in the public. . . . The board members are 'hand-picked' by the school administration. . . . Southside candidates consistently win over better qualified candidates from other sections of the city."[12]

A few others also raised their voices. At All Souls Unitarian Church, the Reverend John B. Wolf ripped Tulsa Public Schools leadership and, specifically, school superintendent Charles C. Mason, for failing to lead the community into the new era of desegregation. Mason had been Tulsa Public Schools superintendent since 1944. In a Febuary 18, 1968, sermon entitled "The Last Days of Dr. Mason," Wolf accused Mason of sloth, playing possum, feigning innocence, deplorable lack of leadership, and operating a façade hiding "galloping mediocrity," among other things.

Tulsa was, in fact, still running dual school systems, which "is against the law," Wolf exclaimed. "It is a scandal. . . . What is holding us back are short-sighted men whose responses are to the prejudices, the pettiness and provinciality of society rather than to the high demands which inspire the mind and enthrall the hearts of men."[13]

Ugly phone calls poured into Wolf's home, accusing him of "mongrelizing the races" and worse. The following Sunday, twenty-two preachers decried Wolf from their own pulpits. Wolf's response was to preach more sermons about school desegregation.

"People who complain that the citizenry lacks a voice in government, in their churches or schools, are likely to be considered radicals [or] Communists," Wolf said. Part of the problem with contemporary society, he said, "is a deep-seated feeling of guilt about race on the part of almost all white people. When [this guilt] is denied or repressed, it can appear in the form of towering hostility against the person one has already wronged. . . . Here is a real live demon in our midst that must be exorcised."

The solution? "We have to tell it like it is," Wolf said. "And we have to repent of it and move to correct it. . . . And that is the only way."[14]

Charles Mason retired. A new school superintendent, Dr. Gordon Cawelti, took over May 1, 1969, saying, "Public education must secure civil rights for all its citizens [and find] ways to overcome widespread racial, religious, and ethnic prejudice and discrimination." The biggest hurdle was Tulsa's segregated housing pattern, Cawelti said.[15]

Nonetheless, Tulsa's progress in desegregating its schools "could truly be described as meager" before August 1971, the U.S. Commission on Civil Rights found. For example, boundary changes added twenty white students to formerly all-black Booker T. Washington High School.[16] At the historically black Carver Junior High, the school board added one white student, bringing the 100 percent black enrollment to 99.8 percent.[17]

By the 1970s, the National Urban League found that Tulsa was now only the sixth most segregated city in America.[18] Nonetheless, the 1970 census revealed troubling trends:

• Tulsa's population was 331,638, of which 10.6 percent (35,277) were black, nearly all still clustered in a few square miles of North Tulsa.[19]

• Average black families had a fraction of the average income of whites. Majority-black schools scored miserably on achievement tests; the black high school had reading scores eight times lower than the highest-ranked white high school.[20]

• White Tulsans were beginning to abandon the north side and were moving, quietly and overwhelmingly, south and east—often outside the Tulsa Public Schools district. More than 200 percent of Tulsa's growth since 1960 had occurred in the lily-white southeast quadrant, while the northern and central sections were losing property value and population.[21] North and central Tulsa were being abandoned, as planner Gerald Wilhite said at the time, like a "Kleenex city."[22]

• At least in part because of white flight, these trends would continue and accelerate in subsequent decades, leaving vacancies throughout north and central Tulsa, eroding the economic health of the entire community in general and the Tulsa Public Schools in particular.

• Tulsa Public Schools enrollment was sagging and by 1974 would be down 14,000 from its 1968 high water mark of 80,000 students. By coincidence, southeast suburban school districts gained nearly 12,000 students in the same time period, and that number did not include the burgeoning private schools. By 1975, the number of TPS white students would drop from 66,000 in 1968 to 49,000, while black enrollment would rise to 11,407. It was, in fact, just the beginning.[23]

• These trends meant that, by the 1970s, Tulsa and its region were assidu-
ously re-segregating neighborhoods and therefore schools. The neighborhood school concept was on a collision course with desegregation and the
demands of modern law. But the school board continued to contend that,
whatever else happened, Tulsa would preserve its neighborhood schools and
avoid the big yellow bus.

On April 20, 1971, the U.S. Supreme Court dropped another shoe and
ruled, in the Swann case, that judges could order busing as a legitimate
means to integrate public schools. The rest, as they say, is history.

Although pale by comparison to what was occurring in other places such
as Oklahoma City, Tulsa's uproar was memorable over the specter of MFB
("Massive Forced Busing"). Forty thousand people signed petitions against
busing, spearheaded by westsider Virgil Hensley and his Coalition for
Neighborhood Schools. They were challenged by the Community Relations
Commission, the League of Women Voters, some churches—and Neighbor
for Neighbor.[24]

Each side put forth school board candidates in the January 1972
election—the first under a new state law, spearheaded by Tulsa's first black
legislator (he always teased that he was just "a soft lavender tan"), the Reverend Ben Hill. Previously, all Tulsa's School Board members were elected at
large district-wide, which meant a minority had no chance of being elected.
Under the new law, school board members would be nominated in district
elections, then elected citywide.

In the first district election under the new law, NFN's Gloria Caldwell
managed the campaign of the pro-integration candidate, Community Relations Commission member Dr. Earl J. Reeves. He lost, overwhelmingly. The
anti-busing candidate won 80 percent of the vote.[25]

But the fight over school integration was far from finished.

rban Blight, Southeast Flight Mean Tax Bite

Two Tulsas: One Thriving

By ANN PATTON
Of the World Staff

Tulsa, a little country town grown up, is showing signs of big city problems. Urban blight and spreading areas where a "crisis of confidence" threaten ...

1st of 3 Parts

are signs which the average Tulsan may not see but which are digging into his tax dollar and threatening to cost him even more.

Tulsans directly involved already are paying dearly, sometimes with their life's savings. Those escaping their encounter with "urban problems" without great financial loss often are still left with a deep residue of bitterness.

... heart of the issue is ... complex ... terns — both a cause and effect of the "central-city" crisis one hears so much about.

BUT IN TULSA'S CASE, rather than creating a doughnut-shaped city with an abandoned heart, experts warn Tulsans are simply moving southeast and throwing away investments in what they have known as America's most beautiful city.

Wherever you live in the city, you already are paying with tax dollars for the areas left behind — plus creation of the new.

It appears there really are two Tulsas, as many have maintained, one booming and one dying. But the dividing line is shifting.

"In terms of present and future housing needs, Tulsa appears to be at a very pivotal juncture," warns a housing study of the Indian Nations Council of Governments credited by some with launching the city's intense study of its growth patterns.

TWO-THIRDS OF THE city's standard housing, in Central, West and North Tulsa, is threatened by weakening market forces left in the wake of the pull of housing ... and population ... southeast, the ... chairs with housing in this corridor of North Tulsa, the INCOG study says.

Whites are vacating houses on the downhill, blacks are getting final wear of the homes and then abandoning them for other houses newly vacated by whites.

In the process, investments evaporate and neighborhoods deteriorate.

Losses ... racial shi... be docum... — Duri... the area ... whites ... about 7,2... known as ... nity (and ... area) los... between ...

First Voluntary Integration Of School Due Here in Fall

AUG 6 1971

By GREG BROADD
Of the World Staff

Tulsa school officials said Thursday they expect 150-160 evenly split black and white children in Burroughs Elementary School's pilot continuous progress program when it opens Aug. 30.

The plan, which became near-reality at a Wednesday night meeting of about 200 black and white parents at Burroughs, is the result of two months of quiet planning by a group of whites led by Tulsa attorney Maynard Ungerman.

This group was encouraged and aided by Dr. Gordon Cawelti, Tulsa schools superintendent, and Burroughs principal Elmer Jenkins. It becomes Tulsa's first voluntarily integrated school.

"We will begin in-service training of the three team teaching leaders this month," J. Morton, director of elementary education, said Thursday.

"THE BALANCE of the teaching staff for the new program will be trained by the middle or end of September. The program should be in full operation in its own 'H-pre-' unit by November," Morton said.

Mrs. Ungerman said Thursday she has "about 75-80 white youngsters signed up and ready for the program." These students would be voluntarily transferred from their home schools to Burroughs under the majority-to-minority transfer policy of the Tulsa Public Schools.

She said "response has been very positive and very good since the Wednesday meeting."

MRS JOE Williams, a black parent of Burroughs students, said: "Many of us have wanted integrated educational experiences for our children. That's why we first moved into this neighborhood in 1964.

"But soon there was a mass exodus of whites from this school attendance zone and the school became all black. This is the first time the whites have wanted to come back here. All our children can benefit," she said.

MRS. UNGERMAN said one of the most important aspects of the program "is its flexibility to conform with the individual needs of the students in it."

The Ungermans have three children — a kindergartener, a third grader, and a fifth grader — who will be bused about 10 miles from near their home to Burroughs for a voluntary integrated education.

"We expect about 75-80 black students to join the whites in the new voluntary integrated curriculum at Burroughs."

HE SAID the three segments — humanities, communications skills, and mathematics-science — would hold about 50-55 children in each segment in two age levels.

In other words, about 25-30 students would be grouped by ages (6 and 7-year-olds; 8 and 9-year-olds; 10 and 11-year-olds) for each of the three segments of the continuous progress curricula.

Mrs. Dale Edmond, director of elementary curriculum for the Tulsa schools, said the three segments would be similar to those being opened Aug. 30 at the new Columbus and Sandburg Elementary Schools.

"This program provides children with the opportunity for continuous growth at their own rates in any subject area," Mrs. Edmond said. "It makes them want to go back for more because they are properly challenged."

Jenkins said he is "elated" over the response and the new program for Burroughs ...

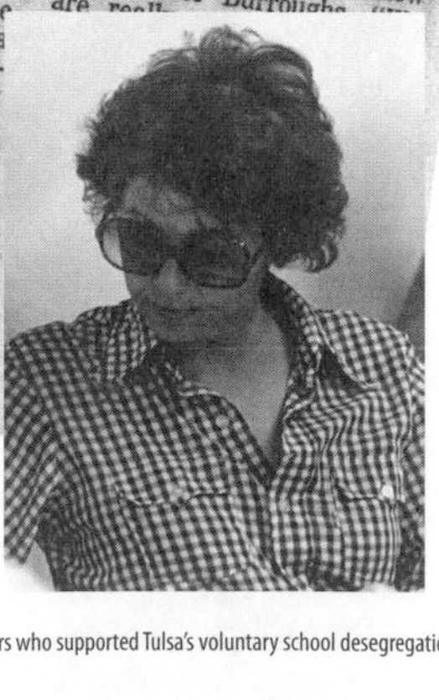

Sandra Downie (now Langenkamp), NFN and civic volunteer, was one of the mothers who supported Tulsa's voluntary school desegregation program.

Chapter 12

Learning To Love
That Big Yellow Bus

"Placing oneself between the oppressor and the oppressed
is the essence of liberation theology which, in my opinion,
is the fundamental message of the New Testament."

—Dan Allen

EVERYBODY KNEW IT WOULD NEVER HAPPEN. BUT IN TULSA IT DID.

Timothy Downie, age 6, is ready.

Tim's name is pinned securely to the pocket of his new blue Oxford-cloth shirt, above his plaid madras pants and prized new Superman belt. His blond hair is carefully parted and slicked to one side above a cherub face. When the big yellow bus lurches to a stop with grinding brakes, Tim eagerly jumps on. Happy to see some of his friends already aboard, he doesn't think to wave goodbye.

Left in a faint dust cloud behind the bus, Tim's mother is definitely not ready. Not ready to send her youngest to first grade, not ready to send him out into the world, and certainly not ready to bus him clear across town. Anxiety is a knot in her stomach: What have I done?

So it is that Sandra Downie runs to her car, day after day, and follows that school bus for an hour, around the graceful curving streets and manicured lawns of her neighborhood, around the neighborhood lake, across the commercial streets, beyond the shopping centers and industrial parks, beside the burned-out hulks of abandoned houses and boarded-up storefronts, and into the mean streets of ghetto poverty. It is not ten miles away, but it might as well be a foreign country.[1]

Everybody knew it would never happen. White mothers would never voluntarily send their little children on buses from their safe neighborhoods clear across town into the black ghetto, trusting them to fates unknown. The kids would be terrified and traumatized. Lord only knows what kind of trouble would ensue. School buses were the enemy, the trigger for anti-busing riots around the country. In Oklahoma City, not so far away, a father bought an old school bus and invited the whole town to bring their hammers and beat it to death.

Clearly, this voluntary idea would never work. But, amazingly, in Tulsa it did.

Tulsa and Oklahoma might be peddling backward as fast as possible, but the future was clear to some: the federal courts would not accept Tulsa's snail-paced desegregation program. The school board responded by desegregating teaching staffs, adding a majority-to-minority transfer option, and establishing a desegregation program on the backs of the black community that would bus black students to white schools. The historic black school, George Washington Carver Junior High, would be closed, as the board promised in a new plan filed with the court in 1971.[2]

It was unthinkable to consider busing white children into black neighborhoods, of course. If bus they must, the only option the school board could envision was to close black schools and bus the black children into white schools.

Community reaction was swift and severe. The closing of Carver set off a firestorm backlash in the black community, with support of sympathetic whites who believed it was fundamentally unjust to make black children bear the entire burden of integrating a society not of their making.[3]

Blacks set up a protest at Carver Freedom School and, with white sympathizers, organized prayer vigils, marches, picketing, boycotts, and demonstration sit-ins. Their leaders included Julius Pegues, Rev. Bob Goodwin, the NAACP, white minister Donald Dallmann, seventy-five-year-old Mable Little, a matriarch of the black community, and many others. Mayor Bob LaFortune was among many petitioning the school board to reopen Carver, to no avail.[4]

The situation came to a head when the school board reaffirmed its decision to close Carver. "You have proved once again the freedom of the poor, the black, the disadvantaged whites really are ignored at this table," Dallmann said. The sit-ins moved to the Education Service Center.[5]

The most memorable sit-in stretched into the night at the Education Service Center. At 10:00 p.m. police moved in, at the direction of acting mayor Anthony Keating (LaFortune was out of town). They arrested the protesters, producing the unforgettable specter of Mrs. Mable Little being hauled to jail in her impeccable tapestry cloche hat and Logan green leather gloves, accompanied by a collection of black and white sitters-in.[6]

It was all too much. Eventually, the school board gave in and agreed to consider a plan to reopen Carver.[7] But how? It was a problem without a solution. If they had to bus and they couldn't bus just blacks—the only other option was unthinkable. It would tear Tulsa apart.

Meanwhile, back at Neighbor for Neighbor, an idea was cooking.

Maybe, said Pat Flanagan, something could be done. Maybe, she told Father Allen, WE could do something. Well, said Dan, let's look at this thing.

"I read that the feds were coming to give us a good busing plan," Pat remembered later, "and I thought, 'This is going to be awful.' I heard about one other city that had done a voluntary plan, and I thought we could do that here and serve everybody's interests. 'Open classroom' was the rage then, and I thought maybe we could do an open classroom in a black school and get the whites to volunteer. What worried me was whether it would offend the black community; would they see it as Lady Bountiful swooping in with salvation baskets?"

She invited a few people into her living room in the spring of 1971 to talk it over, including NFN's Maynard Ungerman and his wife Elsa, Rosie Brown and Estelle Hamilton from the League of Women Voters, and two black educators: Roosevelt Ratliff and Millard House.

"They thought it was a wonderful idea," Pat said. "So we took it to the NFN board. Nobody at NFN cared who got credit, so we went after a network of names to support the idea. We thought maybe NFN was viewed as too radical to sell the idea, so that led us to the League of Women Voters, for respectability."

The only way to proceed with justice would be to bus children both ways—black to white, and white to black, into salt-and-pepper classrooms. Now, how to do that? It would require massive amounts of black patience and parents who were willing to put their most precious commodities— their children—where their social-liberal mouths were. The discussions flowered.

Meanwhile, separately, another group was coalescing around the idea of improving education quality through a new curriculum design: children would learn through individualized lesson plans and progress at their own rates of achievement. Some people called this idea "New Design," and its proponents began talking with the desegregation advocates.

"We would all sit on Pat's floor," Sandra Downie remembered later. "Some people said, 'We have to have the New Design curriculum.' But we were thinking, 'What's that? We have to get these races together.'"

They hit on the right mix: Create a unique classroom New Design that would lure the most thoughtful parents of both races and convince them to bring their children together. Make it so good, that people would volunteer for their children to go there. Let children explore and progress at their own rates, instead of forcing them to stay at the level of the most mediocre student. Treat the bus as a tool, not an enemy, because of the caliber of the prize at the end of the ride. Start young, before society turns the children into racists, and give these children the very special benefits of a diversified education. In the process, let them help our community do the right thing. The children and the parents, black and white, can be part of history and show the way for the rest of Tulsa and the nation.

It was exciting, frightening, daunting. They knew it was important. Could they pull it off? Well, who knows? Maybe. . . . Yes! said Dan, you can do it! You have to do it.[8]

Pat and Maynard went to see Superintendent Cawelti and Assistant Superintendent Bruce Howell. They described their proposal for an integrated, open-classroom elementary school. Cawelti brought in Millard House, from the public schools' staff, who carefully did not show too much enthusiasm. The meetings dragged on into summer 1971.

"Pat and Maynard were not exactly welcomed with open arms," Gloria Caldwell remembered later. "But they were persistent."[9]

"The school staff was enamored by the open classroom concept," Pat remembered, "but they admitted they wanted to try it in an affluent South-side school where they thought it would have a better chance of success. They didn't like any part of our plan. The only stick we had was public opinion. If they turned us down flat, they would look terrible. So their solution was to tell us that if we could get a black principal to agree to our plan, they would reluctantly support it.

"When we left that meeting, I was at rock bottom. We knew the principals' jobs and futures were in the hands of the Education Service Center, and they could just tell them to turn us down. I told Maynard they had us and there was not even any point in calling on the principals. Maynard said I was probably right, but I had to interview them anyway."

So Pat set out to visit the principals of six Northside elementary schools, to see if one would take on an experimental voluntary integration project with open classrooms and a continuous progress curriculum.

"One by one the principals told me the same speech," Pat said, "that they 'appreciated our concern and good intentions, but that budgets were tight and their schools just couldn't handle such a demonstration project at the time.' I will always believe the superintendent told them to turn us down."

It didn't help that the school board had tried to create a voluntary Metro Learning Center magnet program that flopped at Booker T. Washington High School. The black-and-white school within the black school had to be abandoned for lack of volunteer students.[10] None of the principals wanted a failure in his school. Popular wisdom was that white students would never voluntarily go to black schools.

The last of the six principals was in the hospital for surgery and thus not available to meet. But Dan and Pat never gave up. "Five principals, and none of them would take it, and then Pat found poor Mr. Jenkins on his stomach in his hospital bed, and Pat was leaning on her side trying to talk to him up-

side down," Sandra said. Elmer Jenkins, principal of Burroughs Elementary
School, was a captive audience while Pat described their idea for a magnet
elementary school. "I think no one
had told him what to say because they
thought, surely no one would be crass
enough to interview a very sick man
in the hospital," Pat remembered.

"Mr. Jenkins's agreement wasn't just a step, it was the single, defining step in Tulsa's voluntary desegregation program. He was a hero."

"Well," Jenkins said, "my wife
Juanita and I have always wanted our
son to know white people."

"He started in on the Martin
Luther King thing," Pat said. "I think he was still on post-surgery drugs. He
said, 'This is a wonderful idea. Of course I will do it.'

"Mr. Jenkins's agreement wasn't just a step," Pat remembered, "it was the
single, defining step in Tulsa's voluntary desegregation program. He was a
hero," Pat said.[11]

The idea was a natural for Jenkins. "I don't see anything but a better
program," he told parents of the 750 Burroughs students. "I think we have
every benefit to gain and no liabilities."[12]

Things moved quickly after that. "We said we would do it with 12
percent black, but he said, 'No, it will be fifty-fifty,' and we almost lost the
whole room over that," Sandra said. "So we had to find fifty white families.
Half of them were the ones—led by white parent Nancy MacDonald—who
wanted the New Design, and the other half were the civil rights types, but I
don't think either one knew who was what."[13]

Thus was born the Burroughs Little School, a voluntarily integrated, open-
design program for elementary children within the larger black Burroughs
Elementary School on Tulsa's north side.

"It got to be a major project," said Maynard Ungerman, "because we had
to move so quickly. I was co-chair of that group on Burroughs. There were
quite a few people involved, some from NFN and many from other organizations, too. We were put on a timeline that the school board didn't think
we could meet. They were very much opposed to integration, and they
were fighting the federal lawsuit back and forth. That is not how the official
histories read now; we have had a good deal of historical revisionism.

"It was a fascinating thing. We captured a lot of media attention, including the *New York Times* and a lot of international television stations interested in how we were trying to voluntarily integrate Burroughs while at the
same time there were riots over busing in Detroit and elsewhere. They used

us to compare the two approaches.

"One night, we had a meeting at my house," Ungerman remembered. "I was chairman of the Tulsa Democratic Party then. In one room was a meeting of the Tulsa Democratic Party leadership, and they were pretty progressive then. In another room was the Burroughs Little School group. And the head of CBS News International was there, and CBS was filming first one group and then the other, back and forth. Things like that happened pretty often in those years. The NFN Board was an active group, and we all had to work in multiple roles to keep it going."[14]

They didn't really stop to ponder the likelihood of success or failure. "Dan made us think things could be done and we could do them," Pat said. "You didn't have to be a rocket scientist to pull something off, just do it."[15]

They convened a make-or-break meeting of two hundred black and white parents at Burroughs to hammer out the details of what they called a "super school."

"Do you want us?" asked Elsa Ungerman, white parent. "Can our children come and work, learn, interact, and play together?"[16]

"We welcome you. Come and join with us," answered black parent Marcella Pete.

"We are a humble and meek people who want the same quality you want. We want to live together in peace," said black parent Mrs. Joe Williams.[17]

"Many of us have wanted integrated education experiences for our children. That's why we first moved into this neighborhood in 1964. But soon there was a mass exodus of whites from this school attendance zone and the school became all black. This is the first time the whites have wanted to come back here. All our children can benefit."[18]

The idea caught fire and spread from family to family.

"We needed a home run to push the recruiting over the finish line," remembered Pat Flanagan. "And we got one."[19]

In mid August, the public learned that one of the Burroughs volunteers was Rod Beckstrom, ten-year-old son of school board member Bob Beckstrom, who said Rod wanted to go with his best friend, nine-year-old Bill Ungerman. "This is not a peace offering," Rod's mother said. "Rod wants the educational cultural experience."[20] "Rod was afraid he wouldn't get signed up in time," his father said.[21]

In September, the school board almost derailed the Burroughs Little School. When Beckstrom made a motion to use school buses for Burroughs voluntary integration, his motion died for lack of a second.[22]

Ultimately, when the school board was assured they would have enough volunteer students, they eventually agreed to the plan and rushed to convert prefab buildings on the Burroughs grounds, design the curriculum, and select and train teachers.[23]

By November 1971, they were ready, and Burroughs Little School opened with 79 black and 98 white pupils. The black children came from the Burroughs area, and the white children were bused in from all sections of the school district.[24]

Children on those buses included Robby Caldwell, Gloria's son; Wilbert Collins's sons Douglas and Wilbert Jr.; Karla and Rebecca Ungerman, children of Maynard and Elsa Ungerman; Pat Flanagan's children Cathy, Leslie, and Phillip; and Sandra's children Whitney, Allyson, and Timothy Downie.

"I was the first parent to sign the list at the Education Service Center," Sandra remembered. "It was the scariest thing I ever did."[25]

From the time it opened, there was a waiting list to get into Burroughs Little School.

"The Burroughs Little School," the schools reported later, "with its restyled curriculum, has offered a smoothly operating example of how children of different races can study and live together."[26] After Burroughs opened, four hundred parents signed a letter endorsing integration and busing. "We believe education is more than just book learning," said the letter, which was promptly denounced by the citywide PTA. "We are preparing our children to live in a world as different twenty years from now as today's world is from the world that most of us knew when we were in school," the Burroughs parents said.[27]

The waiting list grew, along with pressure to expand the Burroughs experiment for other children.

Burroughs became a model. If it could work for elementary school, maybe it could work for middle and high school, too. Maybe it could provide the answer to the Carver dilemma.

"The success of Burroughs was very important in demonstrating that Carver and Washington could also be integrated voluntarily," the schools reported later.[28]

The school board was desperate for a solution to the Carver dilemma, since they had failed to win community support for closing the historically black junior high school and busing out the black students. Eventually, the school administration and representatives of the black community devised a plan to reopen Carver as a voluntarily integrated middle school. Black parents agreed to close the Carver Freedom School and send those students back to public schools. Mayor Bob LaFortune authorized Model Cities money to remodel the Carver building, and the schools devised a new curriculum design featuring "individualized learning on a continuous progress basis," in school-speak.[29]

The League of Women Voters, Neighbor for Neighbor families, and others once again began their recruiting blitz, spearheaded by parent Nancy MacDonald. They worked the churches with fervor and skill.

When school started in 1973, Carver reopened with 250 students, roughly fifty-fifty black and white. Within a year, the number would be expanded to 450, still fifty-fifty, with a perpetual waiting list of hopefuls.[30] Reopening Carver was a grand victory for liberal education and the black community.

On the day Carver reopened, some remembered the school's proud history. When Carver had first opened in 1928, it was the first Tulsa school named after a living black person and became a most important institution in the community. Black scientist George Washington Carver himself came to speak when the school first opened. Fredi Boone, who was in the first eighth grade graduating class, wistfully remembered opening day in 1928: "We danced around the flagpole, and it rained."[31]

Now came the biggest challenge of all, desegregating Booker T. Washington High School. The school board had absolutely no plan, but the administration stuck with a pattern they had learned: toss the problem to the community and let people chew on it for a while, until the solutions rise up from the community itself. Meanwhile, Maynard dogged the issues in the courts and kept up the pressure.

In 1973 hundreds of Tulsans met to hammer out detailed suggestions for a Booker T. plan. Some would remember a hundred meetings before they were through. In late March, the school board approved a voluntary plan for 1,200 students—600 each, black and white. The curriculum would include the most extensive smorgasbord of electives at any Tulsa high school, plus a top-quality volunteer faculty and a 1 to 17 teacher to pupil ratio.[32]

By the fall of 1974, hundreds of students reported to Booker T., half white, half black. Among the teachers: Elsa Ungerman. The black students who could not be accommodated at Washington were assigned to the other high schools, desegregating them (and giving further proof to the accurate perception that Tulsa busing was voluntary for whites but not for blacks).

From then on, there was no turning back. The magnet schools were a rip-roaring success; not only was recruitment not necessary, but it became a challenge to get admitted, and long waiting lists kept many would-be volunteer students away. The Northside Emerson Elementary became a

Burroughs clone. The magnet schools racked up awards at a dizzying rate over the ensuing years. Booker T. Washington High School began calling itself "a world-class school," with plenty of evidence to back up the claim. Many considered it the leading school in Tulsa if not the state, with an international array of advanced course offerings and a bevy of national merit scholars every year.

Many of the initial Burroughs Little School volunteers went through all levels of the magnet schools.

"Robbie was in the first Burroughs class and also the first Carver class, and then on to Booker T," said Gloria Caldwell. "I was involved with the League of Women Voters then, and I didn't know any black people. NFN volunteer Elsa Ungerman called and asked if I would consider letting Robbie be a student at Burroughs. It was not my decision, it was Robbie's. I asked if he would like to go to a voluntarily integrated school, and he said yes. I don't know why, but a lot of his friends were going, too. The bus picked up Robbie at Lynn Lane and took him to Burroughs. He was ten. It was a very long ride, but you know, he learned the city. He was the first on the bus, and he learned all the streets and knew his way around from then on. I was never worried about his safety, and he had a very happy school life."

Gloria remembered a visit from Henry Bellman, Oklahoma's legendary Republican senator, who was concerned about the idea of busing for racial balance. "Henry Bellman became my hero," Gloria said. "There was this huge uproar about busing, riots, terrible things going on around the country. Henry Bellman dropped in one day, unannounced, without an entourage or any publicity, and said, 'I just want to visit with the kids.' He sat in the little chairs and asked, 'What do you children think about this busing thing?' They told him, 'That's the way we go to school.' They convinced him it was ok, and he always did the right thing on busing after that."[33]

Busing was, said Tim Downie years later, no big deal. "Those schools taught me so much about the realities of life, how communities work, strong values and appreciation of school and learning. They taught me to see people for what they are—tolerance, sure, but also that it's not at all about color."

Given a choice, would he go through those schools again? "Oh, yes. My children are there now, going through the same schools," Tim said. "What does that tell you? They are getting a wonderful education, in every sense of the word."[34]

Chapter 13

To A Man With An Empty Stomach, Food Is His God

"We only had one fundraising campaign in the first 10 years.
We're not interested in building up capital.
If it's not actually needed, then I think we're using the people
instead of serving them.
We started last year with $3,600 in the bank.
I didn't think we could possibly survive.
What's going to happen this year, nobody knows.
If we have another winter like last year
we'll be strained to the depths of our convictions."

—Dan Allen

NFN grocery store. Les McClelland photo, *Tulsa Magazine*, November 1977.

"Will your family eat mock turtle soup?" the reporter asked the woman with the baby. "We'll eat anything," she answered.

The day before Thanksgiving, a Tulsa World reporter visited NFN for an annual food-for-the-needy, feel-good holiday story.

"Is there any food left?" asked a woman with a baby, mistaking the reporter for an NFN volunteer. The reporter shuffled through piles of empty boxes in another room and found only a dented can of mock turtle soup, a ruptured bag of beans, and some unwrapped bars of soap.

"Sorry. . . ."

The food gave out early, but the word was circulating that a church was bringing the fruits of its canned food drive. The walls of the little stone house were lined with people waiting for sacks of groceries. And waiting, and waiting. . . .[1]

NFN was struggling but still, by some grace, alive, Father Allen told the reporter from the relative quiet of his office. The heat might be turned off any day. NFN was operating hand-to-mouth, day-to-day.

There was an erroneous rumor circulating that NFN had too much money now, he said. People were saying NFN had an emergency food and medical grant and didn't need any more help, but the grant could not be used for NFN operations, just passed through to the poor. And it didn't come close to meeting the needs out there.

"Excuse me, Ma'am," said an old man coming in the office door. "Could you stand up a minute?"

"Oh—sure."

"We need it, Dan," the man said, "for a burned-out family." He and a younger man picked up the office sofa and carted it out the door.

Standing now, the reporter asked Dan how the grant was working. Ninety-eight percent of the grants went for food, Dan said.

There was a flurry of excitement from the front room. A school representative brought in thirty frozen hens. "Does NFN have a freezer to store them?" she asked Father Allen. He laughed. The hens were gone before the frost melted from their wrappings.

A volunteer at the reception desk asked simple questions: name, how many in the family, what was needed? Food, money to turn on the heat, food, children's shoes, food, blankets, food.

"A baby bed," said a young woman, blushing. The volunteer looked her over and entered her name in one of the ten books of waiting lists for furniture and said, "By the time you need it, we'll have one."

Thirty-four families had joined an organic gardening co-op that produced more than $100 in food per family plus set-aside funds from the sale of produce for start-up funding next summer, Dan said.

As he spoke, a station wagon filled with food arrived at the back door and volunteers hastily began filling sacks for distribution to those in the waiting room.

"How much food would you give a family of ten?" the reporter asked a volunteer.

"I guess for ten you can fill the sack full," the volunteer said.

A bag of corn meal, canned hominy and tomatoes, some applesauce. "Will your family eat mock turtle soup?" the reporter asked the woman with the baby.

"We'll eat anything," she answered.[2]

People and projects ebbed and flowed at Neighbor for Neighbor, as Dan struggled to meet needs and seize opportunities. But one need was constant over the years: hunger was an every-day visitor, along with its wicked stepsister, malnutrition.

Food was NFN's primary and perennial concern, starting with donated foodstuffs that spilled over the vestibule of St. Jude Catholic Church. Before long, NFN would learn that hunger demanded a far more comprehensive approach.

"It is not extraordinary to find people here who are weak from hunger," Allen said.

Hunger hurts, NFN volunteer Sue Ferguson said at the time. She should know, firsthand. Before she found NFN, Sue was in the habit of going without food so her children could eat.[3] "Hunger is painful," Sue said. "It deprives your mind so you can't think. Your body grows weak. Your heart aches because of the loss of nourishment that your body requires. You can't sleep because of the gnawing pain in your stomach. . . .[4]

"I would go to the cabinet hungry and just look inside," Sue said. "Sometimes, I would make a gravy of powdered milk and flour. Sometimes we would go without electricity so we could eat."[5]

Here are some other recipes favored by poor NFN clients:

• *Fried mush.* Soak corn meal in a little water, pour into a pan and let it set up, then slice and fry in drippings or grease.

- *Grease gravy.* Stir old coffee or water into grease, heat and serve on bread, if you have any.
- *Fried bread.* Fry leftover bread in grease or cook over an outdoor fire as a main dish.
- *Beans.* Soak overnight, then cook all day and eat all week.
- *Fritters.* Add one can of corn to big bowl of flour with water and some salt and baking powder, then fry by spoonfuls. Serves 6–8 if you use enough batter.
- *Soup.* Save scraps and bones (chicken, pork, what-have-you) all week. Boil bones, strain broth, add scraps of whatever is left over from a week's meals.

When people were forced to NFN for help, they brought a litany of woe. Most needed food, first and foremost.

After wandering around NFN one day, a reporter wrote that some people said they hadn't eaten in days. A man in his thirties said he had to leave a clerk's job in another state to come care for a sick family member and was mowing lawns for pocket cash while he looked for work. A young mother was staring at a single can of beans in her kitchen. A disabled man said he had only $80 a month left after he paid rent and utilities. Others in the food line were: A single woman without income, due to give birth. Two families living together while unemployed husbands completed technical school. Young families with only one breadwinner whose income couldn't stretch for adequate food.[6]

After wandering around NFN one day, a reporter wrote that some people said they hadn't eaten in days.

"Most of the people who come here are not receiving any form of state or federal assistance," Dan said. "Their income is minimum wage or below. There's no way to make rent and utility payments and pay for food and transportation. So food loses out."[7]

"My husband was laid off last Friday," one woman told the reporter in the waiting room. "It's a week until payday and we have no food," said another.

"Betty Johnson has been working nights in a laundry to buy food for her family of five," the reporter wrote. "Her husband's unemployment benefit has ended and, for four days, the family had been eating whatever food her parents could spare. 'I take popcorn to work to fill myself up,' said Mrs. Johnson (not her real name).

"The family has been making do with 'lots of fried potatoes and gravy.' A recent supper was eggs given by her mother. 'When we were putting them

away, they got dropped accidentally and broke,' Mr. Johnson said. 'We had
to pick them off the floor and scramble them.'"[8]

Little was known about
hunger in America in
NFN's formative years.
Hunger—and, in fact,
poverty—were largely invisible in an affluent society,

*The sharing of food with those in need
was central to Dan's religious philosophy.*

as documented by Michael Harrington in his landmark book, *The Other
America: Poverty in the United States*. Harrington estimated that fifty million Americans lived in poverty in another America that was "an invisible
land. . . . [Furthermore], there are tens of thousands of Americans in the big
cities who are wearing shoes, perhaps even a stylishly cut suit or dress, and
yet are hungry."[9]

The cruel irony was that, in a land of plenty, so much was wasted while
so many went without, yet were invisible, suffering without a diagnosis or
recognition of their problems.

Certainly the problem was undiagnosed in Tulsa. "[I]t is a bit ironic that
. . . we do not, in Tulsa, have any real, objective information on the extent of
hunger or malnutrition," said Dr. George Prothro, then director of the Tulsa
City-County Health Department.[10]

Fortunately, when he started Neighbor for Neighbor, Dan Allen didn't
need statistics to document hunger. He saw it all around him. It is important to know that when NFN started, no other poverty program provided
food except welfare commodities.

The sharing of food with those in need was central to Dan's religious
philosophy, just as the Eucharist was central to his religious fervor. "To a
man with an empty stomach, food is his God," trumpeted a banner near the
NFN entry.

Father Bill Skeehan remembered that Dan would offer mass in the kitchenette of his little rock rectory, then halt the service halfway through and,
as part of the ceremony, purposely go into Neighbor for Neighbor and do
some specific act such as offering donated food to a needy family. Returning
to the kitchenette, he would offer up this service as a gift to God. Feeding
the hungry and serving the poor were holy acts, in Dan's faith, a logical
and essential extension of the community sharing—communion—of the
Eucharist.[11]

How did it work on the ground? Years later, a young mother named Cindy remembered, her first visit to NFN.

Cindy was ten, the youngest of five girls, and, although she had no words to describe it at the time, she could feel her mother giving up.

"It wasn't as if it had been easy up to then," Cindy remembered later. "First our dad's accident, and then the divorce. He couldn't work. My mom was a nurse, but then illness threw her out of work, too. It was hard to see my mother struggle, but we were getting by. We had limits, how many pieces of bread we could have, how much milk. I could see my mom was losing weight, and it was later that I figured out she was living on whatever scraps we left on our plates."

And then, when there was no other option, her mother applied for food stamps—but she was turned down. Somehow, after that, the mother and girls found their way to Neighbor for Neighbor.

"I could feel her fear as we walked in the door. We were in a big room, with old folding chairs crowded together. I huddled close to my mom, wondering what could be ahead. Why did we have to ask for food? Our family had always been proud and had a strong work ethic. I could tell it was so hard for her, and we were all ashamed.

"And then it hit me: *we were poor.* I never knew it before. It washed over me, a big wave of shame, and somehow I was certain it was my fault.

"I could feel my mother giving way, and it was like my world was dissolving."

By the time they were summoned by a counselor, Cindy and her mom were both crying.

"The lady was so nice, we couldn't believe it. She made us comfortable, gave us kids some toys, and made us feel we were not a burden. Her smile was warm and welcoming, nonjudgmental. She wanted to know all our needs, and she tried to fulfill every one—not just a handout, but trying to help in the long term, trying to take care of your mind, body, and soul."

When Cindy's family left, they were carrying crayons and coloring books, several bags of groceries, a collection of clothes, a voucher for gasoline, and plans for dental care and new eyeglasses. "They even got us counseling, which we needed badly—the divorce was hard." Most important, they had an infusion of self respect.

"We were overwhelmed by the generosity, but even more, we were never made to feel inferior. They never demeaned us or made us feel like we were subhuman. My mom found a pay phone and was telling somebody all about it. She was laughing and crying all at once. They didn't even know us, but they cared enough to say, let us help with whatever you need. It was amazing." Shortly thereafter, her mother was able to return to work and keep her family afloat.

It changed Cindy's life. Grown up now, she is a single mom studying to prepare for a helping career. "I think the way we were treated at NFN showed me there are people who want to help people. I never want anybody to feel that they don't matter. I've been reading about Dan Allen, and it gives me joy to learn how much he wanted to help people. We wouldn't have poverty if we could all help people help themselves, like he did, and that is what I want to do with my life."[12]

It was the endless unmet needs that wearied Father Allen. He developed a short fuse on the lack of understanding on the part of the non-poor. One sore point was holiday-only charity. "It seems only at Thanksgiving and

He developed a short fuse on the lack of understanding on the part of the non-poor.

Christmas are people aware of the needs of the poor," he grumbled. "What sense does it make to decide twice a year to do something about the hunger problem? The poor are hungry all year round."[13] So it was that Dan Allen would angrily reject beautiful Christmas food baskets from the likes of Sandra Downie. If the would-be donors could be led to understand why, Dan would declare them long-term students in his University of Poverty.

NFN volunteers were giving out thousands of grocery bags of donated food a year, Allen said, but it didn't come close to covering the needs. Hundreds had to be turned away. "The churches bring food on Monday, and we never have any left by Tuesday," he fumed.[14]

Something more needed to be done.

The pain of poverty and life on the edge was no stranger to Father Dan Allen and, over time, it created a nagging emotional hunger in him that would not be satiated.

Part of Dan's genius lay in his Neighbor for Neighbor design, which was the antithesis of corporate management. He took literally the Matthew 6:34 counsel to "take no thought for the morrow" and scorned agencies for whom self-perpetuation was a central goal. Dan's goal was to move out everything that came in, as quickly as possible, remembered Dan's niece Judy Allen Hess. If some donation came in the door, he moved it out the door as quickly as somebody needed it. Nothing lingered to build his program; if he gave away more than he took in, he was successful. If NFN was hungry, with a precarious life continually on the edge of collapse, how much more so were the lives of the poor.

A second element of his genius was his empathy, but it also came at a dear price. In his dealings with the poor, Dan took their suffering personally. Their problems became his problems. He took it as a personal failing if he could not solve all their problems in short order. Some would see that he

The needs were so great, compared to the resources he could muster, that depression and rage became Dan's constant companions.

was moving mountains, but Dan saw the greater mountains still unmoved. If he was luring the city's best and brightest into the University of Poverty, what he called an adult education program, Dan saw all those who were yet unmoved and unhelped. The needs were so great, compared to the resources he could muster, that depression and rage became Dan's constant companions. Many saw his flashes of black humor as joy, and zest there was, but it was edged in darkness.

Much of the time, Father Dan was sustained by fervent religious faith and a certainty that came from following his understanding of the gospel, to care for the poor as an act of worship. But there was darkness and continuing pain even in his spiritual life.

No one had a keener wit than Dan, remembered Jeff Nix, "but he always looked pained and sad. It wasn't about the mission. He knew what he was doing was right, but he had a sadness that—my guess is that it really bothered him that some people are so mean and uncaring.

"It was like—life shouldn't be this way. And, 'God, how did you let it get this way? Are you just not paying attention?'

"I think this is where he differed from his church. The church said it's all unfolding the way it should, but Dan thought it should be evolving a hell of a lot faster. He wasn't too interested in the future. He wanted it now."[15]

Father Dan's beloved Catholic Church was retrenching from the humanitarian emphasis of Vatican II, edging back toward a hierarchical religious institution with more traditional leanings. Everything in his heart and family heritage propelled him to devote his life to the church, but Dan agonized because he believed the church was not doing enough to help the poor, which he believed was the heart and essence of religion.

The flow of Oklahoma events is instructive.

In fact, Dan was just one of Bishop Reed's challenges. Having opened the gates for change, Oklahoma's bishop had his hands full with a rising flood of radicalism, including a rebellion led by Father Skeehan, arguably Dan's closest ally in the church.

Father Skeehan's experimental Church of the Resurrection had been established in 1968 as a kind of parish without walls. It grew to be a strong parish of liberal zealots. Resurrection's parish office was in a shopping center, and services were held in a school gym. Resurrection didn't much want a permanent building. Skeehan believed the church should focus on service, not grand church buildings, and he did not mince words in saying so.[16]

Nonetheless, a local benefactor—a very close friend of Bishop Reed, who hailed from Tulsa—offered a quite grand building to the bishop. It was to be, in fact, a cathedral, far into South Tulsa, to replace the one downtown and provide a house for Resurrection.

A heated debate ensued. There may have been no relation to the fact that, on April 30, 1971, Bishop Reed had announced a recommendation to divide the Oklahoma diocese. The next day, probably by chance timing, the simmering Tulsa cathedral issue came to a head, in a fiery public meeting where Skeehan challenged the bishop's plan. Before the evening was over, the bishop's new Tulsa cathedral had been scuttled by Skeehan's argument that the money should go to the poor, not into more Southside church buildings. In short order, the deal was dead. The benefactor withdrew his offer; the cathedral was never built, but the benefactor didn't send the money to the poor, either.[17]

On August 1, 1971, Bishop Reed announced a revised plan that would raise Oklahoma City to the status of an archdiocese and create a separate Diocese of Tulsa (*sans* new cathedral). No

"I regret to inform you that after years of thought and extensive consultation, I have decided to leave the priesthood, effective Feb. 1, 1973."

more than a month later, Bishop Reed was stricken ill and died suddenly on September 8, 1971, at age 65. He had been, by many accounts, the most liberal of the Oklahoma bishops and probably the most supportive of Dan Allen's work.[18] "Bishop Reed was the best bishop we ever had," Skeehan said.[19]

On December 19, 1972, the Holy See created the Tulsa Diocese. This decision also localized control of Tulsa Catholic Charities. A family member recalled that Dan had high hopes that the new order would focus more attention on the poor. She remembered going with Dan to a meeting. She thought it was a board meeting for the new Tulsa Catholic Charities, probably in January 1973.

But the meeting left Dan bitterly disappointed. Nothing was allocated for Neighbor for Neighbor. Nothing. To Dan, that equated to allocating nothing for the poor. She recalled that a terrible dark cloud crossed his face, and he set his jaw "like flint," clenched his teeth, and walked out, furious.[20]

It was shortly thereafter on January 31, 1973, in the dead of that winter, that Dan wrote a letter to the Oklahoma archbishop, John R. Quinn.

"I regret to inform you that after years of thought and extensive consultation, I have decided to leave the priesthood, effective Feb. 1, 1973," Dan wrote. "I find myself progressively at odds with the Church on major issues. I cannot continue to live a life that is hypocritical, both for my own welfare and that of the Church. I can no longer survive as a person and remain in the priesthood. It is my desire to remain

"Dan didn't leave the Catholic Church," said Father Skeehan. "The church left Dan."

as director of Neighbor for Neighbor. Your understanding and prayers are respectively requested."

Dan sent copies of the letter to his board of directors, with a handwritten note: "I sincerely hope that as a board member you will understand and support me in this decision, which I have come to after years of thought and counsel. It is the most difficult life decision I have faced."[21]

Dan had arranged for his resignation to be effective on the day following his letter, clearly intending to be done with the priesthood before Bishop Quinn could even receive the letter, let alone respond. Curiously, there is no record that the bishop ever accepted Dan's resignation or even responded to the letter. The bishop's silence could be taken to mean different things: perhaps Dan's letter was not worthy of notice or reply; or perhaps the bishop so treasured Dan that he refused to accept the idea of his resignation. The silence was all the more remarkable, said Bill Skeehan, because such a letter could well have prompted the bishop to retaliate and excommunicate Dan.

But whatever the reason, the effect was to leave Dan's precise status open to interpretation. Some in the Catholic Church considered Dan an adversary from then on—and indeed he railed against the church he loved. Others admired him and thought he left the priesthood to better serve the poor. Some believed he never really resigned. Others thought, incorrectly, that he left the Catholic Church. But the Catholic Church remained Dan's church of choice, as he once said, "because it is the only one that has the body and blood of Jesus Christ."[22]

"Dan didn't leave the Catholic Church," said Father Skeehan, "The church left Dan."[23]

"The church should put her presence where Christ put his," Dan told a group of friends after he resigned.[24] Years later, he confided to a friend that he threw away his identify when he resigned, in disillusionment, requiring him to start over.[25] It could well be argued that the institutional Catholic Church, which he loved so deeply, broke Dan Allen's heart.

For Dan, none of the legalities seemed to matter in the long haul. He announced in 1973 that he had resigned from the priesthood, yet accept the title when people called him Father Allen. Once his niece, Judy Allen Hess, asked the diocese historian Dan's status; she recalled that he told her, flatly, that of course Dan was still a priest.[26] Certainly he was never "laicized," the Catholic process to remove a priest. Yet in 1995 the diocese noted, in an admiring obituary, that "Dan Allen left the priesthood in 1973 to become fulltime director of Neighbor for Neighbor."[27]

Like many things about Dan Allen, the reality was an enigma, wrapped in contradictions and mystery.

Dan had other things on his mind. NFN was below the bottom of the barrel. More than once in the 1970s, NFN had to shut down because its resources were depleted.

"Exhausted from helping between 30 and 60 families daily and trying to figure out where the agency stands financially," the *Tulsa Tribune* reported at one point, "Allen listed what would be shut down: "The food co-op store—no more food is available. The non-interest loan program—no money is available. The clothing department for children—no more clothing is available." Less than $500 remained in the bank account, Allen said. He said he had no idea when or whether NFN could continue—or, more importantly, where their clients would go for help.

"We have nowhere to send them," he said. "How we'll be able to do it this year, I don't know. To me, the bottom line is this—to all these people complaining about the federal money going into social programs, red tape, and bureaucracy, we offer an alternative way. But we've been here too long to give up now. I'm going to find some way."[28]

The community responded, and NFN did reopen, then and again. Day after day, Dan found a way to keep going, but it all carried a heavy price. He was looking haggard and perpetually exhausted, but his face was set.

Oklahoma Bishop Victor J. Reed, circa 1968.

Pat Flanagan is on the phone in the lower newspaper clipping.

Chapter 14

Hunger and Thirst
After Justice

Companies seek cans

"Not a whole lot can go wrong with a can," Bill Majors, director of the Neighbor for Neighbor Food Bank, said. Consequently, the Food Bank doesn't receive many canned goods from local and national food distributers to give to the needy.

To increase their canned goods supply, the NFN Food Bank is seeking out companies to hold an annual food drive one month out of the year.

"We get a significant volume of canned goods around the holiday season, and very little from January to November." Majors said.

In May, the Transport Workers Union 514 and the employees of the Ford Motor Company-Tulsa Glass Plant proved just that.

The union contributed more than 900 pounds of canned goods and $600 to the Food Bank after a month-long collection. Ford employees contributed more than 1,800 pounds and $500.

Other companies planning canned food drives are QuikTrip, the Bank of Oklahoma, Keystone Pioneers of the Bell Telephone Co. and Public Service.

Any company or organisation interested in participating in this program can call Bill Majors at 425-0220.

LOADING UP — The Neighbor for Neighbor Food Bank, under the direction of Bill Majors has grown 725 percent since it began three years ago.

Food Bank collects mistakes by the millions

"We were combining charity with a sense of social justice—
a two-fold action that's at the heart
of what Christianity is all about. . . .

I believed the purpose of a parish was to care
for the people nobody else gave a . . . damn about."

—Dan Allen

Bill Major at Food Bank. Teresa McUsic photo, *Eastern Oklahoma Catholic,* June 24, 1984.

IT CHANGED BILL MAJOR'S LIFE FOREVER.

Bill Major is stunned.

Bill is a high school student, with close-cropped brown hair. He's handsome, thoughtful, quiet and a little shy.

He has been volunteering with his church youth minister, repairing old cars in the Neighbor for Neighbor back lot, and he's become pretty good at taking apart two or three old cars and reassembling the cannibalized parts into one car that would actually run.

But now comes a real challenge: Booker Washington and his trash truck.

The truck is all that stands between Booker and the starvation of his eight kids. If it doesn't run, he has no income, period. The truck is an accident waiting to happen, an aimless collection of clanking loose bolts and gerrymandered widgets held together, if at all, by spit, string, coat hangers, and desperation.

Working under the truck filled with rancid garbage and maggots is unforgettable, but even more memorable is going home with Booker, who became a friend. Nothing in Bill's Wheeling Avenue Christian Church or East Central High School teachings prepared him for the reality of poverty that he saw at Booker's house.

Never before had Bill seen the raw slash of hunger, the squalor of despair, the cruelty of poverty. "It opened my eyes," Bill said later, in his typical understated way. "And Dan Allen taught me the unforgettable lesson that regardless of a person's standing, they had dignity and self-worth. Just because they didn't have means, there was no reason to take away their decision-making and choices. Everybody who came to the door had the opportunity not only to need something but to help somebody else."

It changed Bill Major's life forever.[1]

Other problems might ebb and flow, but Dan Allen could never escape chronic worry about feeding the hungry.

In time, the "Christmas basket" style of charity evolved into well-organized, year-round projects. There was no reason for anyone in Tulsa to go hungry, declared Mrs. William G. Seal, volunteer director of NFN's food program in 1971, if the city's four hundred churches would help with her program, which she named "Pack a Sack." Each church family should gather a little donated food one Sunday a year and deliver it to NFN, where it was sacked and parceled out to eager families.[2]

On October 1, 1972, Dan promoted a mother of twelve, Pat King, to become director of NFN's emergency food and medical program.[3] Around

the same time, NFN received a lifesaving boost from the Roman Catholic
Church of the Resurrection, Father Bill Skeehan's liberal experimental
parish, which began providing
its sustaining NFN donations in
1972. After Skeehan heard the
saying in New York, Resurrection
adopted a "give a damn about your
fellow man" philosophy to support

*Resurrection adopted a "give a damn
about your fellow man" philosophy
to support NFN.*

NFN. Skeehan designated the first Sunday in December as "Give a Damn"
Sunday, when Resurrection members voluntarily assumed responsibility
for much of NFN's overhead. Without that help, NFN could not function,
Allen said.[4] Resurrection and Bill Skeehan became the firm pillar of support
for NFN, and for Dan.

In tribute to Resurrection's support, a banner over Dan's desk
proclaimed: "Give a damn!"

Dan dreamed that poor people could experience the dignity of selecting
their own food in a grocery-store setting, rather than suffering the indig-
nity of having a sack handed to them without choice or ceremony. He also
dreamed that NFN could form a food cooperative and help the poor get in
the habit of eating balanced meals.[5] In 1977, with an anonymous donation,
NFN remodeled again and created a large food co-op that would allow
NFN "to purchase quality food at the best available price to donate to the
poor, instead of having to pay retail price," said Bill Summers, NFN manager
of the food co-op.[6]

An experimental co-op had served a limited membership, but the new
co-op could expand food service for a $3 annual membership fee plus at
least one hour a month of volunteer service at the store, Summers said. "We
will shy away from prepackaged 'junk' food," he said. "The store will empha-
size fresh fruits and vegetables, whole grains and whole grain breads. There
will be less emphasis on fats."[7]

"We help them with the best buys," he said. "We show how to stretch that
dollar and to eat properly. We see that over half the children who come in
here have dental problems. . . . We see the effect of teenage mothers not
eating well during pregnancy."[8]

In time, Dan's dream produced a full-fledged grocery store at Neighbor for Neighbor, where needy families could shop and choose their own
food with NFN vouchers. The vouchers ranged from $10 to $20 a week,
depending on how much food NFN had available that week. The vouchers were considered loans, to be repaid in cash when possible or in service

at NFN—including the management of the store. One such manager was Sue Ferguson, the mother who had kept her family alive with gravy made of flour and dried milk. "I love my job," Sue said. "I'm giving back for the help I got. Some of these people have worked all their lives and it really slices their pride to have to ask for help."[9]

It was 1979 before Tulsa undertook a systematic analysis on the subject of hunger and malnutrition. One might imagine that by that time the situation had improved, since by then various government programs and many private charities were operating. In the 1979 study, the researchers surveyed a low-income Tulsa neighborhood with 31,000 inhabitants and found that more than 21,000 of them were below nutritional standards for "at least one of the nutrients studied (calories, protein, calcium, iron, vitamin A, or vitamin C)." Diets of more than 5,200 of those Tulsans met less than one-third of the standard for at least one of the nutrients. The problems were especially critical for the young and the elderly. Nearly 10 percent of the households in the survey area "had periodic difficulty in obtaining food for basically economic reasons," according to the study's strained technical lingo.

It was 1979 before Tulsa undertook a systematic analysis on the subject of hunger and malnutrition.

The '79 study was sponsored by Tulsa Metropolitan Ministry's Hunger Task Force. (Was it a coincidence that the Hunger Task Force staff coordinator was a young man named Bill Major?)[10]

By 1980, NFN was still searching for better ways to meet the unmet needs for nutritional food. Volunteers tried an open-air produce market, but it ran afoul of a detail in health regulations and stalled.[11] Then NFN joined with the Tulsa Metropolitan Ministry and Bill Major's TMM Hunger Task Force.

After Major graduated from high school and the ranks of NFN volunteers, he had enrolled in college and studied for the ministry. But like many of his friends who graduated with a degree in religion, he decided the traditional ministry was not for him. Bill bounced from job to job, working in various posts such as utilities customer service trainer, public housing inspector, and corrections officer. ("I lasted a month as a corrections officer," he remembered later.) In 1978 he landed on his feet in a job that fit his idealistic bent, as coordinator of the new Hunger Task Force.

When the Hunger Task Force study showed a tremendous level of need, Major's next step was to find ways to improve nutrition among Tulsa's poor, on a far broader scale than ever attempted before. "The schools had a free lunch program by that time, but no school breakfast program. So one of our first projects was to obtain funding and support to get a breakfast program up and running," Bill said.

"About that time, there was a new movement in the U.S. to create food banks. I worked with Rodney Bivins who was working in Oklahoma City to create a food bank, and we agreed to carve the state into two territories: he would take the middle and western Oklahoma, we could take the north and east."

That was the easy part. Harder would be to actually create a Tulsa food bank, but the rewards could be great. The idea of food banking is to gather food that, for one reason or another, is being discarded or is unneeded, then to store and dispense it to the needy.

Food banking seemed the next logical step for Tulsa's large-scale problems of feeding the hungry, and NFN seemed the logical place to do it, Major said.

"Dan immediately grasped the possibilities and saw how a food bank could really help people, and he was ready to do whatever was necessary to get it started, although in the long haul food banking was not really his issue. So he asked me to come to NFN to run their food co-op and to start a food bank. I started working in a closet off the original food store," Bill said.

An early need was a warehouse. Food banks operate on a mega scale, fed by national and regional networks that may collect entire boxcars of mislabeled canned goods or truckloads of donations from grocery stores and bakeries. Food banks need secure, safe storage for nonperishable and perishable goods that are then assembled and donated to groups, such as soup kitchens, that serve the needy.

QuikTrip donated a refrigerated truck, which was critical for picking up food from grocery stores.

The NFN warehouse came from an unexpected source. Don McCarthy, perennial NFN volunteer, was dissolving his engineering business and donated his metal building, and even provided the concrete slab to place it on.

The next big breakthrough came when NFN obtained a grant to buy a freezer. "It was a huge freezer, in our view at the time," Major remembered. A local convenience-store chain, QuikTrip, donated a refrigerated truck, which was "critical for us in terms of picking up food from grocery stores, including things that needed refrigeration," Bill said.

Don's son, John McCarthy, was in college deciding that petroleum engineering was not his cup of tea. John came on as Bill's assistant. "John and I did everything—drove the truck, managed the warehouse, coordinated the food donations and distribution, and worked with NFN on remodeling the space," Bill said.

"In those early days, we were still also running the NFN food co-op. People could come in and buy food on a wholesale basis plus obtain donations from churches. Dan strongly believed that, to maintain folks' dignity, they should be able to choose from a store, not just receive a handout.

> *"Dan strongly believed that, to maintain folks' dignity, they should be able to choose from a store, not just receive a handout."*

"On the other side, we were establishing the food bank. We were signing up the food pantries and shelters—there were not so many then—to convince them it was worthwhile to work with us and to meet our standards. They would have to pay us maybe 6 to 8 cents a pound and could not resell anything. Meanwhile, we were lining up the national network and local sources of donated food. At that point, the food industry was still very tentative about donating. They had been selling discards to secondary markets overseas, and it took getting the IRS rules changed to give them economic incentives to donate. In those early days, you could not pick and choose what you got, but we were determined to offer the most balanced, nutritious food possible."

Years later, Bill would still wince remembering his first big donation was chocolate syrup. "Not much nutrition there. But soon there was lots of macaroni and cheese and a lot of dried soup mix. There were tons and tons of commodities, cheese and dried milk, dried beans. The federal government was cleaning out their warehouses, offering truckloads of commodities for a while, which allowed us, with the other products, to provide a better balance of nutrition."

"There was a produce house at 10 North Trenton, and we worked hard to convince them it was good for them to work with us," John said. "We would pick up whatever they had. If we got too picky, they wouldn't call. We had a van with the back seat taken out. One time they gave us cabbage, in big net bags, that had been in some guy's pickup for too long, no telling how long. NFN tried to clean it up outside but it was just mush, really foul. We peeled the heads, and they ended up no bigger than baseballs. The back of the van had to be hosed out.

"We got bananas big time, and corn on the cob. Sometimes we would go to the grower farms, too."

As the food bank grew, they were able to tap big food companies in northwest Arkansas, bringing in frozen turkeys, chickens, and Little Debbie snack cakes.

The food bank quickly became a big business. As the industry grew larger and more sophisticated, so did the regulations governing food banks. Predictably, Dan was on a collision course with the burgeoning regulations.

"I remember meeting after meeting with Dan, closed-door meetings crowded into a tiny room, and always he was smoking," Major remembered. "We were worried that his ashes would drop and set him on fire, but never would I have said a word. Dan was way up there in my hierarchy of heroes. We went round and round about the mounting regulations our food bank had to meet.

"His point was—he didn't want to be considered a charitable organization. Help was a loan, not a handout. It was a friend helping a friend, reinforcing the dignity of people—that they were just like everybody else, they were just having a hard time. And, most of all, Dan didn't want the bureaucracy to take over, turning NFN into a welfare organization. He fought tooth and nail about keeping databases, because he thought they just turned the poor into numbers. He wanted to offer universal, unconditional positive regard.

"When I look back," Bill said, "I know I was way too rigid then. He inspired me then, and always will."

In a few years, the food bank moved to independent status, leaving the warm womb of Neighbor for Neighbor and opening the way for tremendous growth. Over many years, the food bank has contributed immeasurably to the health and well being of countless needy families. "And Dan Allen made it all possible," Bill Major said.[12]

"His point was—he didn't want to be considered a charitable organization. Help was a loan, not a handout. It was a friend helping a friend, reinforcing the dignity of people— that they were just like everybody else, they were just having a hard time."
—Bill Major

NFN Director Resigns From Priesthood

FEB. 6, 1973

The Rev. Dan Allen, director of Neighbor for Neighbor, Tulsa's self-help program for economically disadvantaged, resigned from the priesthood of the Roman Catholic Church effective Feb. 1, he announced Monday.

Allen said he hopes to continue as NFN director "because the heart of my ministry is service to the poor."

His resignation raises several questions which presumably will be resolved by the Most Rev. Berard J. Ganter Jr., bishop-elect of the Tulsa diocese, following his elevation to the episcopate Wednesday.

Allen has been serving as priest for the Community of the Living Christ, Tulsa's Roman Catholic parish without boundaries. Presumably another priest will have to be assigned to that group.

IN ADDITION TO SUPPLYing Allen's salary, some support has been provided by the Diocese of Oklahoma City-Tulsa to NFN in the form of physical facilities leased at little or no costs.

This headquarters, at 1506, E. 46th St. North, presumably will become the property of the Tulsa diocese, with its establishment, and to Ganter and his advisers will fall the decision as to whether NFN may continue to use the facilities.

"Through my 16 years priesthood," said Allen, "I have progressively found myself at odds with the church on major issues. My greatest disappointment lies in ... that the church has not ... its power to bear in ... of those who have n...

"Although I am ... the church for the ... leges I have on ... priest, I can not ... change in the 'c...

See Resign

'THE REV. DAN ALLEN'

Resigns

Continued from B-1

tien during my lifetime. So, I have decided on a new life stance, both for my own personal survival and in hopes of a more adequate expression of my Christian concept of man."

ALLEN SAID HE WANTS to continue his work with NFN "and would hope for continued support from those who have given so generously in the past."

A native of Edmond, Allen was reared in Tulsa and attended St. Francis Elementary School and Marquette High School before enrolling at Oklahoma State University. He completed religious studies at St. John's Seminary, Little Rock, Ark.

Allen began the NFN program while a priest at St. Jude's parish on Tulsa's far northside. He was recipient of the Sertoma Club's "Service to Mankind" award in 1969 for his NFN work.

15 years of loaves and fishes

By ANN PATTON

NEIGHBOR FOR NEIGHBOR ...

TULSA WORLD

SUNDAY,
DECEMBER 19, 1982

OPINI[ON]

Light for the Poor: Who Pays the Bills When Charity Fails?

By KEN NEAL
Associate Editor

The plight of the poor in a wealthy (although temporarily economically depressed) society burst into Tulsa news last week as Neighbor for Neighbor announced it will stop using its limited funds to pay its clients' electric bills.

The driving force for Neighbor for Neighbor, a non-government organization which relies on the public for money and services to help those in need, is Dan Allen, a former Roman Catholic priest and seminary professor.

Allen runs what most Tulsans agree is the most efficient charitable organization in town, repeatedly delivering several dollars' worth of services for every dollar collected.

Allen and his board are tired of seeing a big part of the NFN budget go for utility bills. They are particularly unhappy at Public Service Co. of Oklahoma, seeing the money paid PSO as a "subsidy."

While that is an inaccurate assessment, it is an understandable one for a man who has for years dealt with the problems of the poor on a day-to-day, closeup basis. Allen sees poverty in a way that the majority of us never see it and furthermore don't want to see.

NFN's rebellion on paying the electric bills for poor PSO customers raises a question that the more affluent part of society cannot and should not ignore.

Perhaps it is best illustrated by discussing this question: Should utility companies "forgive" their poor customers from paying?

To those who see utilities as greedy, faceless corporations with tremendous profits, the answer is likely to be yes.

That concept of public utilities, is, however, fundamentally in error, although it is often an underlying assumption of those who regularly complain of steadily increasing utility bills.

Simply put, public utilities, in return for the exclusive right to provide a service, are regulated by the public, through its elected representatives, in this case the state Corporation Commission.

The maximum amount of profit is set by the Commission. Contrary to the public perception, utilities have historically earned considerably less than the maximums allowed by the Commission.

This bit of apologia is necessary to make this point: The only way utilities can "forgive" utility bills for the poor is to at some point charge them to the paying customer.

Next question: Is the public willing to pay higher utility bills to allow the poor not to pay?

So far, the answer to that is a resounding "no."

The Corporation Commission has considered such "lifeline" programs. Typically, the debate on them involves spokesmen for the poor and elderly. On the other side are the paying customers, many of whom are paying utility bills equal to monthly house payments.

NEAL,

David Landholt, assistant director, NFN, circa 1977, *Tulsa Magazine*. Newspaper clippings from *Tulsa World*, 1973 and 1982; *Tulsa Tribune*, 1983.

Chapter 15

They Can Either Eat
Or Pay Their Utility Bills

"There's no reason why poor people can't get the help they need
and still keep their dignity. . . .

"Our program isn't for the people it serves.
It's with the people."

—Dan Allen

Digging footings for NFN construction. Tom Gilbert photo, *Tulsa World*, 1994.

"What would happen," Dan mused one Christmas, "if we decided to light up life instead of trees?"

It was a cold winter, with few good options. First the lost job, then the sick babies, then lights and gas turned off. When her man left and the landlord starting talking about evicting them for back rent, Mamie would have moved her family into her car, but she didn't have one. To try to stay warm, she and the children wore all their clothes every day. During one cold snap, hope just ran out. She broke up the chairs and set them afire in a washtub over the dead furnace grate in the middle of her living room floor.[1]

Elsewhere that winter, there was warmth and laughter, where a cluster of women gathered in the old Neighbor for Neighbor building that once housed the food bank. Dan called it "The Women's Project."

Nothing was more important to Dan Allen than protecting home and hearth for families ensnared in the rigors of poverty. Neighbor for Neighbor's attempts to help create safe and secure homes led down first one and then another path to trial-and-error adventures that ranged from organizing women's self-help projects, to fighting for heat and lights, to crusading for safe public housing.

The Women's Project was born as a kind of Christmas present to himself. "What would happen," Dan mused one Christmas, "if we decided to light up life instead of trees?"[2]

Dan knew that women were the lynchpins of healthy homes and families. A sure formula for poverty was to be a single female with children, and he tried many ideas to give women greater economic and emotional security. NFN organized household workers, experimented with home repair co-ops, and developed various experimental cottage industries.

"Dan saw that these women's lives were so dreary," recalled Pat Flanagan. "He wanted to give them self respect and self determination, but even more—what if they could be around something beautiful?"[3] So it was that, by spring, woman of varying ages and life circumstances were working at NFN to create beauty and put it out for sale.

"They just got started before Christmas last year," Allen told a visitor in 1985. "Some of the women working out here have never worked before, but they're making this project go." Dan said he saw incredible changes in their attitudes and self-confidence since they started working with Pat Flanagan and Carol Falletti who codirected the women's economic development project. "Some of them were afraid to drive around town alone before," Dan said. "Now they're making and selling 'GadRags' to retail outlets in Tulsa and Oklahoma City."[4]

Some were designing and producing handmade belts and buckles that were marketed under the brand name "GadRags." Others were crafting jewelry. Some were creating handmade GadRags sales tags that attached to each item and described the women's project and the name of the woman who created it. The

In the fall of 1979, Neighbor for Neighbor closed down again, "with resources exhausted and optimism a luxury."

tags said, "The Neighbor for Neighbor Women's Project provides support, services, and income for poor women."

On the morning in question, the circle of women began a spirited debate over the wording. It produced a kitchen rebellion. "When people say, 'poor,'" exclaimed a young woman named Trisha, "what they really mean is that you're stupid or you can't be as good as anybody else. Well, I'm none of those things, so don't call me 'poor.' I just have a low income and that's all. So call me that.'"

"What was really terrific about this discussion," said Pat Flanagan, "was that the workers weren't trying to avoid the word . . . But in daring to shuck the shackles of other people's labels, in daring to name themselves, they took another giant leap toward freedom."

GadRags changed the tag wording to say "low-income women." "Poor is simply a four-letter word describing society's poor understanding of low-income women," Pat said.[5]

In another attempt to strengthen homes, NFN started a storefront furniture repair cooperative, using a special grant from the United Presbyterian Church.[6] Under the direction of volunteer experts, furniture was repaired by families who received help. "A workable level of labor exchange would be two pieces repaired for each piece received," Dan wrote in his monthly newsletter. "This will provide a definite sense of self-worth [and] education between skilled and unskilled workers."[7] Elsewhere, Dan was also trying to reestablish a gardening cooperative and a solar greenhouse.

But winter fuel crises brought people to NFN in droves, forcing NFN to shut down more than once during the 1970s.[8] In the fall of 1979, Neighbor for Neighbor closed down again, "with resources exhausted and optimism a luxury," Dan reported later. High utility rates were robbing the poor and killing NFN, he said.

But then, with help from the news media, "Tulsa resurrected NFN and sent it into a record year of $198,000 in donations and $184,587 loaned to the poor through family assistance," he said. Thirteen percent of the funds came from local businesses, 27 percent from churches (plus hundreds of volunteer man-hours), and 60 percent from individuals. "Resurrection Church, alone, donated over $26,000 for salaries, and Tulsa Trailer & Body Inc. continued to retire our building loan and salary overhead to the tune of $18,000," giving NFN an unusual nest egg of $26,000 to face the winter.[9]

"When they say somebody thinks outside the box—they can't really imagine how far out of the box Dan was."
—Maynard Ungerman.

It was never easy. One year, a group of college economics students came to NFN during a minimester to work with the poor. Only one returned after the course was over. "They really couldn't take the psychological shock," Dan said. "It depressed them."[10]

They were not alone. Sometime in that era, Pat Flanagan had moved back to Tulsa, after a decade away. She called NFN and arranged to meet Dan Allen at Denny's to begin catching up. "I didn't recognize him," she remembered later. "When I left he was a kind of chunky dark-haired guy, and when I came back he was a heavy gray-bearded old guy. I was gone nine years or so—those were hard years for Dan."[11]

As Dan was trying to help others create homes, he decided to create one of his own: a country retreat that he called The Farm, on land his family had owned for many years.

"One day," Bill Skeehan remembered, "Dan and I were driving south on Lewis and had just turned right on 71st Street when he spotted a roadway construction shack. It looked like a little beat-up Swiss chalet. Without saying a word, he whipped into the site, negotiated, and bought it on the spot. He got it moved to his family's land, up on the Caney River, and it became his home."

The retreat probably saved Dan's life, friends said. It gave him a place to get away from the ever-present needs at Neighbor for Neighbor, to commune with nature, and to regroup emotionally. Soon Father Skeehan and Father Bob Pickett built cabins, too. They would travel to the farm on Sunday afternoons and stay over Monday nights. "We had twenty years of

Mondays together," Bill Skeehan said.[12]

What Dan built was unlike any other place, filled with zany carpentry, handcrafted art, and collections from nature. "When they say somebody thinks outside the box—they can't really imagine how far out of the box Dan was," remembered Maynard Ungerman. "Working with him was a fantastic experience, and nothing was more fun than being at his farm. He loved to play golf, so he decided to build a nine-hole golf course at his farm. But instead of building a course and greens with nine holes, he dug one hole and approached it from nine different directions.

"Then he decided he wanted an eighteen-hole course, so he dug a second hole and approached it from nine more directions. Now that's what I call outside the box. He got the water out of the Caney to water his course. Dan was a rugged individualist, with a mind like you just don't see. If he had wanted, he could have been anything—a multimillionaire—because he was a true innovator. That's why, quirky as he was, a lot of people who were very, very influential believed he could do no wrong. It was always a thrill to work with Dan."[13]

It took Dan five years to build his home in the lush river valley that he loved. It took the river less than five days to wreck it. After twenty-two inches of rain, the river rose, relentlessly, and engulfed it in October 1986. The flood lingered

"I'm going to wiggle my imagination and start over." —Dan Allen

over many days. Dan lost everything but took it with uncharacteristic serenity. "You can put your house where it's good for the house, or you can put it where it's good for you," Allen said. "I chose what was good for me."

What now? "I'm going to wiggle my imagination and start over," Dan said.[14]

Little better off than those it struggled to help, lurching from one fiscal crisis to another during its teenage years, Neighbor for Neighbor continued to attack the root causes of the interlocking problems of poverty, including the continuing struggles of the poor to pay rising utility rates.

Throughout the 1970s, Dan had observed that NFN payments to utility companies were spiraling upward, as NFN struggled to keep heat, power, and water flowing to needy families. The decade saw some progress on the City of Tulsa water and sewer side, where rates had traditionally been skewed to benefit business and industry. With behind-the-scenes help from NFN volunteers, the League of Women Voters helped create a vigorous public debate over City of Tulsa rates. LWV members Norma Eagleton and Patty Eaton both subsequently became elected city officials and helped bring about major changes in the city utilities. The concept of fighting for fair utility rates became part of the local culture.

Nonetheless, by 1977, utility payments, to pay for dramatic increases in power and heating rates, had edged ahead of food assistance as the number one demand at NFN.[15] The more he looked at it, the madder Dan got. "The utility companies are robbing poor people of the necessities of life," he fumed. "Gas, electricity and water are basic rights of people—not rights of companies to be used for excessive profiteering." Neighbor for Neighbor didn't have enough funds to keep helping with emergency bills, he said. "The sources of funds for human improvement are dwindling to nothing. We find ourselves in the same situation as the families we serve. . . . What's going to happen to these people? Where do folks like us go?"[16]

"The utility companies are robbing poor people of the necessities of life."

To fight what Dan considered exploitation of the poor by utility companies, NFN created the Coalition for Fair Utility Rates. The coalition was spearheaded by Jim Martin, who was working as a loaned executive to NFN. Martin's employer, a well-intentioned NFN benefactor, originally sent Martin to NFN to get the organization on a sound business footing. But at Dan's University of Poverty, the archconservative Martin quickly became a radicalized Dan Allen supporter and crusader for the poor.[17]

Jim Martin began poring over the records of Oklahoma Natural Gas Company, the natural gas provider, and Public Service Company of Oklahoma, which provided electric power to the Tulsa area. Martin and the coalition were particularly incensed by PSO's plan to build a nuclear power plant east of Tulsa. The proposed Black Fox nuclear plant stirred up quite a spirited local debate, lasting a decade. A diverse constellation of people and groups challenged the plant. The Sunbelt Alliance favored civil disobedience and triggered mass arrests with its sit-in and break-in tactics. CASE, the Citizens Action for Safe Energy, favored legal intervention and was run by grandmother Carrie Barefoot Dickerson, who financed her CASE crusade by making handmade quilts.

NFN and Carrie Dickerson both focused on the potential economic impact for the poor. The Coalition for Fair Utility Rates took a broader stance, arguing that the Black Fox nuclear plant would be too expensive and would raise rates that would particularly impact the poor, and, even worse, would pose health and safety risks for the entire region.[18]

In 1979 an incensed Dan Allen called a news conference on Black Fox and power rates. Over the past two years, NFN had spent more than $100,000 in no-interest loans to help poor families keep their lights and heat turned on, he said.

NFN was not taking a stand on whether the Black Fox nuclear plant should be built, he said, but NFN and the Coalition for Fair Utility Rates were demanding full disclosure of information relating to the decision. "For anyone to make a decision on the economics of such a plant, as to how it will affect the utility bills of Public Service [Co. of Oklahoma] for consumers, they have to know whether such a plant will in fact reduce or raise consumer bills," Dan said. Allen and the coalition argued that an unsafe plant would bear unknown costs that would fall heavily on those least able to pay.

The average person was being shut out of the process, said NFN's Maynard Ungerman. The Nuclear Regulatory Commission should open its closed-door hearings to the public and release their background information, including a critical analysis called the Reed Report, he said.

The Reed report, Martin said, "is probably the only document related to safety features of nuclear plants. . . . If there are safety problems, steps will have to be taken to correct them and there will be cost factors involved."

At NFN, things were getting worse, Dan said. The utility fight was not without cost to NFN, because many influential Tulsans favored building the nuclear plant and condemned those who were fighting it. Donations dropped at NFN, making things harder for the poor. "We are finding it's one or the other for [NFN clients]—they can either eat or pay their utility bills," Dan said.[19]

In its quest to contain utility rates, NFN also made a decision to intervene in the rate increase hearings before the Oklahoma Corporation Commission. By a quirk of fate, new doors were opened for consumers when Norma Eagleton left her job as Tulsa Finance Commissioner to accept appointment to the Corporation Commission, which regulates gas and electric utilities in Oklahoma. Jim Martin stepped up NFN's continuing analysis of records, aided by two professors at the University of Tulsa, Dr. Cadwell Ray and Dr. Charles Sackrey. Martin reported some Corporation Commission success: rate increases had been scaled back, and PSO received a $22 million increase in rates, not the $29 million requested.[20]

Meanwhile, the Black Fox debate dragged on for years, keeping the issue of utility rates before the public. CASE hired crusading attorneys Tom Dalton and Lou Bullock, and the Coalition for Fair Utility Rates hired Charley Cleveland, a former state representative. The fight continued for a decade, in the courthouse and the state house, with courthouse efforts by CASE attorney Tom Dalton, civil disobedience by the Sunbelt Alliance, relentless research by NFN and the Coalition for Fair Utility Rates, and probing questions from Norma Eagleton at the Oklahoma Corporation Commission. Carrie Dickerson sold her business, Aunt Carrie's Nursing Home in Claremore, and mortgaged her farm to help finance the fight.

Projected costs for Black Fox continued to spiral upward. When they announced the plant in May 1973, PSO estimated it would cost $450 million. By 1979 cost estimates were between $1.5 and $2.5 billion.[21]

On January 15, 1982, the Oklahoma Corporation Commission issued its ultimate licensing decision. It was a shocker: PSO should not proceed with the Black Fox nuclear plant. The OCC said its job was to protect Oklahoma ratepayers from imprudent management decisions and "the Black Fox Nuclear Power Station project is no longer economically viable."

A month later, PSO pulled the plug and scrapped its Black Fox Nuclear project. PSO also booted its hard-shell president, Dick Newman, and placed the electric utility in the hands of a moderate reformer, Martin Fate, who said the protests and delaying tactics were the major factors in losing Black Fox.[22] It was the only nuclear power plant in the U.S. to be canceled by a combination of legal and citizen action after construction had started.[23]

If the crusade over electric utility rates killed Black Fox, crusaders also saved Public Service Company in the process, as confirmed years later by a PSO executive who helped shepherd the Black Fox application. "Black Fox would have bankrupted PSO," he said.[24]

In addition to electric power, equally urgent at NFN was the cost of natural gas to heat homes of the poor.

After Black Fox, debate centered on the need for "lifeline" rates, fixed at a more affordable level for low users at a charge below actual costs so that other users would, in effect, subsidize low-income users. Allen rebelled against NFN continuing to "subsidize" utility companies by paying most of the NFN budget to keep lights and heat turned on for poor families. There seemed to be no good options.

The utilities "have us over a barrel," Dan said. "We can't let people freeze to death for lack of heat, and they can't have their electricity turned off because they'd have no way to keep food and their kids would have no light to study by."[25]

In frustration, Allen briefly stopped making PSO payments with NFN funds. "We couldn't see continuing to subsidize something that keeps going up beyond a reasonable rate, year after year," he said. "It's a simplistic form of saying that we've had it with these rate increases." Nonetheless, NFN pledged to continue to help in other ways, including "all the associated problems people face" that included payment of other utility bills.

A PSO spokesman said the utility had tried to work with NFN, without success. Dan said there was "a natural rub" between NFN and PSO. "We're simply dealing with the people who cannot pay, and they're trying to get them to pay. We can't help but be at conflict with the people who have the product [electricity] that clients need," he said.[26]

On the natural gas side, NFN was finding a little more cooperation from Oklahoma Natural Gas Company, perhaps because—in an ironic twist—the gas company had hired NFN's long-term volunteer, Gloria Caldwell, to develop its consumer affairs programs. Gloria developed what became known as a "Share the Warmth" program. Gas customers could check a box for a donation to the company, and the voluntary proceeds were used to pay bills for customers who could not pay.

Dan Allen was cool to the Share the Warmth program, which he considered more of a band-aid than a cure for poverty. It got off to a slow start, raising only $10 when it began.[27] But over the coming years, Gloria's Share the Warmth program raised millions of donated dollars to help thousands of families.[28]

On January 15, 1982, the Oklahoma Corporation Commission issued its ultimate licensing decision. It was a shocker: PSO should not proceed with the Black Fox nuclear plant.

The OCC said its job was to protect Oklahoma ratepayers from imprudent management decisions and the Black Fox Nuclear Power Station project is no longer economically viable.

TULSA WORLD
FRIDAY
JANUARY 11, 1985

CITY/STATE

SECTION D

Line of People Was Half-Mile Long

2,300 Get Shoes In Giveaway

When Neighbor for Neighbor workers opened their doors for the agency's shoe giveaway at 9 a.m. Thursday, they faced a line of people a half-mile long, said secretary Diane Gower. Some had been waiting since 7 a.m.

By noon, nearly 2,300 pairs of new and used shoes — mostly children's sizes — had been given away to approximately 400 families, Ms. Gower said. Some who came for shoes had to be turned away because the sizes they needed were not available or all shoes had been spoken for when they arrived.

The shoes were the result of the Shoe Shuttle drive held by Trippet's shoe stores during the Christmas season, in which customers donated used shoes and boots and the store promised to match donations pair-for-pair.

Trippet's and Jumping Jacks shoe stores ended up more than matching public donations,

to accompany 656 usable pairs of used shoes given by customers, a Trippet's spokesman said.

The two retailers last year donated 2,256 pairs of shoes to Neighbor for Neighbor, the spokesman said. Distribution took a little over a week last year, compared to a half a day this year, Ms. Gower said. "That lets us know there's definitely a need for shoes," she said.

Byron Franklin, president of Trippet's, started the program last year "because he wanted to do something for the needy of Tulsa using his product," the Trippet's spokesman said. "He hated to see good shoes go to waste and wanted to give them to people who couldn't pay for them.

Neighbor for Neighbor accepts donations of shoes, food and clothing year round at 1506 E. 46th St. North. For more information, call Neighbor for

A near-empty room reflects the need for shoes following Neigh

TULSA WORLD, SUNDAY, SEPTEMBER 27, 1981

TULSA WORLD Opinion

Tulsa's Working Poor In Health Care Trap

That mother of four may make only $28 too much per month to qualify for federal assistance, but she is automatically cut off from the routine medical care most Americans take for granted.

CLINIC

By BRITTON GILDERSLEEVE
World Medical Writer

IT'S NOT only the overcrowded, understaffed facilities.

The other problem with northside Tulsa health care facilities, say those in the know, is financial focus — on the working poor.

Neighbor for Neighbor director Dan Allen cites figures showing Tulsa is the only city of its size in the country without a charity hospital.

Charity patients are not on Medicare/Medicaid reimbursement. They are usually patients with no

barred from using those services if they haven't paid previous bills.

Allen believes the problem lies with longterm ignorance of northside Tulsa needs. And what he calls "prejudice against the northside in general."

"HALF OF our clients have an income less than $200 a month. Almost 90 percent have an income below $500 a month. How the hell can you manage on that, much less pay a medical bill? What are these people supposed to do?" he asked angrily.

Despite the poverty-level status of many NFN clients, only one NFN client in four is receiving public assistance, Social

mother working at a minimum wage job trying to support her children — who aren't making it," Moton director of planning and operations Chon Roure stressed. "They don't qualify for aid, but they can hardly make ends meet. That's who we're seeing now, the ones who are trying to stay off welfare but just can't manage everything."

That mother of four may make only $28 too much per month to qualify for federal assistance, but she is automatically cut off from the routine medical care most Americans take for granted — dental exams for her children, the security that comes from rushing a feverish toddler to the emergency room instead of waiting for Tuesday clinic.

Although NFN does not receive federal funding per se, recent budgetary cuts in several areas are sure to increase the current caseload, according to Allen and NFN clinic director Carol Falletti.

"WE SERVE the people who fall between the cracks," Allen said. "And the cracks are getting a lot bigger.

Most services at NFN are free. They include general practice consultations, fittings for prescription glasses, eye examinations, preventive and restorative dentistry as well as oral surgery and help in obtaining drugs prescribed for a serious medical condition.

Chapter 16

Surely These Hell Holes Should Have A Higher Priority

"Funded by donations, we are free of government rules
and regulations. Every program we start comes out of
our relationship with the poor,
who are coequal participants.
They set the agenda."

— Dan Allen

Life was hard in slum housing.

Thus was born the idea that Dan Allen would conduct his own personal Parade of Homes—Northside edition.

It's time. Dan Allen collects his inner circle of volunteers and heads for the bus, with local officials and news media in tow.

Elsewhere in Tulsa, potential home buyers line up every year to tour captivating new homes in the annual Parade of Homes. These are the finest of Tulsa's new houses, scattered throughout southeast neighborhoods, carefully sited in only the best school districts. For a week every spring, home builders showcase new houses to parades of would-be buyers and shameless gawkers. A hot technique this year is mixing brick, stone, and siding for exteriors, below complex pitched-roof designs. Wood shingles are favored on high-dollar roofs. Three-car garages are standard. Inside, the new homes feature cathedral ceilings that soar above spacious entries and family rooms, which usually open into kitchens lined with furniture-quality cabinets and built-in appliances. All are so beautiful, it is almost impossible to choose.

Why should this experience be limited to southeast Tulsa? Dan asked. True, there is not much new building going on in North Tulsa, where the economy is permanently stalled, but we still have a story to tell. Why not have our own showcase event? Thus was born the idea that Dan Allen would conduct his own personal Parade of Homes—Northside edition.

The bus boarded on a cool spring morning. Heading out from Neighbor for Neighbor headquarters, the bus headed southwest, into what was once the black community.

On your right, remnants of shacks dating back to the '21 Race Riot. Note the creative roof treatments of tar paper scraps, attached in segments over many years; the original siding, weathered wood mended with plywood; and the drafty windows enhanced by cardboard and black plastic trash bags. On your left, note the extensive open-space stretches, cleared by urban renewal but still fallow in the absence of market or financing . . . or hope.

The bus route wound west, through once-grand streets with graying mansions and comfy bungalows hungry for repair. These were the original white-flight neighborhoods. When the laws and banks opened up these neighborhoods, black families began edging this direction—but panicking whites quickly fled, taking home values with them.

Wandering north again, the bus drove through post-war tracts: oceans of mass-produced two-bedrooms framed up as fast as possible after WWII for white factory workers. Many fled as the line of black washed closer, and by the 1980s the houses were coming apart. Home equities were shaky at best, slum landlords were the norm, and bank repossessions were everywhere. Some streets had more boarded-up repos than inhabited homes. It was a cruel joke played on believers in the American dream.

"We're concerned with the management of these projects," Allen said as the bus turned into a bleak public housing project. "The conditions some people are living in are deplorable, and it's time the Tulsa Housing Authority took some responsibility." The projects were no more than holding pens, plagued by drug dealers and crime, and boarded-up apartments were "a mini market for drug dealers"—yet there was a six to eight month waiting list, and many residents paid as much in rent as people living in South Tulsa apartments, he said.

The projects were no more than holding pens, plagued by drug dealers and crime, and boarded-up apartments were a mini market for drug dealers.

Lean stray dogs scattered as the bus drove through. A pretty little girl in a hot-pink coat waved at the bus. She was less than ten yards from a cluster of men sharing some secret stash. Broken window screens flapped in the wind, and a mother hurried across the field, dragging a child by each hand, at the final destination point in Dan's Allen's North Tulsa Parade of Homes tour.[1]

Questions about the Tulsa Housing Authority had lingered for a long time. They came to a head in the 1980s, when Dan Allen declared war on THA.

NFN had successfully challenged THA's racial discrimination policies in the 1970s. About the same time, a newspaper reporter, appalled by conditions in the projects, conducted her own investigation.

In addition to what should have been the obvious problem of stuffing too many challenged people in boxes dropped into already-fragile neighborhoods, there were persistent rumors of corruption in THA operations. Inspectors at THA projects told the reporter that developers of the "turnkey" construction projects were submitting inflated bids, substituting inferior materials and workmanship, then pocketing the difference, with handsome payoffs to THA management; when construction or maintenance problems surfaced, THA blamed the tenants.

The reporter collected affidavits from a number of sources and was warned, "Be sure to check under the hood of your car [to watch for bombs] every day." (The warning was sobering, coming shortly after a political assassin blew up District Court Judge Fred Nelson with a 1970 car bomb.) Ultimately, the reporter was not allowed to print the story, which newspaper lawyers said contained libelous allegations with insufficient documentation. The rumors were never proved.

Nonetheless, as she was wrapping up her investigation, THA Director James Clouse began his own inquiries about the reporter and then, abruptly, resigned.[2]

The 1980s had brought severe recession in Tulsa. The city's oil industry collapsed, as Houston lured many of the companies that had sustained the town for generations. White flight was sucking the economic health out of Northside neighborhoods, which were stigmatized. The advancing line of abandonment moved relentlessly from north to south, but southeast prosperity hid the problem from most Tulsans.

Tenants told NFN over and over again that needy families with no other options were trapped in crime-ridden, vermin-infested units that were coming apart.

Dan and NFN became increasingly frustrated with the impacted problems of the poorest of the poor living in public housing. By the late 1980s, NFN was routinely providing food and other assistance for eight hundred THA tenants a month, giving NFN a pretty good window into the festering housing problems and projects—now including scattered sites as well as the big complexes. Tenants told NFN over and over again that needy families with no other options were trapped in crime-ridden, vermin-infested units that were coming apart.

The Tulsa Housing Authority was funded by the U.S. Department of Housing and Urban Development, with a staff and local board of commissioners; but there was little local scrutiny of THA, which was unresponsive to NFN's concerns. Frustration bubbled over in the fall of 1987, when NFN launched its own investigation into operations of the Tulsa Housing Authority. Point men in the investigation were NFN board members Gloria Caldwell and Pat Flanagan.

The root problem, Dan said, was that THA limited its role to property management, rather than helping the people. Not so, countered THA Director Tom Hares, but Dan dredged up a news story from the previous March quoting Hares: "It's our responsibility to pay off the bonds, maintain the buildings and collect the rent—the functions of a landlord. I think it would be a mistake for the Housing Authority to take care of people from birth to death."[3]

"What is not realized [by the public] is the brutality awaiting those trapped in the projects, due to indifference to their plight," Dan said. "You can't do much until the people charged with managing the facilities do what they're supposed to do. We'll pursue this thing until the rights of the tenants are forthcoming." He said THA was not living up to its legal charge, outlined in the federal Housing Act: "The term 'lower-income housing' means decent, safe and sanitary dwellings assisted under this act."[4]

This time the *Tulsa World* jumped into the fray. An editor visited complexes and found drug dealers and men stripping cars operating in plain sight; she was told the criminals didn't live in the projects but used them as places of business. "The public—if it gives a damn—must demand a massive intervention into the lives of prisoners in these places with all the social services and legal protection available," the *World* wrote in an editorial. "Surely these hell holes should have a higher priority . . . [for] pre-school, day-care and recreation programs that would remove children from the corrupt environment for longer periods. . . . It's time to give occupants of the modern poor house this kind of respect—to recognize their own responsibility and capacity to change. If they are, in fact, no more than helpless victims of a cruel society, then their problem, by definition, is unsolvable. They are condemned forever as non-persons."[5]

THA director Hares responded by proposing to demolish the worst of the Comanche Park housing units, which were so bad THA could not rent them. The idea of demolition was "ludicrous," snapped Pat Flanagan, in an era when hundreds of families were homeless or on waiting lists for THA units. Instead, Pat said, THA should assign a full-time Comanche Park manager who could focus on solving problems, making repairs, and ensuring that drug dealers were not operating out of vacant units.[6]

NFN demanded that THA Director Tom Hares resign. THA must move beyond its "landlord" philosophy, said NFN board member William H. Morris Jr., a former city commissioner.[7]

It got worse. Police were appalled by drug dealers who brazenly set up shop in cars and vacant apartments. As problems multiplied, fear-mongering rumors took on lives of their own, with mounting fear and shunning of housing projects.[8]

Sandra Downie, by that time a vice president of Tulsa's Chamber of Commerce and a member of the THA board, tried to find a middle course to improve operations. Sandra saw that the authority was all about buildings but largely ignored the people living in them. She pressed for social services.

Sandra took direct action twice: when Dan Allen asked her for money to add a case manager to work with THA residents, and when a resident nun named Sister Grace sought to fund a child care center for Sandy Park. In both cases, the money came from a secret angel for NFN with a keen interest in housing projects.[9] But on the THA board, other authority members ignored Sandra's ideas.[10] Frustrated by the inaction and pressured by the nonsupport of Mayor Dick Crawford, Sandra resigned from the THA board.[11]

Since at least October 1987, NFN had been demanding records of THA's "Section 8" housing, a $9.7-million-a-year program to pay private landlords to rent their units to THA tenants. On behalf of NFN's Dan Allen and Pat Flanagan, in January 1988 Maynard Ungerman took THA to court to get the records. It took months.[12]

While Maynard Ungerman and Bill Morris fought THA in court, Pat Flanagan and Gloria Caldwell continued their own sometimes-risky investigations that would consume them for two years.[13] In time, NFN obtained records, piecemeal: the addresses of the Section 8 units, names of the property owners, and amounts paid for rent.[14]

Despite initial skepticism, local news media also jumped into the fray as the records slowly trickled out. When *Tulsa World* reporters analyzed the records, they found plenty to write about. "A taxpayer-funded housing program for the poor is subsidizing rent in Oral Roberts University apartments and paying five property owners more than $100,000 a year," wrote the *World's* Tom Kertscher and Wayne Greene on February 14, 1988. Using federal poverty funds to subsidize ORU's student housing program struck many as odd. To make matters worse, a THA employee who managed part of the program was herself raking in Section 8 payments as landlord for units she owned—but THA said that was not a conflict of interest.[15]

HUD said there was no violation in using Section 8 to pay for student housing if they met the income guidelines, but Dan Allen exploded over the information. Dan blasted the use of funds to subsidize rents for a multimillion-dollar private university. And if there was no conflict for a manager to pay herself from her own program, "I fail to understand what the hell conflict of interest means," he said.[16]

Reporter Kertscher dogged the story. In April, in response to the court-ordered release of more THA records, he wrote that some Section 8 rents were up to 80 percent higher than for comparable nonsubsidized units. Many of the Section 8 units were owned by out-of-state landlords, and others were owned by a few large local firms. Even expensive units were plagued by maintenance problems: at one Southside complex for the elderly, entirely in Section 8 units, water had been leaking into senior citizens' apartments for six years, although the complex received $600,000 a year in Section 8 payments.[17]

"This was a turning point for a lot of people, to learn that students housed at Oral Roberts University were using public funds," Gloria said. ORU was controversial in Tulsa, in its own right, as was the famed televangelist for whom the school was named; so using poverty money for ORU students riled some people. For Dan, who was fighting every day to keep the roof over heads of poor families, it was doubly damnable.

"That really got Rodger's attention. It was a wake-up call for him and lots of people, to think of ORU using federal funds meant for the poor." — Gloria Caldwell

The information blockade finally broke open in May of 1988, when the judge ordered THA to release tenants' addresses. "I'm suspicious," said NFN's Maynard Ungerman, "that they fought so hard to keep us from getting the records. That worries me."[18]

Dan said it was important to get the addresses to evaluate where THA payments were going. "My honest reaction was, [why spend] seven months, all the money and the energy to do the obvious. Enforce the law as it is clearly written. Most laws are not that clear; this one is."[19] As it turned out, some addresses were in the middle of the Arkansas River.

Now the battle moved to City Hall, where officials seemed puzzled at THA operations and struggled to understand what authority they had over THA.

"How does a program allow housing assistance for the poor to become a college scholarship?" wondered Mayor Rodger Randle, who came into office in May 1988.

"We had been working behind the scenes," Gloria remembered. "We wanted a GAO [U.S. Government Accounting Office] investigation, but we got no support from the congressional delegation. We met with every city commissioner, and Gary Watts and J. D. Metcalfe were very supportive. Then Maynard went to the City Commission meeting to talk about THA. And at the very next meeting, here came ORU students saying, 'Don't take away our Section 8 housing,' right across from the campus. That really got Rodger's attention. It was a wake-up call for him and lots of people, to think of ORU using federal funds meant for the poor."

"Meanwhile," said NFN's Bill Morris, "mothers with small children, homeless people and others tell us they have been on a THA waiting list for subsidized housing for over a year. Can any thinking person believe that graduate students fall in the category of those most in need, those in the worst conditions, and those least able to pay?"[20]

Tulsa Housing Authority refused to allow the city auditors access. Director Tom Hares refused to return phone calls.

Mayor Randle did his own fact-finding tour of housing projects on Halloween 1988 and held a series of impromptu meetings with tenants. What he found, in the words of one reporter, were projects "battered by vandalism, littered with broken dreams, . . . a roof and walls but little else for the city's poor [and] a landlord without a heart. . . . At Seminole Hills, Randle walked the cracked sidewalks littered with broken glass to shake hands with tenants leaning against units with broken windows and boarded doors. The only tree in the complex was a wild elm seedling that had survived by twining itself around the rungs of a dilapidated children's slide."

The mayor put out a call for volunteers to refurbish playground equipment at the projects. "It's not acceptable to say we are unable to provide for the homeless when we have at the same time boarded up units sitting vacant in these projects," Randle said. "We have to improve the environment and make it a safe place for families to be raised."[21]

Another member of the City Commission, Street Commissioner J. D. Metcalfe, was more direct. It was time—past time—for the city to replace the entire THA board, Metcalfe said.[22]

"We're trying to keep people from getting hurt or killed" in the worst areas, said Police Chief Drew Diamond.[23]

Mayor Randle responded by sending city auditors to investigate the THA operation and said it was time for a new philosophy on public housing that focused on humane care for the poor, rather than operating like a slum landlord. "The main objective should be to create affordable and high-quality living environments while operating with a tenant-oriented philosophy," Randle said. "I will assume the Housing Authority intends to change its landlord image and follow our new philosophy unless I hear otherwise."[24] Randle got his answer pretty quickly. THA refused to allow the city auditors access. Director Tom Hares refused to return phone calls. "It's just another little flare-up that will soon die down," Hares told the board. The NFN charges are nothing more than "garbage," and news accounts of problems at the projects are "fiction," said THA board member Jack Schuler.[25]

But Rodger Randle had an ace up his sleeve: he knew that as mayor he was the appointing authority for THA board members, and the term of the longtime THA chairman, Sherwin Everding, was expiring.[26] Thus, the next question was, whom could Mayor Randle appoint to take control of the housing program on behalf of the poor?

Dan Allen's folk knew the perfect person, but it was hard to imagine that she might accept. It was a huge long shot.

No one is sure who first thought of Ruth Nelson for the THA board, but when the opening was known, Maynard and Gloria went to Ruth's house one evening to try to convince her to let them put her name before the mayor. "We expected it would be a hard sell, probably hopeless—but to our amazement, Ruth immediately said, 'Yes.' We met with Rodger, outside of City Hall at his request, and he agreed, too," Gloria said.[27]

Ruth Nelson, a Tulsa patron and civic leader, had no reason to consider the needs of the poor. But there was more to Ruth's story. She and her family were holocaust refugees. She grew up with, as she said, "a sense of obligation to return the boon that was presented to my family when an exceptionally generous relative, my father's uncle Sam Miller, signed our affidavit to come to the United States. We were saved. Our family as a whole was reared to pay our dues."

Following her mother's pattern of quiet community service, Ruth volunteered at Tulsa's Center for the Physically Limited. Moved by the difficulties of disabled people struggling to live independent lives, she spearheaded the building of what became known as Murdock Villa to provide safe and sound housing for people with disabilities. It took years. The center chose the Tulsa Housing Authority to build and manage Murdock Villa.

At the time, Ruth was looking for a new focus for her life after her children were grown. She was driving by Murdock Villa one day when the thought hit hard: here she could make a difference. Here were people who needed her. Ruth worked tirelessly to give the vulnerable Murdock Villa tenants secure homes with as much dignity and independence as possible.

But in 1986 she was troubled by police reports from Murdock Villa, "brought to our attention by then-Major Drew Diamond [later to become police chief] who was serving as an outside voice on a policy committee for the center. We could not understand why the police were being called so often to Murdock Villa. There were so many break-ins and robberies."

Police assessment of conditions at Murdock Villa was shocking. Outsiders were freely preying on the vulnerable invalids and people with disabilities, who were living in squalor without apparent consideration by their landlord, the THA.

"We asked Mayor Crawford and THA to assign an on-site manager who could help assure resident well-being," Ruth said. "They told us it was impossible. They only had money for an on-site boiler engineer, as required by law. We didn't think they actually had a boiler in the building, but they said that was all they had money for." It was the beginning of Ruth's education.

"I finally said I would raise money to provide services at Murdock. I thought it should not be under the auspices of anybody viewed as a bleeding heart, so I got the chamber to manage the project, working through Sandra Downie who was chamber vice president then. We started with one coordinator at Murdock Villa, and that went well."

But then things began to snowball. Ruth was working on Murdock Villa with a cluster of people who included Gail Lapidus, director of Family and Children's Services; Nancy Reese, Executive Director of the Center for the Physically Limited; Police Major Drew Diamond and Lt. Carolyn Robinson. They were also troubled by what was happening at other THA projects. "At that time, people in Comanche Park were throwing things at fire trucks, because they didn't trust anybody, and firemen were refusing to make runs to fight fires in housing projects," Ruth said. "Carolyn and I went to a housing authority meeting to call to their attention the amount of crime at some of the complexes. One THA board member got very aggressive and combative because we even brought it up. They pretty much blew us off."

By that time, NFN had launched its own THA investigation, as well.

Ruth was no stranger to NFN, which she had supported for years, in concert with people like her friend Ann Bartlett, the widow of Oklahoma Governor and Senator Dewey Bartlett Sr. (and mother of Dewey Bartlett Jr., who would later become Tulsa's mayor.) "After Gov. Bartlett died, Ann came back to Tulsa and started volunteering at NFN. She was a staunch Catholic and believed so strongly in Neighbor for Neighbor."

Both Ruth and Ann were admirers of Dan Allen and his work. Among Ruth's life treasures is a letter from Dan. "I have to say, meeting in Dan's office was hard; it reeked of cigarette smoke; I would go home and wash my hair," Ruth said. But she returned, over and over again, because "there was no nonsense about him. He didn't try to sweet talk you, but he didn't try to guilt you, either. He walked the walk.

"Dan tried to give dignity to the people he served, and he made them put in sweat equity so they weren't just getting a handout, and he did it arbitrarily and individually in ways you can't do in any big bureaucratic organization. Dan Allen was a unique man. You can't manufacture one like him, you can't even go out and look for one. When they come along, they are gifts to be cherished."

When the moment was right, "I think I expressed the feeling that I could help make positive change at the Tulsa Housing Authority," Ruth said.[28]

In 1989, two years after Neighbor for Neighbor first demanded change in the housing program, Mayor Rodger Randle appointed Ruth Nelson to the Tulsa Housing Authority. It was a watershed moment.

At first, no one listened when she made a motion or raised a question, she said; but in time she began to build a team. After some years, she

"I am a peace officer, and Dan and Ruth taught me that there is no peace without social justice."—Drew Diamond

was elected chair and was reelected over and over again. Ruth had to learn a lot of hard lessons at THA, and housing projects still have no shortage of challenges, but the improvements were remarkable. She worked quietly but relentlessly, expanding social services, luring community support into the housing projects, forcing out some staff members and nurturing others. "Our staff is so superior now," she said. "They are what make the difference."[29]

"Ruth has been the real heroine," Gloria Caldwell said years later. "She stepped up when she was needed and had the stature to make the changes that were needed. None of it was easy, but she has stuck with it all these years."[30]

"Ruth is a 'people' person," said Sandra Downie. "She understood that the housing authority should be about the people, not the buildings. She has made amazing changes but never allows any personal publicity. She always had a sense about these things—she understood community needs and was dedicated to helping, very quietly, to make things better."[31]

"When Ruth came on board, she was a change agent," said Chea Redditt, now THA executive director. "The administration had to change. When Ruth came on, the board changed and the board changed the staff. We sat down and thought about how we can perfect the program so we can do a better job. And it's evaluated every year."[32] Most years, the new and improved THA has earned a federal ranking of High Performer, with nearly perfect scores.

The lessons learned in Dan Allen's housing crusade went far beyond sheltering. "In those years, we were learning so many things together," recalled Drew Diamond, who served as police chief from 1987 to 1991, then became counsel to presidents and world leaders establishing what became known as community policing. "We are changing the way police work with their communities, because we learned that the way to keep communities safe is to engage people in their own well being. We are not in the business of rescuing people; we are helping them survive and gain the skills to create their own higher quality of life.

"I think I speak for others, too—whatever we are today was shaped in those years by people like Dan Allen and Ruth Nelson. They were willing to take risks to make the right changes. They taught us that if you want to organize to make change, you can do it," Diamond said. "The world is hard on social justice because it is about poverty and race and class, and we want to layer over that as if it somehow takes away from the needs of the 'real people.' But their legacy is to show us that even a small group of people can change the world.

"I am a peace officer, and Dan and Ruth taught me that there is no peace without social justice."[33]

Chapter 17

The University Of Poverty

Dan Allen's Inn

God's Angry Man

By Frosty Troy

"In this group, we initially focused on providing food
and other basic services to the poor.
But from the beginning the idea was not to run simply a charity,
but to integrate charity and justice into one.
If you separate them, you end up with paternalism or legalism."

—Dan Allen

Dan Allen obituary. *The Oklahoma Observer*, December 1995.

"DAN DID NOT PRACTICE WHAT HE PREACHED; HE PREACHED WHAT HE PRACTICED...TO DRAW CLOSE TO THE POOR BY COMING TO THEIR AID IS EQUIVALENT...TO DRAWING CLOSE TO GOD."
—FATHER BILL SKEEHAN

"For the white middle-class community, this place is a 'university of poverty.' Volunteers who last three months will remain a part of this community. If they don't last that long, they don't graduate from this school.

"The graduates take back to their own neighborhoods and workplaces a better understanding of what it means to live in poverty and the impact public policies have on poor people.

"This way of bringing communities together is what's kept the program afloat. When people see what has happened to other people—and can happen to them—then they develop a life commitment to the poor.

"I don't know how the hell we've done it, but we have made it—at least this far. Since we don't have a bunch of regulations and stuff, every day I just try to go in the direction Christ leads." —Dan Allen, 1995.[1]

The early 1990s were busy years at Neighbor for Neighbor, as Dan's audacious venture matured in social justice and love—*caritas*—that were the lynchpins for his religion. If Dan's volunteers were living stones, then his University of Poverty was built on those living stones, in the words of Dan's niece Judy Allen Hess. "Caritas means 'love in action,'" she said, and Dan and NFN were living "a journey on the edge of a cliff, always on the edge."[2]

Experiments continued and matured in efforts to help with housing, children, and legal aid. The legal program came of age, with its own building to house pro bono attorneys who saw clients at NFN, fielded phone calls, and offered free legal advice. Sammy Price, a paralegal, served as coordinator.

Volunteer lawyers had been working at NFN from the early days, offering free advice to untangle the Gordian-knotted legal problems of the poor. In the beginning, legal issues were untangled by volunteer lawyers Maynard Ungerman and Jeff Nix. "We'd give advice to folks needing help," Jeff remembered. "At first it was, drop by when we could, and then we got more volunteer lawyers, as we needed more help and more specialties. Then we set up standard hours so people could know when to come for help."

Why did NFN have to offer free legal help to the poor? "Because we didn't have any rules that excluded people," Nix said. "Sure, they could go to Legal Aid, but they would have to fill out entitlement papers and all that kind of thing. We took anybody who walked in the door.

"It was really fun twisting The Man's tail. I can remember dealing with landlords, apartments, credit unions, groups who were hassling people. They just hated us, because we were tireless

> *"They just hated us, because we were tireless and fearless and would spend five days in Small Claims Court over $12."*
> *—Jeff Nix*

and fearless and would spend five days in Small Claims Court over $12. We weren't doing it for the money or to make a living. For me, it was great recreational use of the law. I couldn't wait for the next crazy-ass case."

Dan's principle of offering unconditional positive regard extended to the legal unit. "The self-esteem part was always integral to what we were doing," Jeff said. "People could say, 'I have a good lawyer; I'm in first class. I am important to this lawyer, and I'm somebody."[3]

In the early 1990s, Dan's longtime dream was realized with opening of a freestanding NFN Legal Clinic. NFN volunteers Kelley and Todd Singer garnered donations to underwrite the program, and Dan bought the abandoned Highway Patrol headquarters building and moved it to the NFN grounds to house the new legal clinic.[4]

Dan Allen had revolutionized Todd Singer, a law student at the University of Tulsa working as a legal intern at NFN in 1989. "I came from a very entitled Jewish upper-middle-class upbringing, and Dan totally changed my perspective," Todd remembered. "The legal clinic was a total outgrowth of who Dan was. He was the child at the parade saying, 'The emperor has no clothes.' Legal education then was all about securing silk stocking firms and working for wealthy clients; there was really little or no interest in social justice for the poor."[5]

"About all lawyers do today is research fees and cover their lives with the green grass of corporate greed, [ignoring] the little folk who thirst for simple justice," groused Dan Allen.[6]

Todd became a favorite of Dan's, in part because the entire NFN family enjoyed Todd's in-house romance. It was at NFN that Todd met his future bride, Kelley, who was volunteering at the medical clinic while waiting to start medical school. (Later Dr. Kelley Singer served as NFN's first physician medical director.)

As editor of the TU law newspaper, Todd began to crusade for a charity law clinic, without success. He and Maynard Ungerman drew together a proposal for a legal aid clinic, but the dean repeatedly said no.[7] When Todd's class asked him to speak at his 1990 graduation, he decided "to make this a moment to remember." He quietly rounded up donors: "Alex Singer, Herman Singer, Julius Bankoff, Henry Zarrow, Andrea Schlanger, Ruth Kaiser Nelson, Edwin Ash, Jill Tarbel, Judy Zarrow Kishner, and others." Todd begged Dan Allen to attend the graduation, but Dan said he had learned not to attend

> *"Those events always turned out to be times that I told off important people in front of many people— always—so I stay away," Dan said.*

important occasions. "Those events always turned out to be times that I told off important people in front of many people— always—so I stay away," Dan said.[8]

"My speech was all about how TU had been remiss in not having a law clinic," Todd said. "I called the dean up to the microphone and gave him the $10,000 to start a law clinic. Everybody was excited, but nothing happened." It took another year of negotiations, but the clinic finally got off the ground, at NFN.[9]

Dan Allen's legal clinic worked for social justice on individual levels. Without charge to clients, the volunteer lawyers handled uncontested domestic issues, wills/power of attorney, credit/bankruptcy, guardianships, adoptions, and landlord/tenant issues.[10] A typical case: a father of two young children said his wife was planning to run away with a drug dealer and take the children out of state, to an unknown location. Within an hour, a NFN pro bono attorney was able to get the man temporary custody and, eventually, permanent custody.[11] The legal clinic was at the heart of Neighbor for Neighbor's mission, Dan said, to fight for justice for "the little people [who] need so desperately just to enjoy basic human rights."[12]

In 1993, NFN started its "Circle housing" program. The name comes from a "circle" support system: "family and volunteers working together to create a circle of people who begin as strangers and end as friends," according to a descriptive brochure. Rather than new construction, the program focused on salvaging and renovating existing homes, including houses donated to NFN. Volunteers rehabilitated donated houses and offered them at modest costs, usually in the $15,000 to $20,000 range, to the poor at low rent or with low-interest loans.[13]

In 1994, NFN launched its "safe house" program. Operated by a social worker named Linda Ladeur, NFN's Safe House program helped and tutored children in the homes of community leaders. A typical case: "A 7-year-old when asked to read said he didn't want to. Turns out he could not read because he could not see. He now has glasses and is a model pupil." The safe house project lasted for six years and then was turned over to the community.[14]

Meanwhile, other "Neighbor" programs were growing around the region: Broken Arrow Neighbors, Western Neighbors, Neighbors along the Line, and an Oklahoma City Neighbor for Neighbor, all carrying Dan Allen's vision far afield.

Back at NFN, Carol Falletti was uneasy. She couldn't remember exactly the first time she saw it: a faint shiver that ran over Dan as he seemed to lose focus for an instant. Probably it was in the summer of 1995. As the weeks went on, it became more pronounced and frequent, as she watched him go blank for a few moments at a time. She talked to two nurses at NFN, Joyce Moroney and Dan's sister-in-law Anne Allen, and they were all troubled. He seemed to be drifting into a series of mild seizures.

"When Dan got sick, I was with him at the farm," said Dr. Tim Dennehy, who had been Dan's friend since high school. "He said, 'There it goes again,' and he would stare for a few seconds, couldn't say anything. Then he would say, 'It's gone.'

Carol was there when Dr. Moroney gave Dan the news: a glioblastoma brain tumor. "See there," Dan said to Carol, "you didn't think I had a brain."

It took a lot of delicate talking, but eventually they convinced Dan to go see Ed Moroney, Dan's doctor and friend.

Carol was there when Dr. Moroney gave Dan the news: a glioblastoma brain tumor. "See there," Dan said to Carol, "you didn't think I had a brain." Carol managed a chuckle, but the news was a cold stab into her heart. She knew what it meant.

Glioblastoma brain tumors are notorious. In an MRI, they appear as ringed lesions in the brain. There are many theories about causes but no real answers; probably not inherited; maybe a virus, maybe something in the environment, maybe a mosquito—no one can really say. But this much is certain: glioblastoma tumors are lethal. The usual treatment is surgery, but the tumor usually reappears, and few people live two years longer. "It's the worst tumor you can have," Dr. Dennehy said.[15]

On September 18, 1995, Father Bill Skeehan sent a letter to the NFN board: "Dan Allen, as some of you may not know, underwent brain surgery on Wednesday, Sept. 6. We do not know yet the extent of his problems. If you would like to drop him a card, he is at St. Francis Hospital. . . . Please do not call or visit."[16]

Dan's niece Judy Allen Hess watched over him in the hospital. Judy had worked as a volunteer dental assistant on Wednesday nights and became a graduate of the University of Poverty. Dan's illness was rough. He was losing his short-term memory, could not concentrate, and had combative spells. "He was trapped in a nightmare from which he could not escape," she recalled, "not that he did not try more than once. . . . It was heart-breaking."

Then he pointed to the scrapbook and said, 'Keep the focus there on the poor and not on'—and then he pointed toward himself.

Sometimes he didn't know who Judy was. Once he asked for a pen and paper, then wrote in slow shaky words, "My name is Dan Allen."

"Another night, we spoke of a time in the past when my son, then a young toddler, nearly drowned. Dan saved the life of my son, Dan's great nephew. Dan remembered it and recounted back to me exactly what happened," she said. Dan said, "He made me great."

Another time, Judy showed him the scrapbook of NFN clippings, kept by his sister Frances, and asked if it might be time to tell the NFN story. "How would you tell the story?" she asked.

"He was weak and used few words, but his idea was clear. He said to take someone who was working, then became jobless, a young family in trouble. He took his hand and turned it palm-side down, indicating their world in all aspects would turn upside down as they gradually lost everything, including their dignity and self-respect. . . . Now bring them to NFN, where justice comes first, and where their personhood is respected, simply because they are humans and deserve to be treated with dignity and respect.

"I filled in some of the words, and he nodded his head, yes. 'People lack knowledge,' he said; those were his exact words. Then he pointed to the scrapbook and said, 'Keep the focus there on the poor and not on'—and then he pointed toward himself. And I said, OK."[17]

On November 8, Dan drifted into a coma. A few days later, he opened his eyes when Judy began speaking softly to him, "thanking him for showing us, by how he lived his life, what Christ meant when he said, 'When you clothed the least of these, you clothed me. When you feed the least of these, you feed me.' He listened until I finished, then he closed his eyes again," she said.

He opened his eyes one more time, on Sunday evening, November 12, when his good friend Father James McGlinchey came in and began to pray. His family watched as Dan closed his eyes again and, as McGlinchey prayed, "Dan relaxed and gave up his spirit," Judy said.

"We folded his hands as if he was in prayer. He looked like a saint."[18]

"There was a pretty good argument about how to bury Dan," remembered Father Bill Skeehan. "His family wanted him buried in his priestly vestments. People said Dan had resigned as a priest, and indeed he did send that letter to the bishop in 1973, saying

> *"We folded his hands as if he was in prayer. He looked like a saint." — Judy Allen Hess*

he was resigning. But in fact the bishop never accepted his resignation, and many people still revered Dan as a priest, as if there was no change. Certainly in the eyes of his family, he was a priest to the very end. So what is true—he was a Catholic and liberal Democrat all his life, but was he still a priest? Like a lot of things about Dan, it is a mystery. But it was clear to me that he should be buried as he lived, and eventually I won out. Dan was buried in a plaid sports shirt."[19]

"His casket was lined with cardboard," chuckled his friend Tim Dennehy. "It was only $800—a rent-a-coffin, lined with cardboard so they could use it again. People viewed him the night before the rosary, and then his body was cremated. The casket was closed for the service and—who knew?—Dan wasn't there. Somehow, it seemed just like Dan would have wanted it."[20]

Dan was buried, for all practical purposes, in a flood of eulogies.

"Dan Allen was a voice of conscience for our community," said Russell Bennett, pastor of Fellowship Congregational Church. "This is what is meant by a prophet, one who speaks for God, who calls us to account, who lays it on the line, who helps us understand that there is no life of meaning or purpose apart from life together.... We who knew this man, whose lives have been touched by him, grieve poorly if the best we can do is verbal tributes.... Dan would want us to see for ourselves and hear for ourselves what is going on in the country, fire our tongues, and in the name of God—speak. Dan, we will not fail you. The work will go on."[21]

Maynard Ungerman said: "Dan was not just a great prophet. He was a great activist. He made things happen.... Dan was not just the conscience of this city—he was the guiding light in many ways.... He touched so many people that none of us could count them. Just the whole attitude of Tulsa toward social concerns has changed drastically in the past 30 years— much of which is because of Dan's direction. He was our guru, our hope, our future. Dan—you're the greatest person I've ever known. Of course we'll miss you . . . NFN will go on but we'll always miss you."[22]

Was Dan a revolutionary? "You bet he was," said Jeff Nix. "Absolutely an iconoclast, an insurrectionist, a role model, Che Guevara. His legacy lies in the many lives he touched and changed, including mine. I named my son after him—Tucker 'FatherAllen' Nix. Dan is the person I admire most in life."[23]

Dan worked the churches of Tulsa like a politician searching for votes.

Carol Falletti remembered Dan's sense of humor: "He smoked cigarettes in chains which made his mustache yellow at the nostrils. His words found your shadow child and set her free. His socks rarely matched, but who cares when you have coveralls. Master, teacher of unconditional positive regard. He was a fighter, a good one to have on your side if you were the underdog. He instilled courage with his strength.

"How he loved BBQ ribs—the sauce on his beard displaying his pleasure—a connoisseur of fat enhanced by spices, and a connoisseur of friends. The fire and sharpness of his tongue caused your skin to burn; the gentle times were cool and intimate. Education of the affluent to the problems of the poor—unconditional service—all tattooed on my heart and mind. . . . Go on, Spirit. Go on to the Otherworld. Those who were ready have received your fire. Good-bye, old friend."[24]

Frosty Troy, the firebrand editor of *The Oklahoma Observer* newspaper, wrote:

"Dan Allen, Oklahoma's angry knight-errant of God, has died of a brain tumor at 65. Blunt and fearless, he scorned legalistic language and pietistic psychobabble. He didn't trade soup for sermons. There were no altar calls, only calls for justice. Neighbor for Neighbor of Tulsa, which he created in 1966, is a national model for aiding the poor. . . . His value to Tulsa and the nation was his fiery ability to rip away the mask of ersatz Christianity, getting people involved. . . . Dan worked the churches of Tulsa like a politician searching for votes. . . . He charged the windmills of society's indifference, he lanced the puffed up church-on-Sunday crowd. His angry rhetoric would make a drill instructor blush. . . .

"His missionary zeal was to tap the genuine charity of people, not the vaults of the government. He recognized that you don't build a life by what you get but by what you give of yourself....

"Dan Allen fought his own personal demons along the way, as do most saints. Neighbor for Neighbor existed on the eternal verge of bankruptcy because if there was a dollar left and a poor person who needed help, that person got it—no questions asked. Dan Allen's principal commodity was hope, the poor person's bread—faith holding out its hand in the dark. . . .He operated on the hard edge of reality where the poor are savaged for a condition often not of their making. Dan Allen called us to renew the world. Impossible? Unreachable? No, imperative....

"His woolly beard and sad eyes beggared a gigantic heart. . . . It is the Dan Allens who make this a great country, . . . that define Christianity."[25]

Father Bill Skeehan led a Mass of the Resurrection for Daniel Richard Allen in Tulsa's

"The man who left the institutional priesthood was still able to exercise his priesthood by being himself bread broken and wine poured-out for others, especially the very least of the poor."
—Father Bill Skeehan

Holy Family Cathedral on November 15, 1995, before a packed house. The full complement of Catholic hierarchy was present, gathered in a special section reserved for a sea of priests and other clergy, all in full formal religious garb.

"Dan was above all a teacher," said Father Skeehan, "because he was below it all: streetwise, incarnate among the poor. He was there, present. Dan did not practice what he preached; he preached what he practiced. It came from his very being, and that's why he appeared so authentic, so real, because he was. . . . To draw close to the poor by coming to their aid is equivalent . . . to drawing close to God. . . .

"It could be said that Dan used colorful language. Well, yes, but he swore . . . out of justified anger, because the 'least' were getting less."[26]

"Paradoxically," Skeehan said later, "the man who left the institutional priesthood was still able to exercise his priesthood by being himself bread broken and wine poured-out for others, especially the very least of the poor. . . . Dan didn't do what he taught, he taught what he did."[27]

There no explaining Dan's story, said Father Skeehan. "He was an enigmatic person. Dan was always raspy; he was his own self and never left off listening to the poor, never tried to take over their lives, always was learning from them. He came from the deep end of poverty and remembered stealing food when he was a kid, but the rich and powerful sought him out, too. He was as deeply religious as anyone I ever knew, but I never remember him praying; his private prayers were very private. It was his intimate personal self, and he chose not to share that. Dan was on a mission, and his mission was to reorder society—to change the world around him, to do something about the poor and the question of the rich. He didn't let anything get in his way, and he never wavered from that mission.

"How do you explain a Dan Allen? It is a mystery, and there is no explaining it. He would never have admitted it, but he was moved by the Holy Spirit. . . . You cannot see the spirit, and you cannot explain it, it is just a blessing of the Holy Spirit. When you see the life of someone like Dan Allen, the signs are all too visible. He was a blessing, pure and simple."[28]

"Tulsa's University of Poverty has lost its president, its voice," wrote Janet Pearson in Sunday's *Tulsa World*. "Allen would be concerned that the graduation rate will not plummet. It is up to Tulsa's citizens, the would-be students, to see that doesn't happen. It costs nothing to enroll, and new classes start every day."[29]

Chapter 18

Sowing Seeds For Perennial Harvest

"Quite often I am asked what will happen
when it is time for me to hang it up.
I can tell you that, with the people who do our daily work,
it would probably grow even stronger."

—Dan Allen

Pamela Henderson Vann with sign. Stephen Pingry photo, *Tulsa World*, September 24, 2008.

BLINK AND THEY ARE GONE...

*"Dan sowed ever-bearing seeds for perennial harvest," said Dr. Jim Wolfe,
clinic volunteer. "Now my daughters are interested in volunteering, and I am
sure they will pass that on, and I am just one person, but who can say how
many others are changed, too? How many-folds has it grown from Dan, and
how many times will it continue to multiply and expand? There is no way to
measure it."*[1]

**Dan Allen is dead, but the yeast of his work continues to bubble and
grow.** His undying legacy is continuing good work by changed institutions,
his Neighbor for Neighbor family, and those they continue to educate and
inspire. Some carried Dan's message and methods into significant positions
of community leadership: uncommon "common folk" serving lifetime
sentences of work for the common good.

At Neighbor for Neighbor, the NFN board unanimously elected Diane
Perkins, a board member, grandmother, and Tulsa philanthropist, to serve as
interim executive director. Before the week was out, Diane was on the job,
working for $1 a year for the next five years, to keep NFN alive. "Sometimes
we wonder to whom we shall turn without Dan," she said. "We know that
there is no one else of his stature for us, and that leaves us carrying the load.
No one person will follow Dan; we must all follow Dan.... Dan the vision-
ary is gone, but his legacy remains ever growing."[2]

His followers continued to carry out his mission long after his death.Bill
Major remained head of the Food Bank until 1990, then turned over the
reins and moved on. He joined LIFE Senior Services in 1991, serving senior
citizens for almost two decades through programs such as case management
programs for the elderly, senior centers, caregiver support, adult day services,
and a magazine that became the most important communication vehicle for
seniors in the Tulsa area. And at the same time, as executive director of
Vintage Housing, Inc., Bill developed fifteen affordable elderly housing
projects valued at $51 million. In 2010, he became executive director of the
Zarrow Family Foundations, where he could continue his helping career
leading one of the region's most important and beloved philanthropic organizations, which annually distributes many millions to help the needy and
to social-service community groups.[3]

The food bank exploded in scope over the years. By its thirtieth
anniversary, the Eastern Oklahoma Community Food Bank was big
business, providing 13 million pounds of food annually to 460 partner

organizations. That's enough food to create nearly 7.5 million meals a year. The food bank could claim they were feeding 60,000 Oklahomans the equivalent of 621,000 meals a month, to help grow strong bones and fill empty stomachs.[4]

John McCarthy never left the Food Bank, and—trained by his father Don McCarthy who brought in station-wagon loads of bread in the early days of Neighbor for Neighbor—John spent his working life helping to feed the hungry.[5]

Don McCarthy remained on the NFN Board for years. A charter member of the food bank, Don never stopped creating out-of-the-box ways to serve the poor, always ahead of his time. In 2004, he designed and built what became known as a "Millennium House," a low-cost, prototype house that was energy-efficient, tornado-safe, healthy, and handicapped-accessible, among twenty attributes. Built almost entirely with volunteer labor and donations, his sturdy 1,200-square-foot house could be replicated for around $50,000. Don's house was so efficient that utilities averaged only $20 a month. The house became an inspiration for builders and planners, and Don received the 2006 Green Award for Sustainability, presented by Oklahoma State University's Environmental Institute. The State of Oklahoma gave him a Safe Kids award. In 2006 Tulsa Partners, a local nonprofit, established the Don McCarthy Millennium Award, which is given annually for innovations in safe and sustainable community service. Well into his golden years, Don turned his attention to pursing his capstone vision, to create not just one house but an entire Millennium Village, which he continued to pursue every day with the energy and effervescence of a newborn pup.[6]

Wilbert Collins built a successful real estate firm, among other business endeavors. Dan Allen would have been proud in 1998 when Wilbert was sworn into office, the first black person ever elected to the Tulsa County Commission, where he produced a distinguished record of public service.[7]

Carol Falletti retired from the NFN clinic in 2005 but never stopped volunteering at poverty clinics. She and Don Falletti and their children worked continually in causes that stretch around the globe. The family that wanted to get away from poverty continued to serve the poor as their preeminent passion. Over the years, Carol received a shower of awards including the Tulsa County Medical Society's Community Service Award, a Pinnacle Award by the Tulsa Commission on the Status of Women, the Harmon Foundation Award, and the Sollicitudo Rei Socialis Award from Christ the King Catholic Church. Carol was also honored by a unique "Withered Wallet Award" from the Oklahoma University Pediatrics Department. Most important to her, the NFN free clinic became a model for similar clinics around the U.S.[8]

Health care for the poor remained problematic over the years. In 2006, when things were far better than during the early years of NFN, a study found that people living in affluent South Tulsa still enjoyed an average of fourteen years' longer lives than citizens of north, east, or west Tulsa. In 2010, in the shadow of Neighbor for Neighbor, the University of Oklahoma broke ground for a super clinic to improve health care for the region's poor.[9]

Racial integration proved to be a two-edged sword. The old Greenwood ghetto was largely dismantled, including both its deplorable housing and its thriving black businesses. Poverty re-created another ghetto farther north; but thousands of African Americans moved up to middle-class and scattered throughout the city, wherever their pocketbooks allowed. Many "minority" citizens became community leaders, without respect to race.

Tulsa's flagship desegregated schools and their students continued to thrive and grow. Few remembered the labor pains of desegregation. The specter of white flight, called by other names, continued to haunt Tulsa. But those in the know knew that the place to be for quality education was in what had been a ghetto, at Booker T. Washington High, Carver Middle, and Burroughs Elementary. Their graduated students, citizens of the world, became remarkable ambassadors and carried their life learning around the globe.

Father Bill Skeehan aged well, steeped in the love of a constellation of friends and his parishioners in Resurrection Parish, Bartlesville's Catholic Community of St. James, and St. Catherine in Nowata. He remained on the Neighbor for Neighbor board for many years. Father Bill never stopped stating his opinions, in his captivating voice, with courage, humor, and let-the-chips-fall frankness. As he basked in retirement, his friends formed a company named The Meddlers to publish two books of his homilies and writings. In 2010, friends wrote a book about Skeehan's life and crusades, *Vatican II: A Promise Broken?*[10]

Resurrection Parish remained a stronghold of Dan Allen advocates and never abandoned its original vision to create a family-oriented Catholic community dedicated to a living gospel.

Ruth Nelson remained chairman of the THA for more than two decades, revolutionizing the program with her determination to focus on human needs. Housing projects are never heaven on earth, but thousands of families have lived safer and better lives because of her work. Every year since 1998, when HUD adopted a system to evaluate housing authority

program management, THA has ranked between 85 and 104 percent. Ruth
continues to avoid interviews or any publicity, and few people know about
her work with THA or her continuing support of Neighbor for Neighbor.[11]

Gloria Caldwell served on the NFN board for more than thirty years,
including many years as chairman. She was a backbone in the Tulsa League
of Women Voters and a tireless crusader for social justice and good government. Gloria served for two years as an advocate for the poor on a state legislative task force considering deregulation of electric utilities; deregulation
was eventually defeated, helping to keep prices under control.[12] She worked
for years at Oklahoma Natural Gas Company. Over its first twenty years,
Gloria's ONG Share the Warmth program raised more than $5 million in
donations to pay bills for more than 50,000 needy customers who otherwise
would have had their gas turned off.[13]

Sandra Downie racked up a long list of civic, volunteer, and vocational
activities that range from chairman of the planning commission to community development vice president of the
Tulsa Metropolitan Chamber of Commerce. Her untiring hand has stirred civic
pots over two generations, in Tulsa and
across Oklahoma. Sandra (remarried in
1993 with a new last name of Langenkamp)
spearheaded a community foundation for
indigent health care, created innovations for
health insurance, and served on the state health care authority. She led or
participated in many local and state planning projects, always pushing for a
fair shake for the little guy. She spearheaded a major initiative to integrate
efforts of early childhood education into health programs across Oklahoma.
Most important for Sandra, her children all focused their adult lives around
public service.

*Always mindful of his lifelong
commitment to serve the poor,
Maynard Ungerman never left
the NFN board.*

Always mindful of his lifelong commitment to serve the poor, Maynard
Ungerman never left the NFN board. He served as president or member
of nearly every do-good board in Tulsa, including the Tulsa Metropolitan
Ministry, the Community Service Council, Family and Children's Service,
Tulsa United Way, Urban League, LIFE Senior Services, the Indian Health
Care Resource Center, and B'nai Emunah Synagogue. As chairman of a
task force on the homeless, he spearheaded building the Day Center for the
Homeless. Maynard served as a judge on the Oklahoma Temporary Court
of Criminal Appeals, lectured at law schools, and continued to bring land-
mark legal cases. A grateful community showered him with recognition,

including a truckload of awards for leadership in interfaith understanding, community and race relations, and the law. In 2010 he was named outstanding senior attorney for the Tulsa County Bar Association. One award Maynard prized most highly was the 2009 "Volunteer of the Year" award by Neighbor for Neighbor.[14]

In 2008, Pamela Henderson-Vann, a grateful woman once helped by Neighbor for Neighbor, convinced the City of Tulsa to rename 46th Street North "Dan Allen Boulevard."[15]

Over the years, in Tulsa and elsewhere, interest drifted away from direct, personal, and radical social action, leaving the mission to institutionalized agencies. Some, such as Western Neighbors, were inspired by NFN; in others, the leaders acknowledged how much they had learned from Dan Allen.

Some of his old friends said wistfully that Dan would probably not recognize the new-generation NFN. Perhaps Neighbor for Neighbor had to grow up.

There was, still, nothing else quite like Neighbor for Neighbor, but it became a very different outfit. At its thirtieth anniversary, in 1998, NFN estimated it was providing more than 30,000 client "encounters" a year and had provided more than a half million since NFN was incorporated. "NFN contributed to the community over $2.5 million 'in kind' services in 1998, more than $55 million since NFN was incorporated," according to NFN records provided by current Executive Director Ann Nicholson Smith.[16]

In 2003, the NFN board took a bold step and bought the abandoned 129,000-square-foot Northland Shopping Center at 36th Street North and Cincinnati Avenue, a couple of miles from the original NFN operation. In 2004, NFN moved into 40,000 square feet of newly renovated space.[17]

The agency that evolved became a relatively well-oiled professional endeavor: computerized, audited, operated with efficient business principles, capable of mass-dispensing aid. Some of his old friends said wistfully that Dan would probably not recognize the new-generation NFN. Perhaps Neighbor for Neighbor had to grow up.

Meanwhile, the old NFN buildings fell into disarray. Bad roofs allowed water to flood the abandoned old furniture and priceless stash of records. Then came the inevitable mold, and retrieval became hopeless, NFN said. Shortly thereafter, Dan Allen's NFN was cremated: the Diocese let the Fire Department burn down the old NFN complex, as a training exercise.[18]

In 2010, a group of Dan's disciples created the nonprofit Dan Allen Center for Social Justice, to carry on his advocacy and work to reinvigorate community conscience. Their central goal is to continue Dan's University of Poverty with educational programs about social justice.

A chance visitor these days would find the old Neighbor for Neighbor site bare. Wires stretch across the driveways. St. Jude Catholic Church is still there, still red brick iced with concrete details and its oddly undersized square steeple; but the building is coming apart at the seams, looking small and forlorn. The cross is a bit askew, the roof sagging, the windows long ago boarded up. An abandoned truck trailer is pulled up beside the broken sidewalk littered with leavings of the last tenant, Catholic Charities. Even St. Jude, the patron saint of lost causes and desperate cases, has given up. The neighborhood is dismal.

If there are ghosts there, only a fanciful mind could discern them:

Back here, in a trailer, Wilbert Collins and Jack Helton are dispensing credit advice to a widow. Nearby, in the warehouse, Bill Major and John McCarthy are building a food bank from scratch, one donated box load at a time; and a women's circle is working with Pat Flanagan to fashion art and beauty from castoff goods. In the old rock house, Carol Falletti, Lorraine Lowe, and spectacular volunteer doctors are creating the clinic from sheer imagination. In the driveway, here comes Don McCarthy with a station wagon full of bread to donate, followed by Gloria Caldwell, fresh from a hard day of lobbying for affordable utility rates. Jeff Nix and Maynard Ungerman drop by on their way back from court. A generation of volunteers and patrons waft through, including Ann Bartlett, Sandra Downie, Ruth Nelson, and Diane Perkins. The vestibule of St. Jude church is overflowing with donated canned food and clothes. Bill Skeehan's hearty laugh washes over it all. And on the back lot, the ghosts of Mack Polk and Dan Allen, in flannel shirt and coveralls, are doing wrench-and-hammer surgery on abandoned cars and Booker's garbage truck. Perhaps it's Dan Allen's version of heaven.

Blink and they are gone, like the last wisps of smoke from the cremation fire. A more literal visitor on a cold spring day might find little more than winter-dead grass, scrubby shrubs, and the carcasses of a few gnarled trees. A sparrow lights on a branch, nods, and is gone. Like a shiver, a stray breeze rattles the dry skeleton of a twisted pear tree. On this gray day, it all appears cold and lifeless; but a closer look reveals new buds, no bigger than a baby's tears, sprouting from dead-like branches.

The Spirit Survives...

Dan Allen's "garage," aka "a church." Photo by Gaylord Herron, *Tulsa Magazine*, circa 1972.

Acknowledgments

Writing a book is an odyssey. I am grateful to the fine band of fellow travelers who shared their keen insights and, even more, shared the adventure of writing Dan Allen's story. They are, as St. Peter would say, the living stones who created the superstructure for this book.

Their contributions cannot be ranked; every one is a cornerstone. All are blameless for any errors by the author; whatever is good in this book belongs, first and foremost, to them.

The long list of remarkable folk begins with the Dan Allen Book Committee, ably facilitated by Carol Falletti, the master of support through what Dan called "unconditional positive regard." There would be no book without Carol—or, similarly, without Judy Allen Hess, Dan's niece, the curator of the vision and the faithful gateway to the Allen family's generously shared memories and memorabilia. Carol and Judy devoted hundreds of hours to research and loving support that sustained me as the researcher-writer.

Clustered with Carol and Judy are their families and the book committee, which also includes Father Bill Skeehan, Don and Dana Falletti (Carol's husband and their daughter), and Linda Nicholson. Father Bill, beloved by all, contributed the book's foreword and, even more, provided a north-point star of steady spiritual inspiration. They served as incorporators when the committee morphed into the Dan Allen Center for Social Justice, a 501 (c) (3) nonprofit dedicated to providing education about social justice to continue Dan's University of Poverty. This book has many patrons, beginning with the Dan Allen Center for Social Justice, Inc.

Publication of Dan Allen's story was made possible by generous contributions and grants to the Dan Allen Center for Social Justice. For the names of those individuals and organizations to whom the Center and author are eternally grateful, see www.danallencenter.org. Their help and dedication is key to the future and elimination of injustice.

Many people granted interviews, including Anne Allen, Janet Allen, Gloria Caldwell, Wilbert Collins, Tim Dennehy, Drew Diamond, Timothy Downie, Carol and Don Falletti, Pat Flanagan, Judy Allen Hess, Sandra Downie Langenkamp, Lorraine Lowe, Bill Major, Don and John McCarthy, Father James McGlinchey, Ruth Nelson, Jeff Nix, Frances Allen Pankey, Kathie Pankey Jackson, Dr. George Prothro, former Tulsa Mayor Rodger Randle, Dr. Earl Reeves, Larry Silvey, Todd Singer, Sister Miriam, Father Bill Skeehan, Ann Smith, Frosty Troy, Maynard Ungerman, Clayton Vaughn, Dr. James Wolfe, Shirley Wright, and former Tulsa Mayor Terry Young. Their stories were the best part of the research.

Special gratitude goes to those who opened their archives of information for research. Much of the book's documentation comes from the files of Neighbor for Neighbor and the *Tulsa World* and *Tulsa Tribune*. Particular thanks are due to Gloria Caldwell, Neighbor for Neighbor; Joe Worley, *Tulsa World*; Howard Barnett Jr., *Tulsa Tribune*; Don Sibley, Tulsa Metro Chamber; and Joshua Peck, Tulsa Historical Society. Unsung heroes include *Tulsa World* librarian Hilary Pittman (who should be sainted), Photo Editor Tom Gilbert, and Sunday Editor Debbie Jackson. Judy Allen Hess and Francis Allen Pankey generously shared the extensive Dan Allen family scrapbook and archives. Pat Flanagan and Gaylord Herron donated artwork. Other contributors include David Breed, the Church of the Resurrection, and Dan's friends Tim Dennehy and Lorraine Lowe.

I am particularly grateful to those who reviewed partial or entire drafts of the manuscript along the way. They include Anne Allen, Gloria Caldwell, Drew Diamond, Norma Eagleton, Carol and Don Falletti, Pat Flanagan, Judy Allen Hess, Sandra Downie Langenkamp, Don McCarthy, Teresa Miller, Dr. L. G. Moses, Ruth Nelson, Jeff Nix, Elaine Perkins, Rodger Randle, Larry Silvey, Maynard Ungerman, and Clayton Vaughn. Their reviews in no way constitute endorsements, but their help was invaluable. The final text is far better because of their comments.

I am glad for this opportunity to thank friends who offered encouragement and wisdom throughout the writing process. The list begins but does not end with Gloria Caldwell, Pat Flanagan, Sandra Downie Langenkamp, Judy Finn, Kim Fuller, Deborah Moon, Elaine Perkins, and Juanise Stockdale. No one ever enjoyed more splendid mentors than Teresa Miller, Dr. L. G. Moses, Sandy Leppin, and Jay Dew. Joe Williams designed the book and shepherded it (and the author) through production, greatly improving its quality. Larry Silvey brought his vast expertise to the book as a faithful mentor and friend who spent many days scanning and editing photos and designing the cover. Jo Ann Reece served as guardian of editorial integrity, and Galen Schroeder generously donated the professional index.

Sustaining help came from Liz Colina, Tom Dapice, Jeff DeGuilio, Sandra Ann Patton, Alan Rowland, Jim Sellers, Sonya Wallace, and Cindy Webster. Margaret Tucker's Locating, LLC, and Mary Ruth Schultz provided office space to manage the flood of research material.

Most of all, I want to thank my husband, Bob, and my family and friends for their faithful support and for enduring the peculiar obsession that writing this book demanded. You made all the difference.

To all of you, and those I have neglected to mention—thank you. Your generous help and support enabled Dan Allen's story to be told.

— Ann Patton

Notes

FOREWORD

1. "Father Dan," *Tulsa World,* editorial, November 15, 1995.

PREFACE

1. Community Service Council Special Service Award: Dan Allen, November 1995.

2. Maynard Ungerman, interview with author, Tulsa, Okla., October 19, 2009.

3. Matthew 25:40.

4. Dan Allen notes, untitled, 1981, Allen Family collection.

5. Diane Perkins, quoted by Heidi Pederson, "Neighbor for Neighbor founder Dan Allen Dies," *Tulsa World,* November 14, 1995.

6. Frosty Troy, "God's Angry Man," *The Oklahoma Observer,* December 10/25, 1995.

CHAPTER 1

1. Tom Kerschner, "Give a Damn Dan Fights Poverty in an Unsaintly Way," *Tulsa World*, August 10, 1987.

2. David Monahan, "Profile: Dan Allen," *Salt of the Earth*, November/December 1995.

3. Mike Wyke photo, "Always on the Edge," *Tulsa Tribune*, November 21, 1986.

4. David Monahan, "Profile: Dan Allen," *Salt of the Earth*, November/December 1995; "Tiny Shack Is Home for 5," *Tulsa World*, January 2, 1969.

5. Don McCarthy, interview with author, Tulsa, Okla., October 29, 2009.

6. Bill Skeehan, interview with author, Tulsa, Okla., November 19, 2010.

7. "Decade of Change," a supplement to the *Oklahoma Courier*, March 1, 1968, 8.

8. Maynard Ungerman, interview with author, Tulsa, Okla., October 19, 2009.

9. *Neighbor for Neighbor Newsletter*, October 1980.

10. Wilbert Collins, interview with author, Tulsa, Okla., November 9, 2009.

11. Pat Flanagan, interview with author, Tulsa, Okla., January 18, 2010.

12. Carol Falletti, interview with author, Tulsa, Okla., April 2010.

13. "Our Church Town," Dan Allen editorial in *Neighbor for Neighbor Newsletter,* September 1988.

CHAPTER 2

1. *The Marque,* 1949 Yearbook, Marquette High School, Tulsa, Okla.

2. Dan Allen birth certificate, Dan Allen family collection; Heidi Pederson, "Neighbor for Neighbor Founder Dan Allen Dies," *Tulsa World,* n.d., c. November 14, 1995.

3. Frances Pankey, Kathie Jackson, and Judy Hess, interviews with author, Tulsa, Okla., November 11, 2010.

4. Anne Allen, interview with author, Tulsa, Okla., July 19, 2010.

5. Judy Allen Hess, quoting story from Frances Pankey, conversation with author, May 25, 2011.

6. Maynard Ungerman, interview with author, Tulsa, Okla., October 19, 2009.

7. Anne Allen, interview with author, Tulsa, Okla., July 19, 2010.

8. Tim Dennehy, interview with author, Tulsa, Okla., November 16, 2009.

CHAPTER 3

1. Egan, *The Worst Hard Time*, 8–10, 88, 309; Debo, *Oklahoma Footloose and Fancy-Free*, 76–77.2. Debo, *And Still the Waters Run*.

3. Debo, *Oklahoma Footloose and Fancy-Free*, 10.

4. Gates, *They Came Searching*, xi.

5. Debo, *And Still the Waters Run*, 162–65.

6. Murray, *The Negro's Place*, 29.

7. Ibid., 8.

8. Debo, *And Still the Waters Run*.

9. Debo, *And Still the Waters Run*, x.

10. Goble, *Tulsa!*, 31.

11. Silvey and Drown, *The Tulsa Spirit*, 25–26.

12. Rogers, *Will Rogers Says*, 49.

13. Hamill, *Tulsa: The Great American City*, 43, 49; Goble, *Tulsa!*, 80–111.

14. Hamill, *Tulsa: The Great American City*, 25.

15. Ellsworth, *Death in a Promised Land*, 19; Goble, *Tulsa!*, 124.

16. Goble, *Tulsa!*, 123.

17. Goble, *Tulsa!*, 123, 207.

18. Goble, *Tulsa!*, 117–18.

19. Ellsworth, *Death in a Promised Land*, 17.

20. Ibid., 7.

21. Goble, *Tulsa!*, 130.

22. Amos T. Hall, interview with author, Tulsa, Okla., c. 1969.

23. Goble, *Tulsa!*, 171–72.

24. Egan, *The Worst Hard Time*, 73.

25. Rogers, *Will Rogers Says*, 26.

26. Egan, *The Worst Hard Time*, 62–63.

27. Ibid., 47, 77, 101, 141, 157.

28. Ibid., 162.

29. Goble, *Tulsa!*, 171–73.

CHAPTER 4

1. Dan Allen family collection.

2. "Two Tulsans to Be Ordained as Catholic Priests May 25," *Tulsa World*, April 27, 1957; "Twelve New Priests to Be Added to Diocese," *The Southwest Courier,* May 18, 1957.

3. Tim Dennehy, interview with author, Tulsa, Okla., November 16, 2009.

4. Martin Luther King, Jr., "I Have a Dream" speech, Washington, D.C., August 28, 1963.

5. "Two Tulsans to Be Ordained as Catholic Priests May 25," *Tulsa World*, April 27, 1957.

6. Judy Allen Hess, interview with author, Tulsa, Okla., June 2008, et seq.7. Tim Dennehy, interview with author, Tulsa, Okla., November 16, 2009.

8. "Decade of Change," a supplement to the *Oklahoma Courier*, March 1, 1968, 3, 5.

9. Bill Skeehan, interview with author, Tulsa, Okla., November 19, 2010.

10. Ibid.

11. Judy Allen Hess, interview with author, Tulsa, Okla., June 2008, et seq.

12. Postcard from Dan Allen family collection; Denise Mohr conversation reported to author by Carol Falletti, fall 2010.

13. Gates, *Miz Lucy's Cookies, 2*76; Community edition, *Tulsa World*, July 15, 2007; Luper, *Behold the Walls,* 185.

14. *Oklahoma Courier*, n.d.

15. Postcard from Dan Allen family collection.

16. James McGlinchey, interview with author, Tulsa, Okla., March 27, 2010.

17. Ibid.; "20 Oklahomans in Selma Unrest," *Tulsa World*, March 1965.

18. Martin Luther King, Jr., "Letter from Birmingham jail, April 1963, quoting the prophet Amos from Amos 5:24.

19. Martin Luther King, Jr., "How Long, Not Long" speech, Montgomery, Alabama, March 25, 1965.

20. Bill Skeehan, interview with author, Tulsa, Okla., November 19, 2010.

21. Don McCarthy, interview with author, Tulsa, Okla., October 29, 2009.

22. Undated photo from Dan Allen family collection.

23. Dan Allen family collection.

24. Don McCarthy, interview with author, Tulsa, Okla., October 29, 2009.

25. "Teaching the Teachers," *The Oklahoma Courier*, January 28, 1966.

26. *Oklahoma Courier*, September 9, 1966, from Dan Allen family collection.

27. "The Church Is on Its Way. The Church Is Marching," *Decade of Change,* A Supplement to the *Oklahoma Courier*, March 1, 1968, 23.

28. *Neighbor for Neighbor Newsletter*, February 1979.

29. "2 Tulsans Recognized for Service to Mankind," *Tulsa Tribune*, December 4, 1968.

CHAPTER 5

1. Dan Allen, "Seeking the Common Good," CBS News video for Ford Foundation, June 1993.

2 Jim Henderson, "What Builds a Ghetto? How Do You Flee?" *Tulsa World.*, June 21–27, 1967.

3. David Monahan, "Profile: Dan Allen," *Salt of the Earth*, November/December 1995.

4. Maynard Ungerman, untitled op-ed, *Tulsa Tribune*, April 10, 1978.

5. David Monahan, "Profile: Dan Allen," *Salt of the Earth*, November/December 1995.

6. "Neighbor Project Has Good Year," *Tulsa Tribune*, January 8, 1969.

7. "Putting End to Poverty Not Easy," *Tulsa World*, February 6, 1969.

8. Pat Flanagan, interview with author, Tulsa, Okla., September 21, 2009.

9. Jim Sellars,"Neighborly Plan Used to Solve Problems," *Tulsa Tribune*, July 5, 1968.

10. Pat Flanagan, interview with author, Tulsa, Okla., September 21, 2009.

11. Sandra Downie Langenkamp, interview with author, Tulsa, Okla., November 2, 2009.

12. Gloria Caldwell, interview with author, Tulsa, Okla., November 2, 2009.

13. "Aid to Shoeless Children Sought in City Program," *Tulsa World*, n.d. (c. 1968).

14. "Hunger Brings New Call," *Tulsa World*, September 1, 1968.

15. "Neighbor for Neighbor is Needing Neighbors," *Tulsa World*, November 26, 1970.

16. Don McCarthy, interview with author, Tulsa, Okla., October 29, 2009.

17. "Tiny Shack Is Home for 5," *Tulsa World*, January 2, 1969.

18. "Volunteer Aid Project Needing More Neighbors," *Tulsa World*, October 6, 1968.

19. Jim Henderson, "Experts in Poverty Battle Help Their Neighbors Fight," *Tulsa World*, April 14, 1968.

20. Beth Macklin, "Neighbor for Neighbor Plan Expansion Proposed," *Tulsa World*, November 15, 1968.

21. Jim Henderson, "Experts in Poverty Battle Help Their Neighbors Fight," *Tulsa World*, April 14, 1968.

22. Clayton Vaughn, interview with author, Tulsa, Okla., May 5, 2011.

23. Beth Macklin, conversation with author, Tulsa, Okla., c. 1976.

24. Larry Silvey, e-mail exchange with author, April 25, 2011.

25. Nancy Feldman, conversation with author, Tulsa, Okla., c. 1987.

26. Jim Henderson, "Experts in Poverty Battle Help Their Neighbors Fight," *Tulsa World*, April 14, 1968.

27. Ibid.

28. Bonner, *The Road to Renewal,* 257.

29. Gloria Caldwell, interview with author, Tulsa, Okla., November 2, 2009.

30. Jeff Nix, interview with author, Tulsa, Okla., April 20, 2011.

31. Jim Henderson, "Experts in Poverty Battle Help Their Neighbors Fight," *Tulsa World*, April 14, 1968.

CHAPTER 6

1. Jeff Nix, interview with author, Tulsa, Okla., April 20, 2011.

2. *Neighbor for Neighbor Newsletter*, December 1995.

3. Jim Henderson, "Experts in Poverty Battle Help Their Neighbors Fight," *Tulsa World*, April 14, 1968.

4. "Volunteer Aid Project Needing More Neighbors," *Tulsa World*, October 6, 1968.

5. Pat Flanagan, *Neighbor for Neighbor Newsletter*, September 1988.

6. Jim Henderson, "Experts in Poverty Battle Help Their Neighbors Fight," *Tulsa World*, April 14, 1968.

7. Jim Sellars, "Neighborly Plan Used to Solve Problems," *Tulsa Tribune*, July 5, 1968.

8. Jim Henderson, "Experts in Poverty Battle Help Their Neighbors Fight," *Tulsa World*, April 14, 1968.

9. Dale Speer, "Neighborly Repair of Autos Curbed," *Tulsa World*, April 30, 1969.

10. "Help from Heart—Not U.S. Pocketbook—Project Theme," *Tulsa World*, June 15, 1969.

11. Maynard Ungerman, interview with author, Tulsa, Okla., October 19, 2009.

12. "CBS to Do Program Here on Neighbor-Neighbor," *Tulsa World*, August 8, 1968; "Second Film on Poverty War to Be Made Here," *Tulsa Tribune*, October 26, 1968; "Tulsa's Neighbor for Neighbor Program on CBS," *Tulsa World*, November 16, 1968.

13. Jim Sellars, "Neighbor for Neighbor Project Is Challenged," *Tulsa Tribune*, November 4, 1969; Beth Macklin, "Ban on Project at Church Granted," *Tulsa World*, November 6, 1969.

14. "NFN to Close Service Station," *Tulsa World*, August 24, 1969.

15. *Neighbor for Neighbor Newsletter*, October 1988.

16. Beth Macklin, "Ban on Project at Church Granted," *Tulsa World*, November 6, 1969.

17. *Neighbor for Neighbor Newsletter*, October 1988.

18. Maynard Ungerman, interview with author, Tulsa, Okla., October 19, 2009.

19. Jeff Nix, interview with author, Tulsa, Okla., April 20, 2011.

20. Maynard Ungerman, interview with author, Tulsa, Okla., October 19, 2009.

CHAPTER 7

1. *Neighbor for Neighbor Newsletter,* September 1988.

2. "Neighbor Group Gets New Head," *Tulsa Tribune*, May 7, 1970.

3. Doug Fox, quoted in Jeremy Bonner, *The Road to Renewal,* 257.

4. Jeff Nix, interview with author, Tulsa, Okla., April 20, 2011.

5. "Neighbor Group Gets New Head," *Tulsa Tribune*, May 7, 1970.

6. Bill Skeehan, interview with author, Tulsa, Okla., November 19, 2010.

7. David Monahan, "Profile: Dan Allen," *Salt of the Earth*, November/December 1995.

8. Jim Sellars, "'Neighborly' Plan Used to Solve Problems," *Tulsa Tribune*, July 5, 1968.

9. Isaiah 50:7; Luke 9:51–53.

10. Judy Allen Hess, e-mail exchange with author, Tulsa, Okla., June 3 and 7, 2011, citing letter from Dan Allen to "Mickey," December 19, 1994.

11. Judy Allen Hess, interview with author, Tulsa, Okla., March 3, 2011.

12. Ken Bolton, interview with author, Tulsa, Okla., c. 1972.

13. City of Tulsa, Model Cities program grant application, 1967.

14. Ann Patton, "Black Muslim Has Peace Goal," *Tulsa World*, December 6, 1970.

15. James Hewgley and Robert J. LaFortune, interviews with author, Tulsa, Okla., c. 1972; Ann Patton and David Breed, "The Great American Dream," *Tulsa Magazine*, July 1974.

16. E. L. Goodwin, Jr., "Credit Union Stable Less Withdrawals," *Oklahoma Eagle*, May 29, 1969.

17. Maynard Ungerman, interview with author, Tulsa, Okla., October 19, 2009.

18. Ann Patton, "Poor Will Lose If Credit Union Folds," *Tulsa World*, n.d., 1970; Ann Patton,

"'I Thought This Credit Union Was to Help Poor People,'" *Tulsa World*, June 17, 1970; Ann Patton, "Actions of Ex-Consultant Key to Credit Union Audit," *Tulsa World*, December 30, 1970.

19. Jim Sellars, "Neighbor for Neighbor Project Is Challenged," *Tulsa Tribune*, November 4, 1969.

20. Janet Allen, Colorado Springs, Colo., January 13, 2010, letter to author.

21. Ann Patton, "THA Accused of Racial Bias by Ex-Employee," *Tulsa World*, October 16, 1970.

CHAPTER 8

1. Ann Patton, "Widow Pays 8 Years, Can't Move into Home," *Tulsa World*, March 29, 1971.

2. Ibid.; Ann Patton, "Water Hard to Obtain," *Tulsa World*, April 18, 1971.

3. Don Falletti, conversation with author, Tulsa, Okla., c. 1971.

4. Don Falletti, interview with author, Tulsa, Okla., March 2010; Don McCarthy, interview with author, Tulsa, Okla., October 29, 2009; Jeff Nix, interview with author, Tulsa, Okla., April 20, 2011.

CHAPTER 9

1. Pat Atkinson, "Free Clinic Boon to Needy," *Tulsa World*, March 4, 1973.

2. Ann Patton, "Thanksgiving Supplies Fade, Hungry Keep Coming at NFN," *Tulsa World*, November 25, 1971.

3. Britton Gildersleeve, "Tulsa's Working Poor in Health Care Trap," *Tulsa World*, September 27, 1981.

4. Oscar Ameringer, quoted by Robert H. Henry in the foreword to Morgan, et. al,

Oklahoma Politics and Policies, xii.

5. Goble, *Tulsa!*, 147–48.

6. Goble, *Tulsa!*, 140; Rev. Wilkie Clyde Clock, "Survey of West Tulsa," unpublished paper, 1933.

7. City of Tulsa Model Cities grant application, 1967, I: 26–27.

8. Report on the Health System issued March 11, 1966, by the War on Poverty Project, Part III, cited in City of Tulsa Model Cities grant application, 1967.

9. City of Tulsa Model Cities grant application, 1967

10. Bate, *"It's Been a Long Time."*

11. Ibid., 27

12. Ibid., 245.

13. Ibid. 201, 244.

14. Ibid.

15. Ibid., 143, 222.

16. Ibid., 200, 210, 233.

17. Ibid., 222–23, 226–27, 244.

18. Ibid., 146, 208, 222, 230.

19. Ibid., 222, 232–33, 236.

CHAPTER 10

1. *Neighbor for Neighbor Newsletter*, May 1991.

2. "Neighbor for Neighbor Keeps Its Food Project," *Tulsa World*, March 19, 1971; and "Donated Materials, Labor Aid Poverty Projects Here," *Tulsa World*, June 16, 1971.

3. Carol Falletti, interview with author, Tulsa, Okla., March 2010.

4. Ibid.

5. Pat Atkinson, "Free Clinic Boon to Needy," *Tulsa World*, March 3, 1973.

6. Carol Falletti, interview with author, Tulsa, Okla., c. July 2010.

7. Dr. George Prothro, interview with author, Tulsa, Okla., May 25, 2010; Lynn Somers, "Agency for Poor Assisted," *Tulsa World*, September 14, 1975.

8. Carol Falletti, interview with author, Tulsa, Okla., March 2010.

9. *Eastern Oklahoma Catholic,* 1984.

10. Carol Falletti, interview with author, Tulsa, Okla., March 2010.

11. Britton Gildersleeve, "Tulsa's Working Poor in Health Care Trap," *Tulsa World,* September 27, 1981.

12. Tom Droege, "Nonprofit's Block Party Celebrates Good Neighbors," *Tulsa World*, June 5, 2005.

13. Ina Hall, "An American Enigma: The Poor Still Reach Out," *Tulsa Magazine,* July 1976.

14. Tim Dennehy, interview with author, Tulsa, Okla., November 16, 2009.

15. Kathy Neal, "City Dental Clinic Filling Major Gap, *Tulsa World*, August 7, 1977.

16. Carol Falletti, e-mail to author, March 9, 2011.

17. Ibid.

18. Britton Gildersleeve, "Tulsa's Working Poor in Health Care Trap," *Tulsa World,* September 27, 1981.

19. Lorraine Lowe, interview with author, Tulsa, Okla., September 17, 2010.

20. Carol Falletti, interview with author, Tulsa, Okla., March 2010.

21. Jim Wolfe, interview with author, Tulsa, Okla., May 10, 2011.

22. Lynn Somers, "Agency for Poor Assisted," *Tulsa World*, September 14, 1975.

23. Carol Falletti, interview with author, Tulsa, Okla., March 2010, and e-mail, March 10, 2011.

24. Ann Patton, "Fifteen Years of Loaves and Fishes, *Tulsa Tribune*, November 3, 1983.

25. *Neighbor for Neighbor Newsletter,* May 1991.

26. Cary Aspinwall, "Life Preserver: Clinic Caring for Those with No Insurance," *Tulsa Community World*, c. December 2001.

CHAPTER 11

1. Gloria Caldwell, interview with author, Tulsa, Okla., November 2, 2009.

2. Oklahoma Advisory Committee, U.S. Commission on Civil Rights; Hon. Hannah Atkins, Chair, "School Desegregation in Tulsa, Oklahoma," August 1977, 3.

3. Goble, *Tulsa!,* 208.

4. Bennie Luce, "Racial Segregation in Tulsa: A Statistical Comparison," for City of Tulsa Community Relations Commission, March 1976, 1, 8.

5. Oklahoma Advisory Committee, "School Desegregation in Tulsa, Oklahoma," 4.

6. Goble, *Tulsa!,* 206.

7. Amos T. Hall, interview with author, Tulsa, Okla., c. 1969.

8. Fisher, with Goble, *A Matter of Black and White*, 189–93.

9. "The Resegregated Schools," *Tulsa Tribune,* November 13, 1961.

10. Oklahoma Advisory Committee, "School Desegregation in Tulsa, Oklahoma," 35–36; Richard White, "School Ruling Involves Tulsa," *Tulsa Tribune*, July 2, 1963.

11. Oklahoma Advisory Committee, "School Desegregation in Tulsa, Oklahoma," 37.

12. Kyle Goddard, quoted in Oklahoma Advisory Committee, "School Desegregation in Tulsa, Oklahoma," 44–45.

13. Wolf, "The Last Days of Dr. Mason."

14. Wolf, "Is America Having a Nervous Breakdown?"

15. Oklahoma Advisory Committee, "School Desegregation in Tulsa, Oklahoma," 45.

16. Reeves, *Autobiography of Earl James Reeves*.

17. Oklahoma Advisory Committee, "School Desegregation in Tulsa, Oklahoma," 45–46.

18. Bennie Luce, "Racial Segregation in Tulsa: A Statistical Comparison," for City of Tulsa

Community Relations Commission, March 1976, 8.

19. Ibid.

20. Ibid., 1–13.

21. Oklahoma Advisory Committee, "School Desegregation in Tulsa, Oklahoma," 9–103.

22. Ann Patton, "Two Tulsas: One Growing, One Dying," *Tulsa World*, September 27, 1972.

23. Oklahoma Advisory Committee, "School Desegregation in Tulsa, Oklahoma," 17.

24. "Black Group Suggests Unity Plan for School Integration," *Tulsa World*, July 29, 1971.

25. Reeves, *Autobiography of Earl James Reeves*.

CHAPTER 12

1. Sandra Downie Langenkamp and Tim Downie, interviews with author, Tulsa, Okla., February 15, 2010.

2. Oklahoma Advisory Committee, "School Desegregation in Tulsa, Oklahoma," 48.

3. Paul I. McCloud, "Neither Black nor White: A Progress Report on Integration in the Tulsa Public Schools," ED121889 (Tulsa: Tulsa Public Schools, 1974), 3; see also http://eric.ed.gov; "City Prayer Vigil Urged by Blacks," *Tulsa World*, August 5, 1971; "Black Group OKs Boycott of Schools," *Tulsa World*, August 9, 1971.

4. Ann Patton, "Mayor Urges School Aides to Keep Carver in System," *Tulsa World*, August 11, 1971.

5. Greg Broadd, "Board Refuses in 5-1 Vote to Reopen Carver School," *Tulsa World*, November 18, 1971.

6. Little, with N. Hare and J. Hare, *Fire on Mount Zion*, 103; "Police Arrest Eight School Protesters," *Tulsa World*, December 1, 1971.

7. Greg Broadd, "Plan for Reopening Carver to be Drafted for Board," *Tulsa World*, December 4, 1971.

8. Pat Flanagan, interview with author, Tulsa, Okla., January 18, 2010; Sandra Downie Langenkamp, interview with author, Tulsa, Okla., February 15, 2010; Gloria Caldwell, interview with author, Tulsa, Okla., November 2, 2009.

9. Gloria Caldwell, "The Rest of the Story," unpublished paper, August 1988.

10. McCloud, "Neither Black nor White," 3, 6; see also http://eric.ed.gov.

11. Pat Flanagan, interview with the author, Tulsa, Okla., January 16, 2010.

12. Carol Langston, "Burroughs School Integrated: First Voluntary Mixed Elementary," *Tulsa Tribune*, August 5, 1971.

13. Sandra Downie Langenkamp, interview with author, Tulsa, Okla., February 15, 2010.

14, Maynard Ungerman, interview with author, Tulsa, Okla., October 19, 2009.

15. Pat Flanagan, interview with author, Tulsa, Okla., January 18, 2009.

16. McCloud, "Neither Black nor White," 5; see also http://eric.ed.gov.

17. Greg Broadd, "Leaders Say Burroughs School Meeting 'Positive,'" *Tulsa World*, August 5, 1971.

18. Greg Broadd, "First Voluntary Integration of School Due Here in Fall," *Tulsa World*, August 6, 1971.

19. Pat Flanagan, interview with author, Tulsa, Okla., January 18, 2010

20. "Burroughs School Draws 56 Whites," *Tulsa World*, August 11, 1971.

21. "Non-Graded School Proves Attractive," *Tulsa Tribune*, August 11, 1971.

22. "Burroughs Kindergarten Busing Request Rejected," *Tulsa World,* September 8, 1971.

23. "Burroughs School Integrated," *Tulsa Tribune*, August 5, 1971; "White Count at Burroughs Reaches 79," *Tulsa World*, August 14, 1971.

24. McCloud, "Neither Black nor White," 5; see also http://eric.ed.gov; Oklahoma Advisory Committee, "School Desegregation in Tulsa, Oklahoma," 50, 65–66; Pearl Wittkopp, "Tulsa 'Little School' Opens with 180 Volunteer Pupils," *Tulsa Tribune,* November 15, 1971.

25. Sandra Downie Langenkamp, interview with author, Tulsa, Okla., February 15, 2010.

26. McCloud, "Neither Black nor White," 5; see also http://eric.ed.gov.

27. "Burroughs Patrons Support Integration Student Busing," *Tulsa World*, November 11, 1971.

28. McCloud, "Neither Black nor White," 5; see also http://eric.ed.gov.

29. Ibid., 4; see also http://eric.ed.gov.

30. Ibid.

31. June Tyhurst, "Carver Alumni Elated at Revamp of School," *Tulsa World*, September 28, 1973.

32. McCloud, "Neither Black nor White," 6; see also http://eric.ed.gov.

33. Gloria Caldwell, interview with author, Tulsa, Okla., November 2, 2009.

34. Sandra Downie Langenkamp, interview with author, Tulsa, Okla., February 15, 2010; Timothy Downie, interview with author, Tulsa, Okla., February 15, 2010.

CHAPTER 13

1. Ann Patton, "Thanksgiving Supplies Fade, Hungry Keep Coming at NFN, *Tulsa World,* November 25, 1971.

2. Ibid.

3. Bernadette Pruitt, "Many Oklahomans Going Hungry in Economic Slump," *Tulsa World*, January 5, 1986.

4. *Neighbor for Neighbor Newsletter,* December 1987.

5. Bernadette Pruitt, "Many Oklahomans Going Hungry in Economic Slump," *Tulsa World*, January 5, 1986.

6. Tom Kertscher, "For the Needy, an Indispensable Neighborhood," *Tulsa World,* August

10, 1987.

7. Bernadette Pruitt, "Hunger Now Touches Oklahoma's Working Poor," *Tulsa World*, January 12, 1986.

8. Ibid.

9. Harrington, *The Other America*, 10, 13.

10. "A Study of Nutrition among Tulsa's Poor, Part I: Dimensions of the Problem," by Hunger Task Force of Tulsa Metropolitan Ministry, October 1979, 1.

11. Bill Skeehan, interview with author, Tulsa, Okla., November 19, 2010; Hellwig, *The Eucharist and the Hunger of the World*.

12. Cindy Webster, interview with author, Tulsa, Okla., March 7, 2011.

13. "Neighbors Thankful for Clinic," *Tulsa World*, October 19, 1975.

14. Ibid.

15. Jeff Nix, interview with author, Tulsa, Okla., April 20, 2011.

16. Bonner, *The Road to Renewal*, 395–400.

17. Ibid.

18. Ibid., 400–404.

19. Bill Skeehan, interview with author, Tulsa, Okla., November 19, 2010.

20. Judy Allen Hess, quoting Vivian Allen's story, in interview with author, Tulsa, Okla., May 23, 2011.

21. Dan Allen, letter to Bishop John R. Quinn, January 31, 1973, from Dan Allen family collection.

22. Judy Allen Hess, e-mail to author, May 2, 2011.

23. Bill Skeehan, interview with author, Tulsa, Okla., March 11, 2011.

24. Judy Allen Hess, conversation with author, Tulsa, Okla., June 3, 2011.

25. Dan Allen, letter to Todd Singer, May 4, 1990.

26. Judy Allen Hess, conversation with author, May 31, 2011.

27. "Diocesan: Mass Said for Dan Allen," *Eastern Oklahoma Catholic*, November 26, 1995.

28. Laurie Mower, "Neighbor for Neighbor Shuts for 10 Days; Fund Lack Cited," *Tulsa Tribune*, September 1, 1978.

CHAPTER 14

1. Bill Major, interview with author, Tulsa, Okla., September 11, 2010.

2. "Churches Asked to Help 'Pack-a-Sack,'" *Tulsa Tribune*, December 6, 1971.

3. Beth Macklin, "Kids, Jobs Keep Mom Busy," *Tulsa World*, October 8, 1972.

4. "Still a Neighbor after All These Years: Neighbor for Neighbor," *Tulsa Magazine*, November 1977.

5. "Neighbors Thankful for Clinic," *Tulsa World*, October 19, 1975.

6. Ina Hall, "An American Enigma: The Poor Still Reach Out," *Tulsa Magazine*, July 1976.

7. "Nutrition Center under Construction in Tulsa," *Tulsa Tribune*, September 25, 1976.

8. "Allen is Realistic about Work of NFN," *Tulsa World*, September 16, 1977.

9. Diana Nelson Jones, "Easing the Hard Times," *Tulsa Tribune*, February 20, 1986.

10. Tulsa Metropolitan Ministry, Hunger Task Force, *A Study of Nutrition among Tulsa's Poor, Part 1: Dimensions of the Problem*, October 1979.

11. Beth Macklin, "Produce Co-op Gets Green Light," *Tulsa World*, June 17, 1980.

12. Bill Major, interview with author, Tulsa, Okla., September 18, 2010.

CHAPTER 15

1. Author's personal recollection.

2. Dan Allen, "Director Speaks: Christmas Energy," notes for *Neighbor for Neighbor Newsletter*, n.d., Dan Allen family collection.

3. Pat Flanagan, interview with author, Tulsa, Okla., January 18, 2010.

4. Pat Koontz, "Neighbor for Neighbor Founder Offers Hope for Poor," *Tulsa Business Chronicle*, June 10, 1985.

5. Pat Flanagan, *Neighbor for Neighbor Newsletter,* August 1985.

6. "Presbyterians Fund NFN Furniture Repair Co-op," *Tulsa World,* June 10, 1979.

7. Dan Allen, *Neighbor for Neighbor Newsletter*, Fall 1979.

8. "Allen Is Realistic about Work of NFN," *Tulsa World*, September 16, 1977; "Neighbor for Neighbor Resumes Service," *Tulsa World*, September 10, 1978.

9. "Dan Allen's Report," *Neighbor for Neighbor Newsletter*, Fall 1979.

10. Lynn Somers, "Agency for the Poor Assisted," *Tulsa World*, September 14, 1975.

11. Pat Flanagan, interview with author, Tulsa, Okla., September 21, 2009.

12. Bill Skeehan, interview with author, Tulsa, Okla., November 19, 2010.

13. Maynard Ungerman, interview with author, Tulsa, Okla., October 19, 2009.

14. Ed Eveld, "Flood Cleanup New Nightmare," *Tulsa Tribune*, October 14, 1986.

15. "Allen Is Realistic about Work of NFN," *Tulsa World*, September 16, 1977.

16. Janet Pearson, "Utility Bills Hit Poor Hardest," *Tulsa World*, January 30, 1977.

17. Carol Falletti, interview with author, Tulsa, Okla., November 2011.

18. Dickerson*, Aunt Carrie's War Against Black Fox,* 202–10.

19. "'State Enters Black Fox Hearing," *Tulsa Tribune*, n.d., c. 1979; Coy Hobbs, "Black Fox: 'Neighbor' Says Reed Report Release Could Aid Consumer," *Tulsa World*, February 27, 1979.

20. "Editorial," *Neighbor for Neighbor Newsletter*, n.d., c. 1983.

21. Dickerson*, Aunt Carrie's War Against Black Fox*; Carrie Barefoot Dickerson, "Oklahoma/Citizens Action for Safe Energy Inc.," in *No Nukes, Everyone's Guide to Nuclear Power*, ed. Anna Gyorgy (Boston: South End Press, 1979).

22. Dickerson*, Aunt Carrie's War Against Black Fox,* 272–95.

23. "Energy Officials Say Nuclear Power Comeback Not Likely to Happen in Oklahoma," BNET, September 28, 2005; accessed July 18, 2010, http://en.wikipedia.org/wiki/Black_ Fox Nuclear Power Plant.

24. Private conversation with author, Tulsa, Okla., 2008.

25. Beth Mackin, "Care Agencies See Aid Going to Utilities," *Tulsa World*, n.d., c. 1982.

26. Marilyn Duck and Ron Wolfe, "Service Agency, PSO Split on Bills," *Tulsa Tribune*, n.d., c. December 1982.

27. Ken Neal, "Lights for the Poor: Who Pays the Bills When Charity Fails," *Tulsa World*, December 19, 1982.

28. "Share the Warmth Marks 20 Years of Keeping Oklahomans Warm," Oklahoma Natural Gas news release, February 10, 2003, accessed February 12, 2011, http://ir.oneok.com/ phoenix.zhtml?c=120070&p=irol-newsArticle&ID=1520306&highlight=.

CHAPTER 16

1. Lisa Jackson, "Group Guides Tour of Tulsa Housing Projects," *Tulsa World*, November 21, 1988; Pat Flanagan, letter to Neighbor for Neighbor Board of Directors, October 11, 1987.

2. Author's personal notes, c. 1972.

3. Michael Kerrigan, "Ouster of Housing Authority Chief Pushed," *Tulsa Tribune*, December 10, 1987.

4. Tom Kertscher, "Public Housing Management Criticized," *Tulsa World*, November 5, 1987; Michael Kerrigan, "Charity Hits Public Housing Conditions," *Tulsa Tribune*, November 9, 1987.

5. "The Victims," *Tulsa World* editorial, November 15, 1987.

6. Tom Kertscher, "Housing Chief Says Project's Vacancy Rate Warrants Attention," *Tulsa World*, November 24, 1987.

7. Michael Kerrigan, "Ouster of Housing Authority Chief Pushed," *Tulsa Tribune*, December 10, 1987.

8. Drew Diamond, interview with author, Tulsa, Okla., April 29, 2011.

9. Sandra Downie Langenkamp, interview with author, Tulsa, Okla., March 3, 2011.

10. Tom Kertscher, "Criticism May Spur Action, Says Housing Panel Member," *Tulsa World*, n.d.

11. Tom Kertscher, "Housing Panel Withholds Financial Records," *Tulsa World*, January 14, 1988.

12. Tom Kertscher, "Agency Sues to See Housing Records," *Tulsa World*, January 13, 1988.

13. Gloria Caldwell, interview with author, Tulsa, Okla., September 11, 2010.

14. Tom Kertscher, "Housing Agency Frees Records, Suit to Continue," *Tulsa World*, March 16, 1988, et seq.; David Conley, "Judge Orders Tenants' Addresses Released," *Tulsa Tribune*, May 23, 1988.

15. Tom Kertscher and Wayne Greene, "$9 Million Helps Needy Pay Rent," *Tulsa World,* February 14, 1988.

16. Tom Kertscher, "Neighbor for Neighbor Director Upset over Use of Housing Funds," *Tulsa World*, February 16, 1988.

17. Tom Kertscher, "High Rents at HUD Housing Revealed," *Tulsa World*, April 3, 1988; Tom Kertscher, "Section 8 Ruling Criticized," *Tulsa World*, May 24, 1988.

18. David Conley, "Judge Orders Tenants Addresses Released," *Tulsa Tribune*, May 23, 1988.

19. "Housing Authority to Release Addresses," *Tulsa Tribune*, June 1, 1988.

20. Donna Hoffman, "City Considers Changing Housing Authority Rules," *Tulsa World*, October 26, 1988.

21. Donna Hoffman, "Randle Compares City Housing Projects to New York Slums," *Tulsa World*, October 31, 1988; Donna Hoffman, "Housing Project Tenants Unload Frustrations on Mayor," *Tulsa World*, November 2, 1988.

22. Donna Hoffman, "Metcalfe Calls for Ouster of Housing Authority," *Tulsa World,* November 16, 1988.

23. Donna Hoffman, "Embattled Tulsa Housing Director Loving Number 1 Supporter on Board," *Tulsa World*, n.d.

24. Donna Hoffman, "New Image Sought for Housing Panel," *Tulsa World*, November 2, 1988.

25. Donna Hoffman, "Embattled Tulsa Housing Director Losing No. 1 Supporter on Board," *Tulsa World*, n.d.

26. Ibid.

27. Gloria Caldwell, interview with author, Tulsa, Okla., November 2, 2009.

28. Ruth Nelson, interview with author, Tulsa, Okla., March 10, 2011.

29. Ibid., and April 26, 2011.

30. Gloria Caldwell, interview with author, Tulsa, Okla., November 11, 2009.

31. Sandra Downie Langenkamp, interview with author, Tulsa, Okla., February 15, 2010.

32. Ginnie Graham and Curtis Killman, "THA shakeup in 1980s Brought Reforms," *Tulsa World*, June 6, 2010.

33. Drew Diamond, interview with author, Tulsa, Okla., April 29, 2011.

CHAPTER 17

1. David Monahan, "Profile: Dan Allen," *Salt of the Earth*, November/December 1995.

2. Judy Allen Hess, conversation with author, Tulsa, Okla., June 2, 2011.

3. Jeff Nix, interview with author, Tulsa, Okla., April 20, 2011.

4. Todd Singer, interview with author, Tulsa, Okla., May 2, 2011; *Neighbor for Neighbor Newsletter,* April 1997.

5. Todd Singer, interview with author, Tulsa, Okla., May 2, 2011.

6. Dan Allen, letter to Todd Singer, May 4, 1990.

7. Maynard Ungerman, "University and Community—An Effective Partnership?" *Baculus*, April/May 1989.

8. Dan Allen, letter to Todd Singer, May 4, 1990.

9. Todd Singer, interview with author, Tulsa, Okla., May 2, 2011.

10. *Neighbor for Neighbor Newsletter*, April 1997.

11. *Neighbor for Neighbor Newsletter*, September 1998.

12. Todd Singer, interview with author, Tulsa, Okla., May 2, 2011.

13. *Neighbor for Neighbor 30th Anniversary Newsletter*, 1998.

14. Ibid.

15. Carol Falletti, interview with author, Tulsa, Okla., January 19, 2010, and e-mail to author, February 11, 2011; Tim Dennehey, interview with author, Tulsa, Okla., November 16, 2009.

16. Bill Skeehan, letter to Neighbor for Neighbor Board of Directors, September 18, 1995.

17. Judy Allen Hess, "Life and Times of Dan Allen," unpublished manuscript, June 29, 2008.

18. Judy Allen Hess, personal journal, n.d.; Hess, "Life and Times of Dan Allen."

19. Bill Skeehan, interview with author, Tulsa, Okla., November 19, 2009.

20. Tim Dennehy, interview with author, Tulsa, Okla., November 16, 2009.

21. Russell Bennett, *Neighbor for Neighbor Newsletter*, April 1996.

22. *Neighbor for Neighbor Newsletter,* December 1995.

23. Jeff Nix, interview with author, Tulsa, Okla., April 20, 2011.

24. Carol Falletti, *Neighbor for Neighbor Newsletter*, December 1995.

25. Frosty Troy, "God's Angry Man," *The Oklahoma Observer*, December 10/25, 1995.

26. Bill Skeehan, "Mass of the Resurrection for Daniel Richard Allen," Holy Family Cathedral, Tulsa, Okla., November 15, 1995.

27. Bill Skeehan, letter to Frosty Troy, December 26, 1995.

28. Bill Skeehan, interview with author, Tulsa, Okla., November 19, 2010.

29. Janet Pearson, "University of Poverty," *Tulsa World*, November 26, 1995.

CHAPTER 18

1. Jim Wolfe, interview with author, Tulsa, Okla., May 10, 2011.

2. *Neighbor for Neighbor Newsletter,* December 1995.

3. Bill Major, resume and interview with author, Tulsa, Okla., September 11, 2011.

4. "The Many Faces of Hunger in Eastern Oklahoma," Community Food Bank of Eastern Oklahoma brochure, n.d., c. 2010.

5. John McCarthy, interview with author, Tulsa, Okla., September 18, 2010.

6. Don McCarthy, resume and interview with author, Tulsa, Okla., October 29, 2009; "The Millennium House: "A Strong, Affordable Home for the 21st Century," news release,

accessed January 25, 2011, http://www.pathnet.org/sp.asp?id=12535.7. Wesley Brown, "Business Monday: Dedicated to Community," *Tulsa World*, n.d.; accessed March 14, 2011, http://www.wilbertcollins.com/About.aspx.

8. Carol Falletti, resume and interview with author, Tulsa, Okla., July 2011, et seq.

9. Kim Archer, "Whole Health for North Tulsa," *Tulsa World*, September 17, 2010; Kirby Lee Davis "OU-Tulsa Breaks Ground on North Tulsa Health Facility," *The Journal Record* (Oklahoma City), January 25, 2010.

10. Joseph Dillon and Edward Jeep, *Vatican II—A Promise Broken?* (N.p. [Bartlesville, Okla.?]): Skeehan Project, June 2010.

11. Ginnie Graham and Curtis Killman, "THA Shakeup in 1980s Brought Reforms," *Tulsa World*, June 6, 2010; Ruth Nelson, interview with author, Tulsa, Okla., March 10, 2011.

12. NFN history, acessed July 14, 2011, http://wwwneighborforneighbor.org/NFNHistory40.php.

13. "Share the Warmth Marks 20 Years of Keeping Oklahomans Warm," Oklahoma Natural Gas news release, February 10, 2003, accessed February 12, 2011, http://ir.oneok.com/phoenix.zhtml?c=120070&p=irol-newsArticle&ID=1520306&highlight=.

14. Maynard Ungerman, resume and interview with author, Tulsa, Okla., October 19, 2009.

15. Jarrel Wade, "The Sign of His Nature," *Tulsa World*, September 24, 2008.

16. "A Birthday to Remember: 30 Years of Service to Tulsa's Poor," *Neighbor for Neighbor Newsletter*, 1998.

17. NFN history, accessed July 14, 2011, http://www.neighborforneighbor.org/NFNHistory40.php.

18. Ann Smith, interview with author, Tulsa, Okla., January 26, 2010; Tim Dennehy, interview with author, Tulsa, Okla., November 16, 2009.

Selected Bibliography

BOOKS

Bate, Charles James. *"It's Been a Long Time" and We've Come a Long Way: A History of the Oklahoma Black Medical Providers (The Black Healers)*. Tulsa: Acorn Printing Company, 1986.

Bonner, Jeremy. *The Road to Renewal: Victor Joseph Reed & Oklahoma Catholicism, 1905–1971*. Washington, D.C.: The Catholic University of America Press, 2008.

DeBerri, Edward P., James E. Hug, Peter J. Henriot, and Michael J. Schulthers. *Catholic Social Teaching: Our Best Kept Secret*. 4th ed. Maryknoll, N.Y.: Orbis Books, 2003.

Debo, Angie. *And Still the Waters Run: The Betrayal of the Five Civilized Tribes*. Princeton, N.J.: Princeton University Press, 1940; Norman: University of Oklahoma Press, 1984.

———. *Oklahoma Footloose and Fancy-Free*. Norman: University of Oklahoma Press, 1949.

———. *Prairie City: The Story of an American Community*. Reprint, Tulsa: Council Oak Books, Ltd., 1969.

Dickerson, Carrie Barefoot. *Aunt Carrie's War Against Black Fox Nuclear Power Plant*. Tulsa: Council Oak Publishing Co., Inc., 1995.

Dillon, Joseph, and Edward Jeep. *Vatican II—A Promise Broken?* N.p. (Bartlesville, Okla.): Skeehan Project, 2010.

Egan, Timothy. *The Worst Hard Time: The Untold Story of Those Who Survived the Great American Dust Bowl*. New York: Houghton Mifflin, 2006.

Ellsworth, Scott. *Death in a Promised Land*. Baton Rouge: Louisiana State University Press, 1982.

Fisher, Ada Lois Sipuel, with Danney Goble. *A Matter of Black and White: The Autobiography of Ada Lois Sipuel Fisher*. Norman: University of Oklahoma Press, 1996.

Gates, Eddie Faye. *Miz Lucy's Cookies: And Other Links in my Black Family Support System*. Tulsa: Coman & Associates, 1996.

Gates, Eddie Faye. *They Came Searching: How Blacks Sought the Promised Land in Tulsa*. Austin: Eakin Press, 1997.

Goble, Danney. *Tulsa! Biography of the American City*. Tulsa: Council Oak Books, 1997.

Hamill, John. *Tulsa: The Great American City*. Montgomery, Ala.: Community Communications Inc., in partnership with the Metropolitan Tulsa Chamber of

Commerce, 2000.

Harrington, Michael. *The Other America: Poverty in the United States*. Baltimore, Md.:
Penguin Books, 1963.

Harris, David. *Dreams Die Hard: Three Men's Journey through the Sixties*. New York: St.
Martin's/Marek, 1982.

Hellwig, Monika K. *The Eucharist and the Hunger of the World.* 2nd ed. Kansas City, Mo.:
Sheed & Ward, 1992.

Hoye, Daniel F. Hoye, ed. *Economic Justice for All: Pastoral Letter on Catholic Social
Teaching and the U.S. Economy.* Washington, D.C.: United States Conference
of Catholic Bishops, 1986.

Little, Mabel B., with Nathan Hare and Julian Hare. *Fire on Mount Zion: My Life and
History as a Black Woman in America.* Langston, Okla.: Melvin B. Tolson
Black Heritage Center, Langston University, 1990.

Luper, Clara. *Behold the Walls*. Oklahoma City: Jim Wire, 1979.

The Marque. Yearbook.Tulsa, Okla.: Marquette High School, 1949.

Morgan, David R.,Robert E. England, and George O. Humphries. *Oklahoma Politics and
Policies: Governing the Sooner State.* Lincoln: University of Nebraska Press,
1991.

Murray, William H. *The Negro's Place in the Call of Race: The Last Word on Segregation
of Races, Considered in Every Capable Light as Disclosed by Experience.*
Tishomingo, Okla.: William H. Murray, 1948.

Perella, Frederick J., Jr., ed. *Poverty in American Democracy: A Study of Social Power*.
Washington, D.C.: Campaign for Human Development, United States Catholic
Conference, 1974.

Reeves, Earl James. *Autobiography of Earl James Reeves: My First Sixty-Five Years*.
Columbia, Mo.: Earl James Reeves, 1998.

Rhodes, Jewell Parker. *Magic City*. New York: HarperCollins Publishers, Inc., 1997.

Rogers, Will. *Will Rogers Says . . .* , ed. Reba Neighbors Collins. Claremore, Okla.: Will
Rogers Heritage Press, 1988.

Skeehan, Bill. *At this Time: A Seasonal Walk Through the Liturgical Year.* Bartlesville,
Okla.: Meddlers Books, n.d. (c. 1980s).

———. *To Dance with a Cross on Our Back*: *Reflections on the Word Made Flesh.*
Bartlesville: Meddler's Books, 1982.

Silvey, Larry P., and Douglas S. Drown, eds. *The Tulsa Spirit*. Tulsa: Continental Heritage
Press, 1979.

Viorst, Milton. *Fire in the Streets: America in the 1960s*. New York: Simon and Schuster,
1979.

ARTICLES and REPORTS

Archer, Kim. "A Legacy of Love for Others: Aid Group Completes 40th Year." *Tulsa World,* June 22, 2008.

Brown, Wesley. "Dedicated to Community." (Wilbert Collins story). *Tulsa World*, n.d.

Davis, Kirby Lee. "OU-Tulsa Breaks Ground on North Tulsa Health Facility," *The Journal Record* (Oklahoma City), January 25, 2010. Accessed July 18, 2001, http://findarticles.com/p/articles/tulsaworld.com/site/search/default. aspx?type=Advanced.

Diamond, Drew, and Dierdre Mead Weiss. "Advancing Community Policing through Community Governance: A Framework Document." U.S. Department of Justice, Community Oriented Policing Services, May 2009. Accessed July 19, 2011, http://www.cops.usdoj.gov/files/RIC/Publications/e050919202-AdvCommunityPolicing_final.pdf.

"Decade of Change," A supplement to the *Oklahoma Courier* marking the tenth anniversary of the installation of Victor J. Reed as bishop of Oklahoma City and Tulsa, Okla.. March 1, 1968.

Langdon, Judy. "Like a Good Neighbor," *Tulsa People,* October 2010.

Lewis, Andrew B. "The Sit-Ins that Changed America." From *Los Angeles Times*, reprinted in *Tulsa World,* February 7, 2010, G3. Selected from *The Shadows of Youth: The Remarkable Journey of the Civil Rights Generation* by Andrew B. Lewis.

McCarthy, Don. "A Novel Approach for Housing for Moderate to Low-Income Families." Tulsa: Neighbor for Neighbor, Inc., n.d. (c. 2001).

Monahan, David. "Homelessness/Housing." *Salt of the Earth,*(October 2008). Acessed July 18, 2010, http://salt.claretianpubs.org/issues/homeless/allen.html.

Rosin, Hanna. "Did Christianity Cause the Crash?" *The Atlantic* (December 2009). Accessed July 18, 2011, http://www.theatlantic.com/doc/200912/rosin-prosperity-gospel.

Sackrey, Charles. "Tulsa University: 'The Harvard of the Southwest,'" chapter 7 from *Teaching from the Left.* Creative Commons Copyright, 2009. Accessed July 18, 2010, http://www.awcaonline.org/CharlesSackrey/index.php?title=Tulsa_University%2C_the_Harvard_of_the_Southwest.

Tulsa Metropolitan Ministry, Hunger Task Force. *A Study of Nutrition among Tulsa's Poor, Part 1: Dimensions of the Problem,* October 1979.

Ungerman, Maynard. "University and Community—An Effective Partnership?" *Baculus*, University of Tulsa Student Bar Association newspaper, vol. 2, no.3–4 (April/May 1989).

Wolf, John B. "The Last Days of Dr. Mason," February 18, 1968; and "Is America Having a Nervous Breakdown?" February 25, 1968. Sermons collected in *The Public*

Schools Question: Three Sermons Delivered Feb. 18 & 25 and Mar. 3, 1968. All
Souls Unitarian Church, Tulsa, Okla., 1968.

MANUSCRIPT COLLECTIONS

Dan Allen family collection (courtesy Judy Allen Hess)

Allen Family scrapbooks (courtesy Francis Allen Pankey)
Hess, Judy Allen. "Life and Times of Dan Allen." Unpublished article, and 1995 journal.
Letters, cards, photos, newsletters, reports, clippings, videotapes, and memorabilia
Scrapbooks and family collections of letters, documents, photos, and miscellaneous
        materials, indexed

David M. Breed collection

Breed, David M. "The Early History of Southwest Tulsa." (Based on early research and
        initial drafting by Kent Schell), c. 2010.
City of Tulsa. Model Cities program grant application, 1967, and progress reports. Health
        excerpts, Part III, E., of application.
Clock, Wilkie Clyde. "Survey of West Tulsa." Unpublished report, 1933.

Gloria Caldwell collection

Caldwell, Gloria. "The Rest of the Story." Unpublished paper, August 1988.
———. "Timeline." Unpublished paper, Tulsa, November 3, 2007.
Hoort, Lewis "Bud." "Neighbor for Neighbor." Unpublished paper, Oklahoma History
        class research (for Professor Danney Goble's class), Tulsa, May 10, 1989.
Luce, Bennie. "Racial Segregation in Tulsa: A Statistical Comparison." Tulsa: Community
        Relations Commission, March 1976.
Macaulay, Mary. "Neighbor for Neighbor: From Impossible to Possible." Unpublished
        paper, Tulsa, after 1995.
McCloud, Paul I. "Neither Black nor White: A Progress Report on Integration in the Tulsa
        Public Schools." Tulsa Public Schools, ED121889, 1974. http://eric.ed.gov.
Neighbor for Neighbor Newsletters (October 1980), (August 1985), (September 1988),
        1980s report (October 1990), Dan Allen Obituaries (December 1995), Foreword
        from Dan Allen (November 1996), transcript of Dan Allen interview for CBS
        video "Common Good" (November 1997).
Neighbor for Neighbor Miscellaneous File: NFN Announces Micro-lending for Tulsa—
        Neighbors for Economic Development. Flyer (November 16, no year); one-

page report on legal clinic, n.d.; two-page report on CCVI housing grant, n.d.; "Justice," poem by Dan Allen, n.d.; one-page NFN statement, n.d.; Diane Perkins report on services, n.d.; In-kind-services documentation, FY 1978–79; Statement and petition re: THA, July 8, 1989; Article and backup notes on "Idea to List Pleas by Poor for Aid Called a Sham," *Tulsa Word*, c. May 1987; "The rest of the story," paper about school desegregation. No author, August 1988; PSO letter re: Black Fox, January 1979; "Black Fox Foes Denied Request to Open GE Report Hearings," *Tulsa World*, n.d.; NFN report on "Black Fox and the Reed Report," August 2, 1979; Sackrey, Charles, "Some Economic Implications of Black Fox," unpublished paper by Sunbelt Alliance, c. 1979; NFN flyer, bylaws, and mission statement, n.d.

Oklahoma Advisory Committee, U.S. Commission on Civil Rights; Hon. Hannah Atkins, Chair. "School Desegregation in Tulsa, Oklahoma," August 1977.

Tulsa Metropolitan Ministry, Hunger Task Force. "A Study of Nutrition Among Tulsa's Poor, Part 1: Dimensions of the Problem." October 1979 (from Bill Major).

Ungerman, Maynard. "Why Neighbor for Neighbor?" Unpublished paper, Tulsa, n. d.

ARCHIVAL MATERIALS

Ann Patton collection at Tulsa Historical Society: 16,000 indexed items dating from 1960–2004, including 1,600 indexed relevant clippings from 1969–75.

Ann Patton's scrapbooks and databases: Dan Allen news clippings, NFN newsletters, and other documents, 1970–2000, indexed by author.

Tulsa Central Library archives

Tulsa Historical Society archives

Tulsa World archives

INTERVIEWS

Allen, Anne. Interview by author, July 19, 2010.

Allen, Janet. Interview by author, January 13, 2010.

Caldwell, Gloria. Interviews by author, November 2, 2009, et seq.

Collins, Wilbert. Interview by author, November 9, 2009.

Dennehy, Tim. Interview by author, November 16, 2009.

Diamond, Drew. Interview by author, April 29, 2011.

Downie, Timothy. Interview by author, February 15, 2010.

Falletti, Carol. Interviews by author, February, April, and July 2010–July 2011.

Falletti, Don. Interviews by author, March 2010, et seq.

Feldman, Nancy. Interview by author, c. 1990.

Flanagan, Pat. Interviews by author, September 21, 2009, and January 18, 2010, et seq.

Goodwin, James O. Interview by author, August 13, 2010.

Hall, Amos T. Author's personal interview notes, c. 1969.

Hess, Judy Allen. Interviews by author, June 2008–July 2011.

Hille, Mary Ann. Interview by author, May 10, 2011.

Langenkamp, Sandra Downie. Interviews by author, November 2, 2009,
     and February 15, 2010.

Lowe, Lorraine. Interview by author, September 17, 2010.

Macklin, Beth. Interview by author, c. 1976.

Major, Bill. Interview by author, September 11 and September 18, 2010.

McCarthy, Don. Interview by author, October 29, 2009.

McCarthy, John. Interview by author, September 18, 2010.

McGlinchey, Father James. Interview by author, March 27, 2010.

Nelson, Ruth Kaiser. Interview by author, March 10, 2011.

Nix, Jeff. Interview by author, April 20, 2011.

Pankey, Frances Allen (with her daughter Kathy Pankey Jackson, and Judy Hess). Interview
     by author, November 11, 2010.

Prothro, Dr. George. Interview by author, May 25, 2010.

Randle, Rodger (former Tulsa mayor). Interview by author, November 11, 2010.

Reeves, Dr. Earl J. Interview by author, August 28, 2010.

Silvey, Larry. Interview by author via e-mail, April 2011.

Singer, Todd. Interview by author, May 2, 2011.

Sister Miriam. Interview by author, September 29, 2010.

Skeehan, Father Bill. Interviews by author, September 2009, November 19, 2010, et seq.
     through March 2011.

Smith, Ann. Interview by author, January 26, 2010.

Troy, Frosty. Interview by author, September 29, 2010.

Ungerman, Maynard. Interview by author, October 19. 2009.

Vaughn, Clayton. Interview by author, May 5, 2011.

Wolfe, James. Interview by author, May 10, 2011.

Wright, Shirley Marie. Interview by author, May 2, 2011.

Young, Terry (former Tulsa mayor). Interview by author, Nov. 17, 2010.

MISCELLANEOUS DOCUMENTS, LETTERS, and MULTIMEDIA

Dan Allen. Letter to the Oklahoma Archbishop, John R. Quinn, resigning from priesthood, January 31, 1973.

———. Letter to Todd Singer, May 4, 1990.

"Caritas in Veritate," encyclical letter from Pope Benedict XVI to bishops, et al., n.d.

"Lamp unto My Feet," CBS-TV News Special, November 17, 1968 (DVD from Judy Hess).

Legal document, 656 F2nd 593, Coalition for Fair Utility Rates and NFN vs. Oklahoma Corporation Commission, OBG, PSO: Decision of 10th Circuit US Court of Appeals, August 7, 1981. Accessed February 7, 2011, http://law.justia.com/cases/federal/appellate-courts/F2/656/593/184614/.

"Neighbor for Neighbor: The Year-Round Christmas," KRMG interview of Dan Allen by Richard Dowdell, n.d.

Resumes: Gloria Caldwell, Bill Major, Don McCarthy, Maynard Ungerman; and website bios for book committee members Carol Falletti, Dana Falletti, Judy Allen Hess, Linda Nicholson, and Bill Skeehan.

The Common Ground for the Common Good. Video DVD produced for the Synagogue Council of America, the National Council of Churches, and the United States Council of Churches, as part of the Interreligious Project, The Common Ground for the Common Good. © 1993, National Council of Churches.

"The Many Faces of Hunger in Eastern Oklahoma," Community Food Bank of Eastern Oklahoma, brochure, c. 2010.

WEBSITES AND INTERNET SOURCES

Church of the Resurrection. http://www.resurrection-tulsa.org

Community Food Bank of Eastern Oklahoma. http://www.cfbeo.org.

Eastern Oklahoma Catholic archives. http://www.dioceseoftulsa.org/news.eoc.asp.

"Energy Officials Say Nuclear Power Comeback Not Likely to Happen in Oklahoma, BNET, September 28, 2005; Accessed July 18, 2010, from references at http://en.wikipedia.org/wiki/Black_Fox_Nuclear_Power_Plant.

Neighbor for Neighbor. http://wwwneighborforneighbor.org.

Dan Allen's golden chalice was made by his father, a gold spinner, for Dan's first mass in 1957. Photo by James Aldridge.

Index

L
Ladeur, Linda, 155
LaFortune, Bob (Mayor), 59, 60, 101, 106–07
Landholt, David, 128
Langenkamp, Sandra Downie. *See* Downie, Sandra
Langston University School of Law, 93–94
Lapidus, Gail, 148
Lawton, Okla., 6
League of Women Voters, 97, 102, 133–34, 165
legal assistance. *See* NFN Legal Clinic
Leroy (client), 49, 56
liberation theology, 35, 99
LIFE Senior Services, 162, 165
Little, Mable, 101
Little Rock, Ark., 28–29
Liturgy of the Word, 58
"living baskets" food program, 44
"living stones," Fr. Dan followers as, vii, 152, 169
Lowe, Lorraine, 86–87
Luecke, S. F. (Msgr.), 30
lynchings, 25

M
MacDonald, Nancy, 104, 107
Macklin, Beth, 45
Major, Bill, 121, 122, 124–27, 162
Malcom X, assassination of, 32
Manning, Frank (Rev.), 53
Marano, Phil (Dr.), 87
Marquette Catholic High School, 12, 16
Marshall, Okla., 35
Marshall, Thurgood, 93–94
Martin, Jim, 134–37
Mason, Charles, 95–96
"massive forced busing" (MFB), 97
Matthew 6:34, 115
Maxey, Jim (Dr.), 86
McAuliffe, Mary Ellen. *See* Allen, Mary Ellen McAuliffe
McCarthy, Carmen, 34